CliffsNotes®

GMAT®

CRAM PLAN™

2nd Edition

CliffsNotes®

GMAT®

CRAM PLAN™

2nd Edition

William Ma, Jane R. Burstein, and Carolyn Wheater

WILEY

John Wiley & Sons, Inc.

About the Authors

William Ma was chairman of the Math Department at the Herricks School District on Long Island for many years before retiring. He also taught as an adjunct math instructor at Baruch College, Columbia University, and Fordham University. He is the author of several books, including two calculus review books, an SAT prep book, and an online review course for the New York State's Math A Regents Exam. He is currently a math consultant. **Jane Burstein** is currently an instructor at Hofstra University. Educated at S.U.N.Y. Stony Brook and Hofstra University, she taught English at Herricks High School for 36 years. She is the author of the Cram Plan books for the SAT, the ACT, the GMAT, and the AFQT. **Carolyn Wheater** teaches middle school and upper school mathematics at the Nightingale- Bamford School in New York City. Educated at Marymount Manhattan College and the University of Massachusetts, Amherst, she has taught math and computer technology for more than 30 years to students from preschool through college. She is the author of the Cram Plan books for the AFQT and the GRE.

Editorial

Acquisitions Editor: Greg Tubach

Project Editor: Elizabeth Kuball

Copy Editor: Catherine Schwenk

Technical Editors: Tony Bedenikovic, Stacy Magedanz, Mary Jane Sterling

Composition

Proofreader: Melissa D. Buddendeck

John Wiley & Sons, Inc., Composition Services

CliffsNotes® GMAT® Cram Plan™, 2nd Edition

Published by:
John Wiley & Sons, Inc.
111 River Street
Hoboken, NJ 07030-5774
www.wiley.com

Copyright © 2012 John Wiley & Sons, Inc.

Published by John Wiley & Sons, Inc., Hoboken, NJ
Published simultaneously in Canada

Library of Congress Control Number: 2012934992
ISBN: 978-1-118-13417-7 (pbk)
ISBN: 978-1-118-22518-9 (ebk), 978-1-118-23859-2 (ebk), 978-1-118-26328-0 (ebk)

Printed in the United States of America
10 9 8 7 6 5 4 3 2 1

Table of Contents

Introduction

Congratulations! You've made the decision to take charge of your future and apply to graduate school to get that prestigious MBA degree. You're ready for the exciting opportunities available to those who enter the business world armed with management and leadership skills. Beginning in June 2012, the test will change, and you'll have to take the Next Generation GMAT for admission to most graduate business programs and submit your scores. Your first step is to prepare yourself for this important exam. No problem. With motivation and discipline you can prepare yourself to do your very best on all parts of this test. All you need to begin work is a helpful study plan, one that is simple, organized, and feasible. Whether you have two months, one month, or one week, follow the plan in this book and you can achieve GMAT success.

About the Test

The purpose of the Graduate Management Admission Test (GMAT) is to give graduate business or management schools more information as they evaluate candidates for admission to their programs. The test is designed to assess the mathematical skills, critical thinking abilities, and writing skills that are necessary for success in a graduate business or management program.

The test is administered only in a computer-adaptive testing (CAT) format, except in very isolated areas outside the United States. CAT tailors the test to each student's ability level. (That's what the *adaptive* part of *computer-adaptive testing* refers to.) All multiple choice sections are computer adaptive except the new Integrated Reasoning section. You don't need high-level computer skills to complete the test; you just have to know how to use a mouse and how to scroll up or down a page.

The test begins with easy or easy-medium questions. You're asked to use the mouse to select your answer choice; then you must confirm your answer by clicking Confirm. After you've confirmed your answer, you can't go back and change it. If you answer a question correctly, the computer presents a more difficult question. If you answer a question incorrectly, the computer presents an easier question. In this way, you should receive very few questions that are either too easy or too difficult for you. Because difficult questions are worth more points than easy questions, the more difficult questions you can answer correctly, the higher your score will be. In CAT, the computer pinpoints your ability level and arrives at an accurate assessment of your performance using fewer questions than are necessary on a paper test.

When you sit down at the computer in the testing room, before you begin the test, you'll go through a computerized CAT tutorial. The tutorial will explain:

- How to use the mouse
- How to select an answer and how to change it before you confirm
- How to scroll up and down the screen
- How to use the toolbars on the screen
- How to use the built-in word processing program for the essay section

The computer times each section with a countdown clock at the bottom of the screen. When you have five minutes left in the section, the clock blinks several times. This blinking is the only warning you get that time is about to expire.

The GMAT is comprised of four sections:

- **Section 1: Analytical Writing: Analysis of an Argument:** The computer presents you with a brief argument and evidence to support that argument. You have 30 minutes to compose an essay in which you critique the logic of the argument and the evidence supporting it, using the built-in word processing program. Remember: The word processor program has no built-in spell check or grammar check, so be sure to proofread carefully.

- **Section 2: Integrated Reasoning:** This new 30-minute section includes approximately 10 questions and is designed to measure your ability to evaluate information from different sources as you solve challenging problems. The problems may require you to interpret data on graphs and charts, to predict likely outcomes, and to convert quantitative data from graphic to verbal formats. You'll receive a separate score on this section, one that will not count toward your total score.

- **Section 3: Quantitative Ability:** You're given 75 minutes to complete 37 multiple-choice questions. There are two types of quantitative questions: problem solving and data sufficiency. The computer adjusts the questions to your ability level. You can't skip questions; the computer can't determine the correct level for your next question if you skip one, so not answering is not an option. If you don't finish all 37 questions within the 75-minute limit, the computer determines your score based on the number of questions you answered. Warning: If you skip a question, you'll receive no score (NS) for the entire section.

- **Section 4: Verbal Ability:** You're given 75 minutes to complete 41 questions. There are three types of verbal questions: reading comprehension, critical reasoning, and sentence correction. Just as in Section 3, the computer adjusts the questions to your ability level. You can't skip questions; the computer can't determine the correct level for your next question if you skip one, so, again, not answering is not an option. If you don't finish all 41 questions within the 75-minute limit, the computer determines your score based on the number of questions you answered. Warning: If you skip a question, you'll receive no score (NS) for the entire section.

The total test time is 3 hours and 30 minutes. *Note:* There is an optional five-minute break after Section 2 and another optional five-minute break after Section 3. There is no break after Sections 1 or 4.

The Next Generation GMAT score report is comprised of five scores:

- **Integrated Reasoning score** is based on your answers to the 10 Integrated Reasoning questions. This IR score will not count toward your total score.

- **Verbal scaled score** reflects your score on the 41 verbal questions on a scale from 0 to 60 (more points possible than number of questions due to CAT).

- **Quantitative scaled score** reflects your score on the 37 quantitative questions which again is converted to a scale of 0 to 60 due to the use of CAT.

- **Total scaled score,** on a scale from 200 to 800, which reflects your score on all the multiple-choice questions (the total of your verbal and quantitative scores).

- **Analytical writing score,** on a scale from 0 to 6, which reflects the score on your Analysis of an Argument essay.

The scaled scores on the verbal and quantitative sections are configured using a formula that factors in the total number of questions you answered, the number of questions you answered correctly, and the levels of difficulty of the questions you answered correctly.

On the testing day, after you've completed the entire test, *before you see your scores,* you can decide whether to keep the test. If you decide to keep the test, you can immediately view your unofficial scores on the verbal and quantitative sections of the test; official scores, including the analytical essay score, are mailed to you about 10 days after you take the test. When you get your official score report, you'll be able to see how well you did in comparison to other students by using the percentile rankings chart. *Note:* If you decide *not* to keep this test, you aren't allowed to see your scores.

About This Book

The first step in getting ready for the Next Generation GMAT is determining exactly how much time you have and following the appropriate plan: the two-month plan, the one-month plan, or the one-week plan. Each plan has a schedule for you to follow along with the approximate time you'll need to allot to each task. In addition, each chapter gives you strategies for that part of the test. Included in each chapter are practice exercises to assist you in the areas in which you're weakest and to help you continue to maximize your strengths.

Begin by taking the diagnostic test to pinpoint your strengths and weaknesses. The explanation of answers will guide you to the specific chapters that cover the topics in which you need the most help. At the end of the diagnostic test, you'll find a scoring guide that will give you an indication of your current score on each section of the GMAT. Then you can begin to focus on the subject-review chapters. At the end of the book, you'll find a practice test, a simulated GMAT with a scoring guide to give you an authentic test-taking experience.

To prepare for the GMAT, keep the following general guidelines in mind:

- **Know what to expect.** Familiarize yourself with the CAT format, the instructions for each section, and the types of questions. This preparation will save you precious time during the test.

- **Read each question very carefully, and know exactly what you're being asked to solve.** Correctly identifying what the question asks enables you to effectively eliminate responses that may be true, but don't correctly answer what was being asked.

- **Read every answer choice before you select the one you think is correct.** You'll find distracters among the choices—answers that are appealing, but wrong.

- **Move at a steady pace, but don't rush, especially with the first few questions.** The computer will use your answers to adjust the difficulty level of subsequent questions. Wrong answers may keep you at a lower level until you prove yourself able to answer correctly.

- **Use process of elimination to make educated guesses if you don't know the answer to a question.** Don't make random guesses; a wrong answer will move you down the difficulty scale.

- **Stay mentally active.** It's easy to get lulled into rethinking and rereading. Read actively, think logically, narrow your choices, select the best one, and move on.

- **Use the note boards and pencils provided to help you figure out the problems and to plan your essays.** You can't use the computer to take notes.

Beginning in April 2012, you'll be able to download the new GMATPrep test-preparation software free from the official GMAT website. Just go to www.mba.com/mba/thegmat and click the Free Test-Preparation Software link. (Or go directly to the software page at www.mba.com/mba/thegmat/download-free-test-preparation-software.)

I. Diagnostic Test

This diagnostic test is equivalent to a full-length GMAT. It has four sections, which are identical to the four sections on the GMAT:

Number	Section	Number of Questions	Time
1	Analysis of an Argument	1 question	30 minutes
2	Integrated Reasoning	10 questions	30 minutes
3	Quantitative	37 questions	75 minutes
4	Verbal	41 questions	75 minutes

When you take this exam, try to simulate the test conditions by following the time allotments carefully. Use word-processing software (such as Microsoft Word) to write the analytical essay. Do not use the spell-check and grammar-check functions of your software. If you don't have access to a computer, use the answer sheets provided. For Section 2, mark your answers in the spaces provided. You may use a simple calculator. For sections 3 and 4, use the answer sheets provided and fill in the corresponding circles. (On the actual CAT GMAT, you will select your answer on the computer and then click Confirm.)

Remember: On the actual CAT GMAT, the questions in sections 3 and 4 will begin at a fairly easy level and then become gradually more difficult as you answer questions correctly. If you answer a question incorrectly, your next question will be an easier one. On this diagnostic test, the questions vary in difficulty level.

Answer Sheet

Section 1

CUT HERE

Section 2

Fill in answers with questions.

Section 3

1 Ⓐ Ⓑ Ⓒ Ⓓ Ⓔ		21 Ⓐ Ⓑ Ⓒ Ⓓ Ⓔ	
2 Ⓐ Ⓑ Ⓒ Ⓓ Ⓔ		22 Ⓐ Ⓑ Ⓒ Ⓓ Ⓔ	
3 Ⓐ Ⓑ Ⓒ Ⓓ Ⓔ		23 Ⓐ Ⓑ Ⓒ Ⓓ Ⓔ	
4 Ⓐ Ⓑ Ⓒ Ⓓ Ⓔ		24 Ⓐ Ⓑ Ⓒ Ⓓ Ⓔ	
5 Ⓐ Ⓑ Ⓒ Ⓓ Ⓔ		25 Ⓐ Ⓑ Ⓒ Ⓓ Ⓔ	
6 Ⓐ Ⓑ Ⓒ Ⓓ Ⓔ		26 Ⓐ Ⓑ Ⓒ Ⓓ Ⓔ	
7 Ⓐ Ⓑ Ⓒ Ⓓ Ⓔ		27 Ⓐ Ⓑ Ⓒ Ⓓ Ⓔ	
8 Ⓐ Ⓑ Ⓒ Ⓓ Ⓔ		28 Ⓐ Ⓑ Ⓒ Ⓓ Ⓔ	
9 Ⓐ Ⓑ Ⓒ Ⓓ Ⓔ		29 Ⓐ Ⓑ Ⓒ Ⓓ Ⓔ	
10 Ⓐ Ⓑ Ⓒ Ⓓ Ⓔ		30 Ⓐ Ⓑ Ⓒ Ⓓ Ⓔ	
11 Ⓐ Ⓑ Ⓒ Ⓓ Ⓔ		31 Ⓐ Ⓑ Ⓒ Ⓓ Ⓔ	
12 Ⓐ Ⓑ Ⓒ Ⓓ Ⓔ		32 Ⓐ Ⓑ Ⓒ Ⓓ Ⓔ	
13 Ⓐ Ⓑ Ⓒ Ⓓ Ⓔ		33 Ⓐ Ⓑ Ⓒ Ⓓ Ⓔ	
14 Ⓐ Ⓑ Ⓒ Ⓓ Ⓔ		34 Ⓐ Ⓑ Ⓒ Ⓓ Ⓔ	
15 Ⓐ Ⓑ Ⓒ Ⓓ Ⓔ		35 Ⓐ Ⓑ Ⓒ Ⓓ Ⓔ	
16 Ⓐ Ⓑ Ⓒ Ⓓ Ⓔ		36 Ⓐ Ⓑ Ⓒ Ⓓ Ⓔ	
17 Ⓐ Ⓑ Ⓒ Ⓓ Ⓔ		37 Ⓐ Ⓑ Ⓒ Ⓓ Ⓔ	
18 Ⓐ Ⓑ Ⓒ Ⓓ Ⓔ			
19 Ⓐ Ⓑ Ⓒ Ⓓ Ⓔ			
20 Ⓐ Ⓑ Ⓒ Ⓓ Ⓔ			

Section 4

1 Ⓐ Ⓑ Ⓒ Ⓓ Ⓔ	21 Ⓐ Ⓑ Ⓒ Ⓓ Ⓔ	41 Ⓐ Ⓑ Ⓒ Ⓓ Ⓔ
2 Ⓐ Ⓑ Ⓒ Ⓓ Ⓔ	22 Ⓐ Ⓑ Ⓒ Ⓓ Ⓔ	
3 Ⓐ Ⓑ Ⓒ Ⓓ Ⓔ	23 Ⓐ Ⓑ Ⓒ Ⓓ Ⓔ	
4 Ⓐ Ⓑ Ⓒ Ⓓ Ⓔ	24 Ⓐ Ⓑ Ⓒ Ⓓ Ⓔ	
5 Ⓐ Ⓑ Ⓒ Ⓓ Ⓔ	25 Ⓐ Ⓑ Ⓒ Ⓓ Ⓔ	
6 Ⓐ Ⓑ Ⓒ Ⓓ Ⓔ	26 Ⓐ Ⓑ Ⓒ Ⓓ Ⓔ	
7 Ⓐ Ⓑ Ⓒ Ⓓ Ⓔ	27 Ⓐ Ⓑ Ⓒ Ⓓ Ⓔ	
8 Ⓐ Ⓑ Ⓒ Ⓓ Ⓔ	28 Ⓐ Ⓑ Ⓒ Ⓓ Ⓔ	
9 Ⓐ Ⓑ Ⓒ Ⓓ Ⓔ	29 Ⓐ Ⓑ Ⓒ Ⓓ Ⓔ	
10 Ⓐ Ⓑ Ⓒ Ⓓ Ⓔ	30 Ⓐ Ⓑ Ⓒ Ⓓ Ⓔ	
11 Ⓐ Ⓑ Ⓒ Ⓓ Ⓔ	31 Ⓐ Ⓑ Ⓒ Ⓓ Ⓔ	
12 Ⓐ Ⓑ Ⓒ Ⓓ Ⓔ	32 Ⓐ Ⓑ Ⓒ Ⓓ Ⓔ	
13 Ⓐ Ⓑ Ⓒ Ⓓ Ⓔ	33 Ⓐ Ⓑ Ⓒ Ⓓ Ⓔ	
14 Ⓐ Ⓑ Ⓒ Ⓓ Ⓔ	34 Ⓐ Ⓑ Ⓒ Ⓓ Ⓔ	
15 Ⓐ Ⓑ Ⓒ Ⓓ Ⓔ	35 Ⓐ Ⓑ Ⓒ Ⓓ Ⓔ	
16 Ⓐ Ⓑ Ⓒ Ⓓ Ⓔ	36 Ⓐ Ⓑ Ⓒ Ⓓ Ⓔ	
17 Ⓐ Ⓑ Ⓒ Ⓓ Ⓔ	37 Ⓐ Ⓑ Ⓒ Ⓓ Ⓔ	
18 Ⓐ Ⓑ Ⓒ Ⓓ Ⓔ	38 Ⓐ Ⓑ Ⓒ Ⓓ Ⓔ	
19 Ⓐ Ⓑ Ⓒ Ⓓ Ⓔ	39 Ⓐ Ⓑ Ⓒ Ⓓ Ⓔ	
20 Ⓐ Ⓑ Ⓒ Ⓓ Ⓔ	40 Ⓐ Ⓑ Ⓒ Ⓓ Ⓔ	

Section 1: Analysis of an Argument

Time: 30 minutes

Directions: Write an essay in response to the prompt:

The following appeared in a memorandum from the CEO of Superb Company to the head of human resources:

"We should employ more part-time workers because employees who work part time instead of full time have better morale and fewer absences due to illness. In our Centerville store, which has many part-time employees, attendance is up 14 percent over last year's attendance. In our Fringeville discount outlet store, however, which has only full-time employees, the figures for sick days used are up slightly. In addition, an employee survey shows that more Centerville employees reported higher job satisfaction than those at the Fringeville outlet."

Discuss the logic of this argument. In your discussion, be sure to analyze how well reasoned you think it is and evaluate the use of evidence in the argument. For example, you may need to consider what faulty or questionable assumptions underlie the thinking and what alternative explanations or counterexamples might weaken the conclusion. In your response, you may want to discuss what sort of evidence would strengthen or refute the argument, what changes in the argument would make it more logically sound, and what information would help you more accurately evaluate its conclusion.

IF YOU FINISH BEFORE TIME IS CALLED, CHECK YOUR WORK ON THIS SECTION ONLY. DO NOT WORK ON ANY OTHER SECTION IN THE TEST.

Section 2: Integrated Reasoning

Time: 30 minutes

10 questions

Directions: This section contains four types of questions. Answer each question in the space provided. You may use a calculator.

The table below shows the U.S. Trade Deficit (value of exports - value of imports) in millions of dollars by month for the years 2005 to 2010.

	2005	2006	2007	2008	2009	2010
January	−60,396.00	−72,364.00	−65,153.00	−70,148.00	−45,587.00	−46,229.00
February	−62,736.20	−67,061.00	−66,166.00	−71,432.00	−36,507.00	−50,670.00
March	−58,108.70	−67,460.00	−68,929.00	−68,973.00	−38,232.00	−51,072.00
April	−61,638.80	−68,090.00	−67,082.00	−72,817.00	−39,469.00	−51,709.00
May	−60,591.10	−70,403.00	−66,720.00	−72,755.00	−35,945.00	−53,581.00
June	−62,663.90	−68,847.00	−67,793.00	−72,511.00	−38,135.00	−60,888.00
July	−62,734.60	−71,904.00	−67,906.00	−76,879.00	−43,255.00	−53,785.00
August	−62,974.30	−73,123.00	−65,892.00	−70,757.00	−41,544.00	−57,805.00
September	−69,730.50	−70,403.00	−66,818.00	−69,125.00	−45,876.00	−55,644.00
October	−72,439.80	−65,147.00	−67,359.00	−68,555.00	−43,218.00	−49,610.00
November	−68,905.50	−64,840.00	−70,804.00	−51,953.00	−46,931.00	−50,444.00
December	−69,454.80	−68,328.00	−68,143.00	−50,293.00	−48,885.00	−52,471.00

Consider each of the following statements about the trade deficit. For each statement, indicate whether the statement is true or false, based on the information provided in the table.

True	False	
		1. The year in which the largest monthly deficit occurred in November was also the year in which the smallest monthly deficit occurred in December.
		2. The two consecutive years with the smallest change in the median monthly deficit were 2006 and 2007.
		3. The greatest percent change in the trade deficit from January to December was an increase of 28 percent in 2008.

The following scatter plot shows 12 points, one for each month of 2009. Each point represents the price of a single barrel of crude oil and the amount of crude oil, in thousands of barrels, imported to the United States during that month. The solid line is the regression line for the points. The dotted line connects the points representing January 2009 and December 2009.

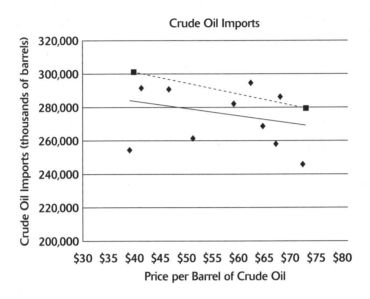

Use the choices provided to fill in the blanks in each of the following statements based on the information given by the graph.

4. The quantity (in thousands of barrels) of crude imported to the United States in 2009 was _____ (*positively, negatively, not*) correlated to the price of a barrel of crude.

5. As compared to the regression line, the line connecting the data points for January and December suggests a _____ (*slightly steeper, slightly flatter, significantly steeper, significantly flatter, equal*) decline in the quantity imported as the price per barrel increases.

Three sources of information are provided below. Examine each entry, and use the information in the sources to judge the validity of the statements that follow.

The following is an excerpt from a policy memo on Transit-Oriented Affordable Housing in the State of California.

There is a lack of supply in the housing market compared to the demand to occur due to projected population growth in the near future. The California Department of Housing and Community Development (HCD) expects the population of California to grow approximately 500,000 annually over the next decade. According to the Los Angeles Housing Department, the area's median income for a family of four is $59,500, while the median income for an individual is $41,560. Unfortunately, the California Association of Realtors claims that the minimum household income needed to purchase a median-priced home in Los Angeles County was more than $106,000. High rental costs add to further frustration of California residents. It is apparent that the high cost of living in California is not compensated appropriately by median wages. This dilemma is forcing an urban sprawl among California residents, leading to longer commutes.

With longer commutes, California residents are spending more time on the roads, rather than with their families. In 1990, the Southern California Association of Governments (SCAG) reported that the average work-trip travel time in Los Angeles was 23 minutes; they estimate that by 2020, it will increase to 29 minutes. This means that in 2020, with a total of 260 workdays in a year, Los Angeles residents will be spending 7,540 minutes, or about 5.2 days, a year on the road, travelling to work alone. This time can be minimized with the building of more transit-oriented affordable housing in California.

The lack of transit-oriented affordable housing in California would lead to traffic congestion due to further commutes; consequently, there would be an increase of environmental hazards and wasted time. As previously mentioned, the population in the state of California is expected to grow exponentially in the next decade. In Los Angeles, new residents may be forced to move into housing developments proposed for Antelope Valley or Riverside and San Bernardino counties; however, the further sprawl would have a tremendous effect on traffic and air quality. The Environmental Protection Agency claims that mobile sources, such as cars, are a major source of air pollution. Because of this, environmentalists are trying to encourage growth in smaller areas in an effort to prevent sprawl and preserve open space.

The following graph is based on data from the U.S. Census Public Use Microdata Sample, and breaks down the pool of commuters in the state of California into income levels.

Percentage of Commuters by Income Level

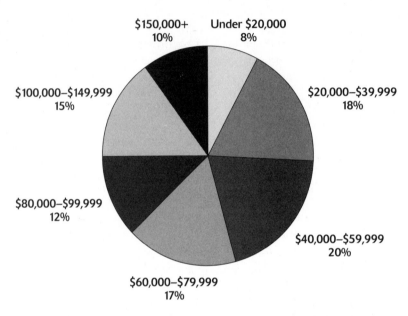

The following graph shows the percentage of workers choosing various options for their commute, and contrasts the responses for the United States as a whole with those for the state of California. Data is derived from the 2000 U.S. Census.

Commuter Options

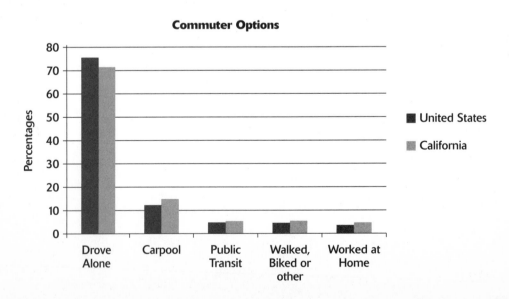

Consider each of the following statements. Does the information in the three sources support the inference as stated?

Yes	No	
		6. California commuters choose to drive alone less frequently than U. S. commuters as a whole, indicating that commuting time is not a significant factor in their decision.
		7. Because more than 70 percent of California commuters choose to drive alone, the environmental concerns that could follow from urban sprawl are a serious concern for the state.
		8. Because more than 50 percent of commuters are above the median income cited by the Housing Department, the concerns about housing are unfounded.

9. The best estimate of the percent of California commuters who can afford to buy a median-priced home in Los Angeles County is

   A. less than 25%.
   B. more than 25% but less than 45%.
   C. more than 45% but less than 65%.
   D. more than 65% but less than 85%.
   E. more than 85%.

10. A small business owner is considering two possible warehouse rentals. The riverfront location requires a security deposit of $16,000 and equal monthly payments for the course of a five-year lease. The downtown facility demands a security deposit of $25,000 and equal monthly payments over the course of a three-year lease. The business owner prefers the shorter lease and the downtown location, but is unwilling to invest more money over the three year period to achieve that. Determine the monthly rents for each location that will result in equal outlay over the first 36 months.

    In the table below, mark the rent for the riverfront warehouse and the downtown warehouse.

Riverfront	Downtown	
		$1,900
		$2,000
		$2,100
		$2,259
		$2,350
		$2,500

IF YOU FINISH BEFORE TIME IS CALLED, CHECK YOUR WORK ON THIS SECTION ONLY. DO NOT WORK ON ANY OTHER SECTION IN THE TEST.

Section 3: Quantitative

Time: 75 minutes

37 questions

Directions (1–22): Solve the problems and indicate the best answers. All given figures lie in a plane and are drawn accurately unless otherwise indicated. All numbers used are real.

1. Rebecca has twice as much money as Rachel. If Rebecca gives Rachel $60, then the two of them will have the same amount of money. How much money does Rebecca have?

   A. $60
   B. $90
   C. $120
   D. $180
   E. $240

2. Janet and Karen are meeting at a library to work on their math project. Because there are five libraries in town, they have decided to choose the library that would result in their traveling the smallest total distance. The accompanying scatter plot graph shows the distances that Karen would have to travel to go to each of the five libraries and the distances that Janet would have to travel to go to each of the five libraries. Which library should they choose?

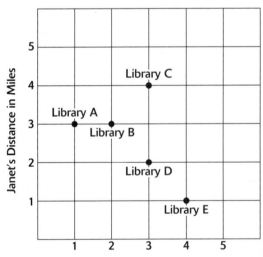

Distance in Miles from Library for Janet and Karen

   A. Library A
   B. Library B
   C. Library C
   D. Library D
   E. Library E

3. What is the arithmetic mean (average) of the set of consecutive integers $\{-2, -1, 0, 1, \ldots, 99, 100\}$?

   A. 47
   B. 49
   C. 50
   D. 51.5
   E. 53

4. If $\sqrt{x} = 4$, what is the value of x^2?

   A. 4
   B. 8
   C. 16
   D. 64
   E. 256

5. If the local post office only has three denominations of stamps available, 1¢ stamps, 10¢ stamps, and 20¢ stamps, how many different sets of stamps can be used to form 41¢?

   A. 4
   B. 5
   C. 8
   D. 9
   E. 10

6. If Michael drove from home to school at 30 miles per hour, and then drove from school back home using the same route at 20 miles per hour, what was his average speed in miles per hour for the round trip?

   A. 10
   B. 24
   C. 25
   D. 26
   E. 50

7. The distribution of a certain test is a normal distribution. If two standard deviations more than the mean is 88 and one standard deviation less than the mean is 76, what is the value of the mean?

   A. 78
   B. 80
   C. 82
   D. 84
   E. 86

8. The Cohen family consists of two parents and three children. If the average height of the five people in the family is 5 feet 8 inches, and the average height of the two parents is 5 feet 5 inches, what is the average height of the three children?

   A. 5 feet, 8.5 inches
   B. 5 feet, 9 inches
   C. 5 feet, 10 inches
   D. 5 feet, 11 inches
   E. 6 feet

9. What is the value of $\left(\sqrt{5} + 2\right)\left(2 - \sqrt{5}\right)$?

   A. −21
   B. −1
   C. 0
   D. 1
   E. 21

10. What is the value of $1 - \dfrac{1}{10} + \dfrac{1}{100} - \dfrac{1}{1,000}$?

   A. $\dfrac{91}{100}$
   B. $\dfrac{99}{100}$
   C. $\dfrac{900}{1,000}$
   D. $\dfrac{909}{1,000}$
   E. $\dfrac{98}{1,000}$

11. Katie, Cristen, Johnny, and Juliet have all been promoted to senior management positions in a company. They are to be assigned to four new offices, of which only one is a corner office with a panoramic view. How many different ways can the four of them be assigned to their new offices with either Cristen or Johnny having a corner office?

   A. 6
   B. 12
   C. 16
   D. 24
   E. 36

12. As part of the high school physical fitness program, each of the 180 students in a school was required to sign up for exactly one activity: soccer, baseball, table tennis, or volleyball. If half the students signed up for soccer, one-third signed up for baseball, and, of the remaining students, twice as many signed up for volleyball as signed up for table tennis, how many students signed up for table tennis?

   A. 5
   B. 10
   C. 15
   D. 20
   E. 30

13. Two rounds of auditions were being held to select 40 students for a new chorus that was being formed. In the first round of auditions, 30 students were selected, 80% of whom were girls. If 25% of the members of the chorus had to be boys, how many boys had to be selected in the second round of auditions?

   A. 2
   B. 3
   C. 4
   D. 8
   E. 10

14. If all the integers greater than or equal to 500 and less than or equal to 600 were written on a list, how many times would the digit 5 appear?

   A. 20
   B. 110
   C. 119
   D. 120
   E. 160

15. Mr. Cohen bought a box of individually wrapped chocolates and decided to give the chocolates to his students. If he gave each student 2 pieces of chocolate, 25 pieces would be left in the box. If he gave each student 3 pieces, 5 pieces would be left in the box. How many students are in Mr. Cohen's class?

   A. 6
   B. 15
   C. 20
   D. 25
   E. 30

16. If the kth term of a sequence is defined as $5k - 1$, what is the value of the smallest term greater than 100?

   A. 20
   B. 21
   C. 104
   D. 109
   E. 504

17. There are 30 cups of coffee on a table. If 16 have milk added, 14 have sugar added, and 10 have both milk and sugar added, how many cups of coffee have neither milk nor sugar added?

   A. 0
   B. 2
   C. 4
   D. 6
   E. 10

18. If you hire Mary's Car Service to drive you across town, you will be charged $10 plus an additional $2, for each $\frac{1}{4}$ mile. Which of the following represents the total number of dollars that you would be charged if the trip is n miles?

   A. $2n$
   B. $10 + 2n$
   C. $10 + 4n$
   D. $10 + 8n$
   E. $12n$

19. If $3^n + 3^n + 3^n = 9^6$, what is the value of n?

   A. 2
   B. 3
   C. 4
   D. 11
   E. 12

20. In a printing company, if one machine can print 600 copies in 12 hours, how long would it take to print 1,200 copies with three identical machines working together?

   A. 4
   B. 8
   C. 12
   D. 18
   E. 24

21. Starting from home, Mary drove 5 miles due east to Bill's house. She then drove 6 miles due south to Karen's house. Mary then drove 3 miles due east to Janet's house. What is the direct distance, in miles, between Mary's house and Janet's house?

   A. 4
   B. 8
   C. 10
   D. 14
   E. 16

22. Line l intersects $\overline{AB}$ and $\overline{BC}$ at D and E, respectively. What is the value of x?

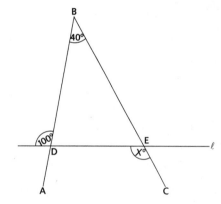

   A. 60
   B. 80
   C. 100
   D. 120
   E. 140

Directions (23–37): Each question is accompanied by two statements labeled (1) and (2). Decide whether the data provided in the statements are sufficient to answer the question, and then choose the correct answer choice. When a data sufficiency question asks for the value of a quantity, it is considered sufficient *only* if it is possible to determine exactly one numerical value for the quantity.

23. What is the value of $2x - y$?

   (1) $y = 2x + 1$
   (2) $2y - 4x = 2$

   A. Statement (1) *alone* is sufficient, but statement (2) alone is not sufficient.
   B. Statement (2) *alone* is sufficient, but statement (1) alone is not sufficient.
   C. *Both* statements *together* are sufficient, but *neither* statement *alone* is sufficient.
   D. *Each* statement *alone* is sufficient.
   E. Statements (1) and (2) *together* are *not* sufficient.

24. What is the area of square $ABCD$?

   (1) The perimeter of $ABCD$ is 12.
   (2) $BD = 3\sqrt{2}$.

   A. Statement (1) *alone* is sufficient, but statement (2) alone is not sufficient.
   B. Statement (2) *alone* is sufficient, but statement (1) alone is not sufficient.
   C. *Both* statements *together* are sufficient, but *neither* statement *alone* is sufficient.
   D. *Each* statement *alone* is sufficient.
   E. Statements (1) and (2) *together* are *not* sufficient.

25. Is the positive integer n divisible by 12?

   (1) n is divisible by 6.
   (2) n is divisible by 4.

   A. Statement (1) *alone* is sufficient, but statement (2) alone is not sufficient.
   B. Statement (2) *alone* is sufficient, but statement (1) alone is not sufficient.
   C. *Both* statements *together* are sufficient, but *neither* statement *alone* is sufficient.
   D. *Each* statement *alone* is sufficient.
   E. Statements (1) and (2) *together* are *not* sufficient.

26. The radius of a circle with center O is 4 and points A, B, C, and D are on circle O. Is $\overline{AB}$ a diameter of circle O?

   (1) $\overline{AB} \perp \overline{CD}$
   (2) $\overline{AB} = 8$

   A. Statement (1) *alone* is sufficient, but statement (2) alone is not sufficient.
   B. Statement (2) *alone* is sufficient, but statement (1) alone is not sufficient.
   C. *Both* statements *together* are sufficient, but *neither* statement *alone* is sufficient.
   D. *Each* statement *alone* is sufficient.
   E. Statements (1) and (2) *together* are *not* sufficient.

27. What is the mean of the set of numbers a_1, a_2, a_3, . . . , a_{20}?

   (1) The sum of $a_1 + a_2 + a_3 + \ldots + a_{20}$ is 100.
   (2) The standard deviation of the set is 2.

   A. Statement (1) *alone* is sufficient, but statement (2) alone is not sufficient.
   B. Statement (2) *alone* is sufficient, but statement (1) alone is not sufficient.
   C. *Both* statements *together* are sufficient, but *neither* statement *alone* is sufficient.
   D. *Each* statement *alone* is sufficient.
   E. Statements (1) and (2) *together* are *not* sufficient.

28. Is △*ABC* a right triangle?

   (1) $AB = 10$, $BC = 24$ and $AC = 26$

   (2) $m\angle A + m\angle C = 90°$

   A.   Statement (1) *alone* is sufficient, but statement (2) alone is not sufficient.

   B.   Statement (2) *alone* is sufficient, but statement (1) alone is not sufficient.

   C.   *Both* statements *together* are sufficient, but *neither* statement *alone* is sufficient.

   D.   *Each* statement *alone* is sufficient.

   E.   Statements (1) and (2) *together* are *not* sufficient.

29. In Karen's math class, there were four tests during the first semester. If the average of her first three tests was an 84, what was her average for all four tests?

   (1)   The grades for the first three tests were 80, 83, and 89.

   (2)   The grade for the fourth test was 92.

   A.   Statement (1) *alone* is sufficient, but statement (2) alone is not sufficient.

   B.   Statement (2) *alone* is sufficient, but statement (1) alone is not sufficient.

   C.   *Both* statements *together* are sufficient, but *neither* statement *alone* is sufficient.

   D.   *Each* statement *alone* is sufficient.

   E.   Statements (1) and (2) *together* are *not* sufficient.

30. If x is an integer, what is the value of x?

   (1) $y = x^2$

   (2) $y = x + 2$

   A.   Statement (1) *alone* is sufficient, but statement (2) alone is not sufficient.

   B.   Statement (2) *alone* is sufficient, but statement (1) alone is not sufficient.

   C.   *Both* statements *together* are sufficient, but *neither* statement *alone* is sufficient.

   D.   *Each* statement *alone* is sufficient.

   E.   Statements (1) and (2) *together* are *not* sufficient.

31. Is $3^{x+1} > 9$?

   (1) $3^x > 1$

   (2) $x < 1$

   A.   Statement (1) *alone* is sufficient, but statement (2) alone is not sufficient.

   B.   Statement (2) *alone* is sufficient, but statement (1) alone is not sufficient.

   C.   *Both* statements *together* are sufficient, but *neither* statement *alone* is sufficient.

   D.   *Each* statement *alone* is sufficient.

   E.   Statements (1) and (2) *together* are *not* sufficient.

32. What is the value of $x - y$?

   (1) $x^2 - y^2 = 9$

   (2) $x + y = 3$

   A.   Statement (1) *alone* is sufficient, but statement (2) alone is not sufficient.

   B.   Statement (2) *alone* is sufficient, but statement (1) alone is not sufficient.

   C.   *Both* statements *together* are sufficient, but *neither* statement *alone* is sufficient.

   D.   *Each* statement *alone* is sufficient.

   E.   Statements (1) and (2) *together* are *not* sufficient.

33. How many real roots does the equation $y = ax^2 + b$ have?

   (1) $a = 2$

   (2) $b = -8$

   A.   Statement (1) *alone* is sufficient, but statement (2) alone is not sufficient.

   B.   Statement (2) *alone* is sufficient, but statement (1) alone is not sufficient.

   C.   *Both* statements *together* are sufficient, but *neither* statement *alone* is sufficient.

   D.   *Each* statement *alone* is sufficient.

   E.   Statements (1) and (2) *together* are *not* sufficient.

34. If *V* is the volume of a cube with sides *S* what is the value of *V*?

(1) The total surface area of the cube is 24.

(2) $1 < S < 3$

A. Statement (1) *alone* is sufficient, but statement (2) alone is not sufficient.

B. Statement (2) *alone* is sufficient, but statement (1) alone is not sufficient.

C. *Both* statements *together* are sufficient, but *neither* statement *alone* is sufficient.

D. *Each* statement *alone* is sufficient.

E. Statements (1) and (2) *together* are *not* sufficient.

35. An urn contains 7 red balls and 12 blue balls. If *x* balls are removed from the urn, and afterwards a ball is picked at random from the urn, what is the probability of picking a red ball?

(1) $x = 3$

(2) After *x* balls are removed, the ratio of red balls to blue balls is 3 to 5.

A. Statement (1) *alone* is sufficient, but statement (2) alone is not sufficient.

B. Statement (2) *alone* is sufficient, but statement (1) alone is not sufficient.

C. *Both* statements *together* are sufficient, but *neither* statement *alone* is sufficient.

D. *Each* statement *alone* is sufficient.

E. Statements (1) and (2) *together* are *not* sufficient.

36. If *n* is 20% of 50% of *x*, what is the value of *n*?

(1) $\frac{2}{3}x = 12$

(2) $\frac{3}{2}x = 27$

A. Statement (1) *alone* is sufficient, but statement (2) alone is not sufficient.

B. Statement (2) *alone* is sufficient, but statement (1) alone is not sufficient.

C. *Both* statements *together* are sufficient, but *neither* statement *alone* is sufficient.

D. *Each* statement *alone* is sufficient.

E. Statements (1) and (2) *together* are *not* sufficient.

37. If *k* is a number of the set {8, 15, 20, 25, 52}, what is the value of *k*?

(1) *k* is a multiple of 5.

(2) *k* is an even number.

A. Statement (1) *alone* is sufficient, but statement (2) alone is not sufficient.

B. Statement (2) *alone* is sufficient, but statement (1) alone is not sufficient.

C. *Both* statements *together* are sufficient, but *neither* statement *alone* is sufficient.

D. *Each* statement *alone* is sufficient.

E. Statements (1) and (2) *together* are *not* sufficient.

IF YOU FINISH BEFORE TIME IS CALLED, CHECK YOUR WORK ON THIS SECTION ONLY. DO NOT WORK ON ANY OTHER SECTION IN THE TEST.

Section 4: Verbal

Time: 75 minutes

41 questions

Directions (1–14): These questions test your ability to recognize correctness and effectiveness of expression. In each sentence, part of the sentence or the entire sentence is underlined. Underneath each sentence, you'll find five ways of phrasing the underlined material. Choice A is the same as the original sentence in the question; the other four choices are different. If you think the original sentence is correct as written, select Choice A; if not, carefully consider choices B, C, D, and E and select the one you think is the best.

In making your selection, follow the requirements of standard written English. Carefully consider the grammar, *diction* (word choice), sentence construction, and punctuation of each sentence. When you make your choice, select the most effective sentence—the one that is clear and precise, without any awkwardness or ambiguity.

1. While the Tokyo String Quartet has been performing together for almost 40 years, its their latest incarnation is renowned for <u>a warm richness of tone, an elegant phrasing, and their playing avant-garde pieces.</u>

   A. a warm richness of tone, an elegant phrasing, and their playing avant-garde pieces.
   B. a warm richness of tone, an elegant phrasing, and their being willing to play an avant-garde repertoire.
   C. using a warm richness of tone, having an elegant phrasing, and their willingness to play avant-garde pieces.
   D. a warm richness of tone, their phrasing elegantly, and their playing avant-garde pieces.
   E. a warm richness of tone, an elegant phrasing, and an avant-garde repertoire.

2. <u>Each of the scientists involved in studying the brain have found that memory is stored in neurons</u> and may be retrieved by stimulating the same neurons that fired when the recalled event first occurred.

   A. Each of the scientists involved in studying the brain have found that memory is stored in neurons
   B. Each of the scientists who studies the brain have found that memory is stored in neurons
   C. Each of the scientists involved in studying the brain has found that memory is stored in neurons
   D. Each scientist involved in studying the brain have found that memory will be stored in neurons
   E. Scientists involved in studying the brain has found that memory is stored in neurons

3. Usually busy transporting needed supplies to international sites, <u>as the demand for fuel has declined the huge supertankers filled with oil are currently floating offshore.</u>

    A.   as the demand for fuel has declined the huge supertankers filled with oil are currently floating offshore.

    B.   and floating offshore, the huge supertankers are filled with oil as the demand for fuel has declined.

    C.   huge supertankers filled with oil are currently floating offshore as the demand for fuel has declined.

    D.   huge supertankers, as the demand for fuel has declined, filled with oil are currently floating offshore.

    E.   the decline in the demand for fuel has left huge supertankers filled with oil currently floating offshore.

4. <u>The birds of New Zealand had no natural predators, wings became unnecessary, and many varieties, including the kiwi and the kakapo parrot, became flightless.</u>

    A.   The birds of New Zealand had no natural predators, wings became unnecessary, and many varieties, including the kiwi and the kakapo parrot, became flightless.

    B.   The birds of New Zealand had no natural predators; wings becoming unnecessary and many varieties, including the kiwi and the kakapo parrot, becoming flightless.

    C.   Because the birds of New Zealand had no natural predators, wings are becoming unnecessary, and many varieties, including the kiwi and the kakapo parrot, are becoming flightless.

    D.   Since the birds of New Zealand had no natural predators; wings became unnecessary and many varieties, including the kiwi and the kakapo parrot, became flightless.

    E.   Because the birds of New Zealand had no natural predators, wings became unnecessary, and many varieties, including the kiwi and the kakapo parrot, became flightless.

5. To portray an accurate portrait of deceased rapper Notorious B.I.G. for a documentary film, fellow rapper Jamal Woolard learned everything he could about the murdered singer, memorizing the words to all his songs, studying videotapes of his mannerisms, and he worked closely with acting coaches to capture the subtleties of character.

   A. fellow rapper Jamal Woolard learned everything he could about the murdered singer, memorizing the words to all his songs, studying videotapes of his mannerisms, and he worked closely with acting coaches to capture the subtleties of character.

   B. fellow rapper Jamal Woolard learned everything he could about the murdered singer, memorizing the words to all his songs, studying videotapes of his mannerisms, and he was working closely with acting coaches to capture the subtleties of character.

   C. fellow rapper Jamal Woolard is learning everything he could about the murdered singer, memorizing the words to all his songs, studying videotapes of his mannerisms, and he worked closely with acting coaches to capture the subtleties of character.

   D. and to learn everything he could about the murdered singer, fellow rapper Jamal Woolard is memorizing the words to all his songs, studying videotapes of his mannerisms, and he worked closely with acting coaches to capture the subtleties of character.

   E. fellow rapper Jamal Woolard learned everything he could about the murdered singer, memorizing the words to all his songs, studying videotapes of his mannerisms, and working closely with acting coaches to capture the subtleties of character.

6. Encouraged by the government to develop alternative-energy vehicles, an energy-efficient electric car will be available to consumers by 2011 by many of the major automobile companies who are committed to creating it.

   A. Encouraged by the government to develop alternative-energy vehicles, an energy-efficient electric car will be available to consumers by 2011 by many of the major automobile companies who are committed to creating it.

   B. Encouraged by the government to develop alternative-energy vehicles, many of the major automobile companies who are committed to creating it, an energy-efficient electric car will be available to consumers by 2011.

   C. Encouraged by the government to develop alternative-energy vehicles, many of the major automobile companies are committed to creating an energy-efficient electric car that will be available to consumers by 2011.

   D. Many of the major automobile companies are encouraged by the government to develop alternative-energy vehicles and as a result they are committed to creating an energy-efficient electric car that will be available to consumers by 2011.

   E. Being encouraged by the government to develop alternative-energy vehicles, many of the major automobile companies are committed to creating it, an energy-efficient electric car available to consumers by 2011.

7. The world's best-known photographer of Native Americans, a powerful and evocative collection of Edward S. Curtis is available for sale in New York.

   A. The world's best-known photographer of Native Americans, a powerful and evocative collection of Edward S. Curtis is available for sale in New York.
   B. The world's best-known photographer of Native Americans, Edward S. Curtis's powerful and evocative collection is available for sale in New York.
   C. Edward S. Curtis's powerful and evocative collection are available for sale in New York, and he is the world's best-known photographer of Native Americans.
   D. The world's best-known photographer of Native Americans, Edward S. Curtis's collection, powerful and evocative, is available for sale in New York.
   E. A powerful and evocative collection of photographs by Edward S. Curtis, the world's best-known photographer of Native Americans, is available for sale in New York.

8. The wall gives the cell its shape and surrounds the cytoplasmic membrane, protecting them from the environment, helping to anchor appendages, which originate in the cytoplasm membrane and protrude through the wall to the outside.

   A. protecting them from the environment, helping to anchor appendages, which originate
   B. protecting them from the environment, help to anchor appendages, which originates
   C. protecting them from the environment and helping to anchor appendages, which originates
   D. protecting it from the environment and helping to anchor appendages, which originate
   E. protecting it from the environment to help it to anchor appendages, which originates

9. With at least $120 billion per year spent on outsourcing and much more at stake when considering productivity improvements and savings, ensuring that outsourcing works has become a top priority for management professionals.

   A. With at least $120 billion per year spent on outsourcing and much more at stake when considering
   B. To spend $120 billion per year spent on outsourcing, and much more on
   C. Spending least $120 billion per year on outsourcing, and much more at stake when considering
   D. Having at least $120 billion per year spent on outsourcing, and much more at stake when considering
   E. Needing to spend at least $120 billion per year on outsourcing, and much more at stake when considering

10. Faced with unemployment, lower home equity, and shrinking 410(k) portfolios, many Americans are not only struggling to keep up with payments, with some relying on credit cards to carry them over difficult financial times.

    A. many Americans are not only struggling to keep up with payments, with some relying
    B. it is many Americans who are struggling to keep up with payments, some even rely
    C. many Americans who are struggling keeping up with payments, relying
    D. many Americans who are struggling to keep up with payments rely
    E. are many Americans struggling to keep up with payments, with some relying

11. Some venture capitalists, despite the appeal of clean energy, is putting more effort into developing technology specifically geared to improve the efficacy of existing energy sources.

    A. Some venture capitalists, despite the appeal of clean energy, is putting more effort into developing technology specifically geared to improve the efficacy of existing energy sources.

    B. Some venture capitalists resist the appeal of clean energy, are putting more effort into developing technology specifically geared to improve the efficacy of existing energy sources.

    C. Despite the appeal of clean energy, some venture capitalists are putting more effort into developing technology specifically geared to improve the efficacy of existing energy sources.

    D. Some venture capitalists, consider the appeal of clean energy, are putting more effort into developing technology specifically geared to improve the efficacy of existing energy sources.

    E. Putting more effort into developing technology specifically geared to improve the efficacy of existing energy sources is being done by some venture capitalists, despite the appeal of clean energy.

12. That increased income from advertisements was necessary to defray the losses incurred by the magazine's decline in readership quickly became apparent to the publisher.

    A. That increased income from advertisements

    B. Increasing the income from advertisements

    C. To increase income from advertisements

    D. Increasing advertising income

    E. They felt increased income from advertisements

13. An annual increase in emission of global warming gases, from 2.9 percent to 3.1 percent, have been reported in several Asian countries, particularly in the coal sector.

    A. from 2.9 percent to 3.1 percent have been reported in several Asian countries, particularly in the coal sector.

    B. particularly in the coal sector, from 2.9 percent to 3.1 percent, have been reported in several Asian countries.

    C. particularly in the coal sector, from 2.9 percent to 3.1 percent, has been reported in several Asian countries.

    D. from 2.9 percent to 3.1 percent being reported particularly in the coal sector in several Asian countries.

    E. from 2.9 percent to 3.1 percent have been reported, particularly in the coal sector, in several Asian countries.

14. The Seaming Sisters, a highly respected women's apparel store known as a purveyor of clothing of rare quality—in style, in workmanship, in fit—which has been a family-operated business for 65 years.

    A. a purveyor of clothing of rare quality—in style, in workmanship, in fit—which has been a family-operated business for 65 years.

    B. a purveyor of clothing of rare quality—in style, in workmanship, in fit—has been a family-operated business for 65 years.

    C. a purveyor of clothing of rare quality not only in style, in workmanship, and fit, but also has been a family-operated business for 65 years.

    D. being a purveyor of clothing of rare quality—in style, in workmanship, in fit—which has been a family-operated business for 65 years.

    E. a purveyor of clothing of rare quality, in style, in workmanship, in fit; which has been a family-operated business for 65 years.

Directions (15–28): These questions are based on the content of the accompanying passages. Carefully read each passage in this section and answer the questions that follow each passage. Answer the questions based on the content of the passages—both what is stated and what is implied in the passages.

Questions 15–17 are based on the following passage.

Network marketing is a business that relies heavily on communication, so every advance in communication technology has a positive effect on its bottom line. These advances have made network marketing an international business, moving billions of dollars of products and services each year.

When the industry began, the telephone was the only form of instant communication. The advent of fax machines, conference calling, and computers in the early 1970s and 1980s were significant factors in the growth of the industry. These technologies lowered the cost of getting information from one place and person to another and sped up the time needed to get this information to the public.

In the 1990s, fax-on-demand, prerecorded conference calling, cellular phones, and portable computers became increasingly popular, less expensive, and faster than ever, greatly aiding the growth of network marketing. But all of these advancements combined don't equal the impact of the Internet on the networking industry. The Internet is making network marketing a powerful and profitable business force in the 21st century.

One major advantage of the Internet is the implementation of targeted e-mailing. With a single click of a button, a sender can transmit a message to a prearranged list of recipients, all of whom have in some way been targeted as potential clients. The sender can broadcast new products or services, publicize important information, and set up a system for ordering products. In addition to its advantage of instantaneous speed, e-mail is inexpensive and accessible to most households in the United States.

Passage adapted from Network Your Way to Millions *by Russ Paley*

15. The primary purpose of this passage is to

  A. tout the advantages of using technology to create new products that will appeal to a select target customer.

  B. chronicle the role of new communication technology in a business that relies on networking.

  C. introduce the concept of network marketing as a viable and profitable alternative to Internet sales.

  D. qualify the generalization that innovative communication systems have expedited sales of new products.

  E. define and dispel the conception of network marketing as a competitive force in the commercial sector.

16. It can be inferred from the passage that

  A. transactions that involve communication technology can increase consumer insecurity.

  B. the government has adopted a laissez-faire policy toward businesses that derive more than 40 percent of their incomes from Internet sales.

  C. it is not fiscally responsible for a networking business to spend more than 30 percent of its budget on new product development.

  D. the identification of a specific target consumer is expedited by more efficient communication technology.

  E. the rate at which a company incurs debt can be slowed by reducing reliance on fossil fuels, a cost-cutting measure that will markedly reduce energy demands.

17. With which of the following statements would the author most likely agree?

    A. More than any other piece of technology, the fax machine has revolutionized network marketing.

    B. Those companies that rely on print material for communication will incur increased costs in the 21st century.

    C. The impact of the Internet on the communication industry is insignificant when compared to the combined effects of the cellular phone and the fax-on-demand.

    D. Expanding a business to include international sales is a risk during a period of economic decline.

    E. The growth of the networking industry increased exponentially as communication technology evolved.

Questions 18–21 are based on the following passage.

When Antonie van Leeuwenhoek in 1675 first discovered bacteria, he thought they were animals. Indeed, under a microscope, many of them bear a close resemblance to those minute worms found in vinegar that are known as "vinegar-eels." The idea that they belonged to the animal kingdom continued to hold ground until after the middle of the 19th century; but with the improvement in microscopes, a more thorough study became possible, and they were classified as vegetable. Now scientists classify them as neither plant nor animal, but as prokaryotes, single-cell organisms with no internal structures.

So far as structure is concerned, the bacteria stand on the lowest plane of life. The single individual is but a single cell composed of a protoplasmic body, which is surrounded by a thin membrane that separates it from neighboring cells that are alike in form and size.

In size, the bacteria are among the smallest organisms that are known to exist. Relatively, there is considerable difference in size between the different species, yet in absolute amount, this is so slight as to require the highest powers of the microscope to detect it. Bacteria are measured in units called micrometers, usually called microns. The average size of bacteria is 1 micron. One millimeter is equal to 1,000 microns; 25,000 microns make up 1 inch. It is difficult to comprehend such minute measurements, but if 100 individual bacteria could be placed side by side, their total thickness would not equal that of a single sheet of paper. Each cell has a large surface area–to–volume ratio, and this determines how fast substances can enter and leave. Nutrients can enter, and wastes can leave these tiny cells very rapidly.

Bacteria are often divided into aerobic bacteria, which require oxygen to live, and anaerobic bacteria, which die when exposed to oxygen. Bacterial infections are often caused by toxins released by bacteria. Antibiotics have been used to fight bacterial infections, but some disease-causing organisms have become resistant to drug therapy. Because they are adaptable, bacteria have developed ways to resist the effects of antibiotics. Adding to the problem, the public has a tendency to overuse these drugs and pressure physicians into over-prescribing them.

18. Which of the following characteristics of bacteria are discussed in the passage?

   A. Thickness of the cell wall and reproductive processes
   B. Vegetative properties of bacteria and structure of the nuclei
   C. The variety of internal structures and the history of the discovery of bacteria
   D. Surface area–to–volume ratio and cell size
   E. Drug-resistant adaptations and locomotive structures

19. Which of the following can be inferred from the passage?

   A. The author extrapolates from Antonie van Leeuwenhoek's findings that prokaryotes have characteristics of both plant and animal cells.
   B. If scientists can discover a method of sealing prokaryotic cell membranes to make them impermeable, antibiotic use can be reduced.
   C. Because bacteria range in size from 0.5 millimeter to 1 millimeter, most are not visible to the naked eye.
   D. The larger the surface area–to–volume ratio of an organism, the less permeable the membrane.
   E. The nucleus of the bacteria cell is a membrane-enclosed organelle that acts as the control center for cell functions.

20. All of the following are true according to the information in the passage *except:*

   A. The development of drug-resistant bacteria is a corollary of over-prescribing antibiotic drugs to treat illnesses that may or may not be bacterial infections.
   B. Structural differences between plant cells and animal cells led biologists to create a new classification for single-cell organisms.
   C. The development of high-powered microscopes uncovered sub-cellular disclosures that spawned a revision of prior classifications.
   D. The environment that is conducive to the growth of one type of bacteria may cause the death of others.
   E. Prokaryotes evolved from proto-organisms that had well-formed nuclei and discrete internal structures.

21. The main purpose of this passage is to

   A. trace the history of bacteria from primeval times to modern-day mutations.
   B. ridicule the fallacious thinking that led early scientists to misclassify single-cell organisms.
   C. discuss a plan for the investigation of the role bacteria play in causing infections.
   D. challenge a popular theory about the evolution of prokaryotes.
   E. present an overview from original misconception to modern understanding.

Questions 22–23 are based on the following passage.

Of no English poet, except Shakespeare, can we say with approximate truth that he is the poet of all times. The subjective breath of their own epoch dims the mirror that they hold up to nature. Missing by their limitation the highest universality, they can only be understood in their setting. It adds but little to our knowledge of Shakespeare's work to regard him as the great Elizabethan; there is nothing temporary in his dramas, except petty incidents and external trappings—so truly did he dwell amidst the elements constituting man in every age and clime. But this cannot be said of any other poet, not even of Chaucer or Spenser, far less of Milton or Pope or Wordsworth. In their cases, the artistic form and the material, the idea and its expression, the beauty and the truth, are to some extent separable. We can distinguish in Milton between the puritanic theology, which is per-ishable, and the art whose beauty can never pass away. The former fixes his kinship with his own age, gives him a definite place in the evolution of English life; the latter is independent of time, a thing that has supreme worth in itself.

22. In the passage, the assertion that "there is nothing temporary in his dramas" is best understood to mean that

 A. Shakespeare's great tragedies focus on leaders whose downfall was brought about through their own tragic flaws.

 B. the themes of Shakespeare's works are universal and require no understanding of the Elizabethan setting to be meaningful.

 C. the Elizabeth Age, often called the Golden Age of Drama, lasted but a few years.

 D. the great poets of the Elizabethan Age, although popular in their time, are no longer read with the same intensity as when they were alive.

 E. poets who reflect the specific conception of beauty and truth in their lifetimes will stand the test of time.

23. The author mentions Chaucer, Spenser, Milton, Pope, and Wordsworth as examples of poets

 A. who are notable for their puritanical philosophy.

 B. whose work has transcended the time period in which they lived.

 C. whose artistic form is completely inseparable from their content.

 D. who are linked inextricably with the epoch in which they lived.

 E. whose talents are diminished by comparison to those of Shakespeare.

Questions 24–28 are based on the following passage.

So what exactly do we mean when we say "environmental markets" and how are these markets going to impact the business landscape? First, the basics: Anytime a unit of exchange arises from an underlying activity that is perceived to benefit the environment by either the buyer of that unit or the governing body that created the units of exchange, the main ingredients of an environmental market are present. In a cap-and-trade system, the governing body places a cap on the total amount of air or water pollution that may be emitted by issuing an equivalent number of allowances, denominated in units of pollution. These allowances may be issued by the government to the business entities that are regulated by the program in amounts similar to their expected production, to lessen the economic impact, or those entities may have to purchase the allowances from the government in an auction. At the end of each specified period, usually a year, the business entities will have to surrender a number of allowances, or permits, equal to their generation of pollution during the period. As the governing entity reduces the supply of allowances available to the market in each subsequent year, the price will go up unless the regulated businesses invest in technologies that will reduce their pollution per unit of output, thereby reducing their demand and the overall market demand for allowances. Environmental markets that are not set up as cap-and-trade markets in the United States include the state-level markets for renewable energy credits, which are granted to producers of renewable energy and given value because utilities must purchase an amount of these credits determined by the state, and the voluntary market for greenhouse-gas emissions, in which credits arising from a unit of greenhouses gas emissions avoided are granted to owners of qualifying project activities by accredited third-party verifiers and sold to voluntary buyers, primarily to conform with the buyer's goal of becoming "carbon neutral." Companies can claim to be carbon neutral if they purchase an amount of these credits for avoided greenhouse-gas emissions equivalent to the total amount of emissions they produce. This is increasingly important from a public relations and corporate responsibility perspective in the United States, even in the absence of federal legislation governing greenhouse-gas emissions.

Adapted and reprinted with permission of the author, Jonathan Rappe.

24. When the author uses the word *allowances,* he is referring to

   A. the amount of pollution an entity is permitted to emit.
   B. the funds a business must set aside to pay for pollution cleanup.
   C. the total government penalty issued to those companies that pollute the air and water.
   D. the economic impact of the reduction of emissions in a given year.
   E. a system by which allowable pollution units are increased as pollution increases.

25. The author believes that it is important for a company to become carbon neutral because

   I. The company will benefit from a good public image.
   II. The company will demonstrate its awareness of accountability.
   III. The company will be complying with government regulations.

   A. I only
   B. II only
   C. I and II
   D. I and III
   E. I, II, and III

26. The author of this passage most likely would agree that

   A. government regulations that control allowable greenhouse-gas emissions are too stringent.

   B. the United States has a history of refusing to address environmental problems, a position that will adversely affect the growth of business in this country.

   C. renewable resources in the United States are so abundant as to make regulations that govern their use superfluous.

   D. in the future, more value will be placed on any activities that lessen the impact of development on natural systems.

   E. the realistic goal of the environmental movement should be to completely eliminate air and water pollution in the United States.

27. Which of the following, if true, would most weaken the author's argument?

   A. Even those companies that invest in pollution-reducing technologies will see a substantial increase in their demand for allowances.

   B. Insufficient data exist, as of yet, to make conclusive claims about the efficacy of "green" programs in the corporate sector.

   C. Researchers attempting to quantify the less-tangible benefits of green construction believe investment in water technologies and a renewed interest in solar-energy innovation will reward Wall Street investors.

   D. A major U.S. bank recently announced that its new building will employ a heat exchange system that will gather heat from groundwater and use it to help heat the building in the winter.

   E. The Climate Security Act of 2008 proposes a reduction in allowable carbon emissions but will allow a facility to use the allowances itself, sell them on a public carbon allowance exchange, or transfer them to another company for a negotiated price.

28. The author's attitude toward the companies that "claim to be carbon neutral" can best be described as

   A. skeptical of the validity of their claim in light of continued noncompliance with government regulations.

   B. indignant toward their refusal to change policy from abusive practices to voluntary compliance.

   C. cautiously appreciative of their willingness to accept responsibility in the absence of government regulations.

   D. totally detached and dismissive, as he rejects any arguments that run counter to his position.

   E. resigned, as he accepts the postponement of the companies' acquiescence to the government regulations currently in effect in the United States.

Directions (29–41): Analyze the situation in each question and select the answer that is the best response to the question.

Questions 29–30 are based on the following passage.

As the price of fossil fuels rises in response to increasing demands, ecologically responsible scientists are looking for alternative sources of energy. Wind turbines may be the answer. Currently, wind power provides about 1.5 percent of electricity use in the United States. However, unlike generating plants that use fossil fuels, which can have consistent output, wind turbines are naturally limited by the highly variable properties of wind. Still, some countries, notably Denmark, are deriving 15 percent to 20 percent of their power from wind turbines. Especially appealing are the negligible fuel costs and low maintenance needed to run the turbines. Wind energy will become the international power source of the 21st century.

29. The conclusion in the passage depends on which of the following assumptions?

   A. A forecasting system that predicts the velocity of available wind has proven to be a boon to countries now depending on wind energy.

   B. Power transmission from offshore turbines is generally through undersea cable, which is more expensive to install than cable on land.

   C. Around the world, governments are increasingly interested in renewable energy that uses local resources and reduces greenhouse-gas emissions.

   D. Wind power generates three categories of environmental impacts—visual impacts, noise pollution, and wildlife impacts—all of which vary from site to site.

   E. The normal way of prospecting for wind-power sites is to directly look for trees or vegetation that are permanently deformed by the prevailing winds.

30. The conclusion in the argument would be most weakened if it were true that

   A. wind turbines can be utilized in offshore installations where the winds are constant.

   B. winds in zones that are within 3 kilometers of a shoreline share wind-speed characteristics of both onshore winds and offshore winds.

   C. wind power is the world's fastest-growing electricity-generation technology because wind is an inexhaustible and renewable resource.

   D. because wind turbines are often mounted on the top of tall towers in rural areas, they can be seen for a long distance.

   E. because wind is an intermittent resource, providing power only when it blows, it is unreliable as a source of constant energy.

Questions 31–32 are based on the following passage.

To promote its new product, an over-the-counter calcium supplement, Wellco can sign with G Publications, a company that puts out one high-fashion magazine, two sports magazines, and one car-enthusiast magazine, for two-thirds the cost of signing with H Publications, which has only one print medium, a women's health and beauty magazine targeted at women ages 40 to 65. Because signing with G Publications will get its advertisement into four publications (versus one with H Publications) and will cost less, Wellco has decided to use G Publications.

31. Which of the following, if true, would most support the Wellco decision to sign with G Publications rather than H Publications?

A. The calcium supplement is designed to compensate for the loss of calcium in bones, which occurs most frequently in women ages 45 to 60 who, surveys show, are most influenced by magazine articles in publications that emphasize women's health issues.

B. According to medical authorities, the preferred way for women of all ages to get adequate calcium is through a healthy, well-balanced diet, rather than through dietary supplements.

C. Magazine advertising can be more expensive than other advertising, but it's a highly effective way of promoting products or services, because people often save magazines and reread them multiple times or pass them on to friends, allowing for additional exposure to advertisements.

D. Studies show that an effective marketing technique to increase revenue from sales of a new product is to scatter an intended message through multiple diffuse outlets rather than to limit focus and target a specific audience.

E. Because they spend billions of dollars annually on advertising, many product owners have a say in the content of the magazine in which they place ads, even stipulating what may or may not be included in a particular edition.

32. Which of the following, if true, would most undermine the Wellco decision?

    A. Because of the staggering diversity of magazines available, it is crucial for those with limited advertising budgets to identify a target market using up-to-date demographic and psychographic information.

    B. Because buyers have unprecedented access to information, they form a group of more informed consumers who are prepared to evaluate new products with discerning eyes.

    C. Although the initial cost of placing advertisements in specialty magazines may be much higher than blanket advertising in several publications, specialty magazines tend to be more thoroughly read and attended to by a select audience and, thus, are cost-effective.

    D. Developing brand loyalty is a powerful goal of advertising, because advertising is often the largest expense of most marketing strategies.

    E. The right type of advertising strategically placed in the right magazine can boost a magazine's sales as much as 20 percent.

33. The Classy Car Manufacturer has a plan to include automatic fire extinguishers in all the new models. Although the installation of the extinguishers will cost the company $1,000 and reduce its profit accordingly, the extinguisher is worth the cost in saved lives because it will automatically deploy when the air bags are triggered by an impact in a collision. According to the company's calculations, fires from accidents can be contained in less than a minute after the accident by the automatic extinguisher, an action that will greatly reduce the total number of deaths and injuries from car fires each year.

Which of the following would most seriously weaken the conclusion?

    A. Because the forward motion of the vehicle will force air into the engine and increase the intensity of the fire, the car must be stopped before the extinguisher can be deployed.

    B. Adding safety features to new cars increases their appeal to consumers who seek to reduce risks.

    C. Although some air bags have failed to deploy in front-impact collisions, statistics show that air bags have reduced deaths in front-impact collisions by 30 percent.

    D. The largest percentage of automobile fires that result in injuries (77 percent) is caused by poor maintenance rather than by accidents.

    E. The technology used to reduce gas consumption is a safety benefit, because slower-moving vehicles have lower crash rates.

34. Consumers who purchase big-ticket luxury goods want to feel exclusive when they shop. Therefore, a retailer who spends huge sums for furniture, artwork, and accessories to create an opulent setting for his or her products is making a wise decision because

   A. even those who are willing to spend extravagantly on purchases of luxury goods like to feel that they are getting merchandise at a discounted price.

   B. in an economic slump, fewer customers are willing to pay exorbitant prices, so luxury-goods retailers must attract more middle-income consumers who are looking for bargains.

   C. the growth of niche brands is helping to cultivate the growth of the luxury market.

   D. an atmosphere of elegance increases the sensation of acquiring something few others can afford, which feeds the aura of superiority desired by many affluent consumers.

   E. the luxury retailer is offering the consumer a product the quality of which is far superior to that offered by mass markets.

35. The government has hired a construction company to build affordable housing for low-income families. One of the conditions required by the government is that the homes be built so that the families will be able to afford to maintain them. The planners are attempting to make the homes as energy efficient as possible, using materials that will keep down heating costs. They are also taking into consideration the laws of physics: The rate of heat loss through a wall is directly proportional to its area and its thermal conductivity. It is inversely proportional to its thickness.

Which of the following would be the best construction plan?

   A. Build apartments with small rooms using inexpensive $\frac{1}{4}$-inch-thick plywood walls that are highly conductive.

   B. Build medium-size houses with one large all-purpose room with 1-inch-thick walls made of semi-conductive sheet rock.

   C. Build apartments with small rooms with 1-inch nonconductive plaster walls.

   D. Build apartments with large rooms using $\frac{1}{2}$-inch-thick nonconductive plaster walls.

   E. Build small houses with sliding fabric panel walls that can be reconfigured into multiple rooms.

36. Drug M, the usual protocol for the treatment of osteoporosis, is administered every three months because the effect of the drug leaves the patient's bloodstream at a rate of 1 percent each day. The Wellness Pharmaceutical Company has developed a new product, Drug P, to treat osteoporosis. This medication is designed to be administered only once a year, because the effect of this drug dissipates at a rate of 0.36 percent each day.

Assuming that all of the following are true, a physician would be more likely to prescribe Drug M rather than Drug P under all of the following conditions *except:*

A. The cost of administering Drug P is approximately $160 per dose; the cost of Drug M is $28 per dose.

B. Studies have shown that patient compliance is directly proportional to the frequency of dosage.

C. The primary side effect of both Drug M and Drug P is bone pain, which is most severe in the first 48 hours after the drug is administered.

D. Although there is substantial data confirming the efficacy of Drug M, no data is available on the long-term benefits of Drug P.

E. Doctors are reimbursed $35 by insurance companies or Medicare for each office visit at which any osteoporosis medication is dispensed.

37. For years, scientists who studied the laws of physics depended on two major theories to explain the physical properties of the universe: relativity, which deals with the universe on a large scale, and quantum mechanics, which deals with the smallest particles of the physical world. These theories, however, presented a problem for physicists because they are incompatible: The universe does not consist of only either large parts or small parts; thus, to have two sets of laws makes no sense. The study of physics had reached a roadblock until development of super-string theory resolved the dilemma.

In order for super-string theory to have been a viable reconciliation of the impasse, which of the following must be true?

A. The physical laws governing the universe must rely solely on the size of the system under consideration.

B. Subatomic particles like quarks and fermions exist outside the realm of gravity, upon which relativity rests.

C. As the universe expands, the laws of relativity expand to encompass stars, the universe, and whole galaxies.

D. At its most fundamental level, the universe dissolves into mathematical equations that can only be solved using quantum mechanics.

E. Super-string theory must propound a set of laws that work for both the large elements of the universe and the most minute.

38. A local hospital uses two brands of equal-quality baby formula to feed infants: Formula X and Formula Z. Babies fed Formula X had an average weight gain of 8 ounces each month, while babies fed Formula Z gained an average of 6.5 ounces each month.

Which of the following best explains the discrepancy in weight gain?

  A. Formula Z is a hypoallergenic formula designed especially for babies who have compromised digestive systems and disorders that hinder their ability to absorb nutrients.

  B. Formula Z is supplied in a ready-to-use bottle, while Formula X is a concentrated powder that must be mixed with water.

  C. The average weight of babies fed Formula X is 7 pounds 2 ounces, while the average weight of babies fed Formula Z is 6 pounds 8 ounces.

  D. In contrast to babies fed formula, babies who are breast-fed gained an average of 7.4 ounces each month.

  E. More Formula Z than Formula X is exported to third-world countries to feed children who are malnourished.

39. The school nurse in Quizzer School District recently noted a decrease in the number of flu cases reported by parents. She attributed this decrease to a new campaign in the school that put tissue boxes in every classroom and encouraged students to wash their hands more thoroughly and frequently.

Which of the following, if true, most weakens the conclusion of the school nurse?

  A. An epidemic of flu 10 years earlier infected almost two out of every three households in the community.

  B. The tissues distributed by the school have a middle layer specially treated with antibacterial and antiviral agents.

  C. Because of better countywide precautions, county health officials do not expect an increase in cases of flu this year.

  D. Students in the district have been taught to sing "Happy Birthday to You" two times while they wash their hands to ensure that they are washing thoroughly.

  E. County health officials have sent to every household a pamphlet comparing the specific symptoms of flu to those of the common cold.

40. Velocardiofacial Syndrome (VCFS) is a syndrome that affects 1 in 2,000 live births. It is caused by a partial deletion of chromosome 22. Included in its effects are 180 possible symptoms involving every system in the body. Among the most common symptoms are cardiac abnormalities, distinctive facial structure, and palate deformities. The National VCFS Organization is lobbying to include the syndrome in routine prenatal screening.

Which of the following is the most persuasive argument for the National VCFS Organization to put forth in order to convince medical authorities to include VCFS in routine prenatal testing?

A. Because of the range of psychological effects and the variable physical manifestations of the syndrome, a diagnosis of VCFS is often not made until the patient is 18 years or older.

B. Amniocentesis can provide a complete genetic analysis, including chromosome duplications and deletions.

C. Symptoms of the syndrome can range from mild enough to be undetectable to profoundly severe, including cleft palate and schizophrenia.

D. Although some of the physical anomalies are not curable, many of the symptoms of VCFS can be ameliorated by early intervention.

E. Surgery to correct cardiac deformities cannot be performed until the patient is at least 5 years old.

41. Statistics show a steady increase in the number of mail-order DVDs rented over the past year. However, a recent survey of American households indicates that fewer families reported watching rental DVDs at home this year than last year.

All of the following would account for this discrepancy *except:*

A. Families who rent two DVDs each month pay the same shipping charges as those who rent one.

B. Some survey respondents admitted that they feel that staying home and watching rental DVDs indicates social unpopularity.

C. A new promotion allows families to get two rentals for the price of one in their birthday months.

D. After six months of rental use, DVDs may be purchased by customers through a mail-order catalog.

E. Many DVD rental companies have increased the number of available titles suitable for infants and toddlers.

IF YOU FINISH BEFORE TIME IS CALLED, CHECK YOUR WORK ON THIS SECTION ONLY. DO NOT WORK ON ANY OTHER SECTION IN THE TEST.

Scoring the Diagnostic Test

Answer Key

Section 1: Analysis of an Argument

See the "Answer Explanations" section.

Section 2: Integrated Reasoning

1. False
2. True
3. False
4. Negatively
5. Slightly steeper

6. No
7. Yes
8. No
9. A
10. Riverfront $2,350; Downtown $2,100

Section 3: Quantitative

Note: PS = Problem Solving, DS = Data Sufficiency, Arith = Arithmetic, Alg = Algebra, Geom = Geometry

1. E (PS, Arith)
2. A (PS, Alg)
3. B (PS, Arith)
4. E (PS, Alg)
5. D (PS, Arith)
6. B (PS, Arith)
7. B (PS, Arith)
8. C (PS, Arith)
9. B (PS, Arith)
10. D (PS, Arith)

11. B (PS, Arith)
12. B (PS, Alg)
13. C (PS, Arith)
14. D (PS, Arith)
15. C (PS, Alg)
16. C (PS, Arith)
17. E (PS, Arith)
18. D (PS, Alg)
19. D (PS, Alg)
20. B (PS, Arith)

21. C (PS, Geom)
22. D (PS, Geom)
23. D (DS, Alg)
24. D (DS, Geom)
25. C (DS, Arith)
26. B (DS, Geom)
27. A (DS, Arith)
28. D (DS, Geom)
29. B (DS, Arith)
30. E (DS, Alg)

31. B (DS, Alg)
32. C (DS, Alg)
33. C (DS, Alg)
34. A (DS, Geom)
35. B (DS, Arith)
36. D (DS, Alg)
37. C (DS, Arith)

Section 4: Verbal

Note: SC = Sentence Correction, RC = Reading Comprehension, CR = Critical Reasoning

1. E (SC)	11. C (SC)	21. E (RC)	31. D (CR)
2. C (SC)	12. A (SC)	22. B (RC)	32. C (CR)
3. C (SC)	13. C (SC)	23. D (RC)	33. D (CR)
4. E (SC)	14. B (SC)	24. A (RC)	34. D (CR)
5. E (SC)	15. B (RC)	25. C (RC)	35. C (CR)
6. C (SC)	16. D (RC)	26. D (RC)	36. C (CR)
7. E (SC)	17. E (RC)	27. A (RC)	37. E (CR)
8. D (SC)	18. D (RC)	28. C (RC)	38. A (CR)
9. A (SC)	19. B (RC)	29. C (CR)	39. E (CR)
10. D (SC)	20. E (RC)	30. E (CR)	40. D (CR)
			41. D (CR)

Answer Explanations

Section 1: Analysis of an Argument

Note: To score your essay, see the rubric in Chapter V, Section B.

As you consider the logic of the argument, you should note several illogical assumptions. To support the conclusion that the company should employ more part-time employees, the CEO makes a leaping generalization: Part-time employees have better morale and fewer illnesses. He uses questionable data to support this generalization and doesn't consider other possible explanations for the statistics. In addition, he uses a survey as evidence, but no information is given about how this survey was conducted, what questions were asked, and who conducted it. All these pieces of information are necessary in order to judge the validity of the survey.

Sample Essays

Essay A

The CEO of Superb Company makes an important decision based on illogical conclusions and untenable evidence. Careful analysis of the validity of the evidence and consideration of the information that is lacking reveal serious flaws in this argument.

To begin, the argument states a conclusion and then presents the questionable evidence upon which this conclusion has been drawn. The decision to hire more part-time workers than full-time workers is based on an evaluation of a faulty comparison between two stores. The first criterion is job satisfaction, which is higher in Centerville than in Fringeville. How does the CEO know this? The argument mentions a survey, but no further information is given. Some serious concerns are omitted here and must be addressed. It is crucial to know who conducted the survey and what questions were asked. For example, if the manager conducted an informal survey and asked each employee if he or she is happy, the results might be very different from an anonymous survey filled out by each employee at home. It is also not stated whether the surveys were conducted in exactly the same manner in the two stores, another factor that would influence the results.

There are several other reasons job satisfaction at the Centerville store can't be compared to that at the Fringeville store. First, the Fringeville store is an outlet store. Often, outlet stores are less well-appointed than regular stores. An outlet store might not have the same employee amenities that a regular store has, such as a lounge, a private locker area, or a place to eat. Second, the clientele may not be as easy to deal with as the shoppers at Centerville store. Outlet stores may attract bargain-hunters from afar, while a centrally located store may have a more familiar group of customers. Third, the location of the stores might account for the discrepancy in morale. A store in the center of town might be more pleasant to work at than one on the outskirts, another factor that might account for lower morale. Finally, we know nothing about the managers and staff of the respective stores. Surely they have an impact on working conditions.

In addition to questionable evidence, the argument uses vague and faulty statistics. The information that attendance in Centerville is up 14 percent is given, but up from what? The baseline attendance figure is missing from both stores. It is possible that the Fringeville store's attendance started out much higher than that of Centerville. Then there is the difference in sick days used. It is important to clarify what "up slightly" means. One more day is very different from 19 more days. To know what "up slightly" means, it is necessary to know the exact figures.

The CEO draws a conclusion that all the evidence points to the difference in full-time versus part-time working hours, but no evidence exists connecting attendance and job satisfaction to the difference in working hours. Unless this direct correlation can be made, this argument is unpersuasive and illogical.

This essay received a score of 6.

Explanation of score: This essay is an outstanding critique of the argument. It clearly analyzes the weak points in the evidence and questions the validity of the conclusion. In addition, it offers counterexamples ("A store in the center of town might be more pleasant to work at than one on the outskirts") and indicates vague assumptions (the survey results). The analysis also questions the ambiguous terms used in the argument ("up slightly") and points out essential information that is missing ("we know nothing about the managers and staff of the respective stores"). Finally, the essay questions the final conclusion: that the evidence points to the difference in working hours, an obviously faulty conclusion. The essay is well written in clear, precise prose; transitional phrases are used effectively; and the structure shows a logical organizational plan.

Essay B

This argument is not a convincing one. The evidence is weak and some of it is very vague. If the head of the company makes a decision to change every worker to part-time based on this argument, he or she may be making the wrong decision.

In the first place, who knows why the workers in Centerville have higher job satisfaction then in Fringeville? The differences between the stores is not explained. It could be that the people who work in Centerville are friendlier and easier to get along with than in Fringeville. There could be more differences between the stores also. Maybe the manager in Centerville is nice and caring and the manager in Fringeville is cold and unsympathetic. Also, the survey is an unidentified piece of information. All the argument says is that a survey was done. Surveys are notorious for being able to be swayed one way or another. The argument does not explain the questions that were asked or who asked them.

If the CEO really wants to change everyone's hours, he or she has to have more accurate information. He or she needs to know if job satisfaction will be improved in the Fringeville store if he changes the hours. Maybe it will get worse. The CEO needs to know why the attendance got better in Centerville. It may have nothing to do with the hours.

There is a lot of missing information in this argument that the CEO needs before he or she makes a well-informed decision. As it is, the argument is not all that convincing.

This essay received a score of 4.

Explanation of score: This essay is an adequate analysis of the argument. It states a position—that the argument is unconvincing—and then lists several weaknesses in the argument. The response questions the evidence accurately but not thoroughly. What is lacking is an incisive and complete analysis. The examples tend to be a bit obvious and even vague ("Surveys are notorious for being able to be swayed one way or another"). It begins to focus on the central issue, the faulty conclusion, but never gets to the specifics of the illogic. The writing is adequate with some errors that don't hinder understanding: unbalanced comparison "people who work in Centerville are friendlier and easier to get along with than in Fringeville") and subject-verb agreement error ("differences between the stores is not explained"). There is not much sentence variety and the vocabulary level is just satisfactory.

Essay C

This argument is not so convincing. I don't think people want to work part-time. The economy is bad, people need more money. How can they make money if you cut there hours.

The company owns two stores. Why can't they just ask the people if they want to work full-time or part-time? That will solve there problems.

Also attendance. Maybe the people who work in Fringeville just get sicker. Maybe one of them got really sick and everyone else caught it.

They took a survey about job satisfaction. Lots of people don't pay attention to surveys and just answer anything. When I get a phone call with a survey, sometimes I say the opposite of what I believe. Who knows if they are telling the truth.

In the end, the argument is not convincing.

This essay received a score of 2.

Explanation of score: This response has serious flaws and fits the criteria for a score of 2. The writer does not appear to have the analytical skills necessary to evaluate the argument effectively. There is some evidence of critical thinking in that the writer understands that the argument is flawed and tries to locate the weaknesses. However, the essay lacks focus; no ideas are fully developed, and the writer relies on questions rather than on analysis. All the paragraphs are underdeveloped, rely on personal opinion rather than analysis, and lack specific examples and references. The writing is flawed by many grammatical errors (notably, vague pronouns, use of *there* instead of *their,* run-ons, and fragments).

Section 2: Integrated Reasoning

1. **False** Sort the table until you find the year in which the largest monthly deficit was in November. The year in which the largest monthly deficit occurred in November was 2007 but in 2007, the smallest monthly deficit occurred in January. *(See Chapter VI, Section A1.)*

2. **True** Sort the table for a year. Calculate, or estimate, the median. Repeat for each year, recording the medians, and then calculate or estimate the change from year to year. The change from 2006 to 2007 was only 1,367 million. *(See Chapter VI, Section A1.)*

3. **False** Calculate the percent change by finding the change and dividing by the January value. But note that while the deficit changes approximately 28 percent from January 2008 to December 2008, it was a deficit reduction, not an increase. *(See Chapter VI, Section A1.)*

4. The quantity (in thousands of barrels) of crude imported to the United States in 2009 was *negatively* correlated to the price of a barrel of crude. As the price increases, the number of barrels imported tends to decrease. *(See Chapter VI, Section B1.)*

5. As compared to the regression line, the line connecting the data points for January and December suggests a *slightly steeper* decline in the quantity imported as the price per barrel increases. The January/December line drops a little more sharply than the regression line. *(See Chapter VI, Section B1.)*

6. **No** The percentage of California commuters choosing to drive alone is slightly smaller than the U.S. figure, but the reason for the choice is not clear. Lack of feasible alternatives may be an issue. *(See Chapter VI, Section C1.)*

7. **Yes** With more than 70 percent of commuters driving alone, commuting times increasing, and congestion on the roads all feeding air pollution, the effects of urban sprawl are serious. *(See Chapter VI, Section C1.)*

8. **No** More than 50 percent of commuters earn more than median income for an individual ($41,560) but only about 37 percent earn more than the median for a family of four ($59,500) and neither of those incomes are adequate for the purchase of a median-priced home in the city of Los Angeles. *(See Chapter VI, Section C1.)*

9. **A** According to the memo, "the minimum household income needed to purchase a median-priced home in Los Angeles County was more than $106,000." From the circle graph, 25 percent of commuters earn $100,000 or more, so fewer than 25 percent earn $106,000 or more. *(See Chapter VI, Section C1.)*

10. **Riverfront $2,350; Downtown $2,100** For the Downtown location the business owner will invest $25,000 + 36 payments of the monthly lease amount. In the same period of time, for the Riverfront property, he'll invest $16,000 + 36 payments of the monthly rent. (Although the term of the lease is five years or 60 months, you only need to examine what happens in the first three years.) A little algebra can help you estimate.

$$\$25,000 + 36D = \$16,000 + 36R$$
$$\$9,000 + 36D = 36R$$
$$\frac{\$9,000 + 36D}{36} = R$$
$$\$250 + D = R$$

The Riverfront rent can be $250 per month higher than the Downtown location, and the two costs will be equal. *(See Chapter VI, Section D1.)*

Section 3: Quantitative

1. **E** Let x be the amount of money that Rachel has. Then $2x$ represents the amount of money that Rebecca has. Because Rebecca gave Rachel $60 and they have the same amount of money, you can write the equation $2x - 60 = x + 60$. Subtracting x from both sides of the equation, you have $x - 60 = 60$, or $x = 120$. Thus, Rachel has $120, and Rebecca has $240. *(See Chapter X, Section B.)*

2. A According to the scatter plot, the distance from Library A to Karen's house is 1 mile and the distance from Library A to Janet's house is 3 miles. Thus, the total distance from Library A, to their houses is 4 miles, the smallest.

	A	B	C	D	E
Distance to Karen's house	1	2	3	3	4
Distance to Janet's house	3	3	4	2	1
Total distance	4	5	7	5	5

(See Chapter XI, Section B.)

3. B Because the given set contains consecutive integers, the average of the set is the middle integer. From –2 to 100, there are 103 integers. (Don't forget that 0 is included in the set.) Therefore, the middle integer of the set is the 52nd integer. The 1st integer of the set is –2; thus, the 52nd integer is 49. Another approach is to find the sum of the integers from –2 to 100 by using the formula $\text{sum} = (a_1 + a_n)\left(\dfrac{n}{2}\right)$, where $a_1 = -2$, $an = 100$, and $n = 103$, and then divide the sum by n (that is $n = 103$). *(See Chapter XI, Section A.)*

4. E Squaring both sides of the equation $\sqrt{x} = 4$, you have $\left(\sqrt{x}\right)^2 = (4)^2$ or $x = 16$. Thus, $x^2 = 16^2$ or $x^2 = 256$. *(See Chapter XI, Section B.)*

5. D This problem involves not only selecting from three subgroups of stamps, but also factoring in the values of these stamps. This is not a permutation or combination problem. One way to do this problem is to list all the possible outcomes. Summarizing the outcomes, you have the following table:

1¢	10¢	20¢
1	0	2
1	2	1
11	1	1
21	0	1
1	4	0
11	3	0
21	2	0
31	1	0
41	0	0

There are nine possible sets of stamps to make 41¢. *(See Chapter XI, Section A.)*

6. B Let d be the distance between Michael's house and his school. Because distance = rate × time, which is equivalent to $\text{time} = \dfrac{\text{distance}}{\text{rate}}$, $\dfrac{d}{30}$ is the number of hours it took Michael to drive from home to school, and $\dfrac{d}{20}$ is the time he took to drive home. The time for the round trip is $\dfrac{d}{30} + \dfrac{d}{20}$ and the total distance is $2d$. Therefore, the average speed for the round trip is $\dfrac{\text{distance}}{\text{time}} = \dfrac{2d}{\dfrac{d}{30} + \dfrac{d}{20}}$. Simplifying the complex fraction, you have $\dfrac{2d}{\dfrac{2d}{60} + \dfrac{3d}{60}} = \dfrac{2d}{\dfrac{5d}{60}} = 2d\left(\dfrac{60}{5d}\right) = 24$. *(See Chapter X, Section B.)*

7. **B**

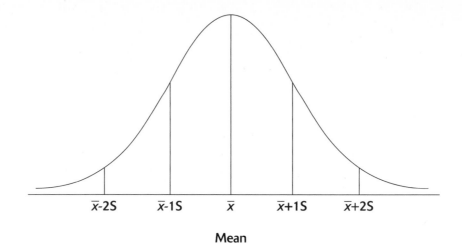

Mean

Because $88 = \bar{x} + 2S$ and $76 = \bar{x} - 1S$, $88 - 76 = (\bar{x} + 2S) - (\bar{x} - 1S)$. Therefore, $12 = 3S$ or $4 = 1S$. Substitute $1S = 4$ in $76 = \bar{x} - 1S$, you have $76 = \bar{x} - 4$ or $\bar{x} = 80$. The mean is 80. *(See Chapter XI, Section A.)*

8. **C** The average height of the five people is
$$\frac{(\text{sum of heights of 2 parents}) + (\text{sum of heights of 3 children})}{5} = 5 \text{ feet 8 inches. Multiply both sides of}$$
the equation by 5, and you have: (sum of heights of 2 parents) + (sum of heights of 3 children) = 25 feet 40 inches. The average height of the two parents is: $\dfrac{\text{sum of heights of 2 parents}}{2} = 5 \text{ feet 5 inches}$, or the sum of heights of two parents is 10 feet 10 inches. Therefore, the sum of heights of the three children is (25 feet 40 inches) – (10 feet 10 inches) = 15 feet 30 inches. Thus, the average height of the three children is $\dfrac{15 \text{ feet 30 inches}}{3}$ or 5 feet 10 inches. *(See Chapter XI, Section A.)*

9. **B** Applying the distributive property to $\left(\sqrt{5} + 2\right)\left(2 - \sqrt{5}\right)$, you have $\left(\sqrt{5}\right)(2) + \left(\sqrt{5}\right)\left(-\sqrt{5}\right) + (2)(2) + (2)\left(-\sqrt{5}\right)$, which is equivalent to $2\sqrt{5} - 5 + 4 - 2\sqrt{5}$ or –1. Note that $\sqrt{5} + 2$ and $\sqrt{5} - 2$ are conjugate pairs, and their product is an integer. *(See Chapter XI, Section A.)*

10. **D** The lowest common denominator of 10, 100, and 1,000 is 1,000. Converting, you have $1 = \dfrac{1,000}{1,000}$, $\dfrac{1}{10} = \dfrac{100}{1,000}$, and $\dfrac{1}{100} = \dfrac{10}{1,000}$. Thus, $1 - \dfrac{1}{10} + \dfrac{1}{100} - \dfrac{1}{1,000} = \dfrac{1,000}{1,000} - \dfrac{100}{1,000} + \dfrac{10}{1,000} - \dfrac{1}{1,000} = \dfrac{909}{1,000}$. *(See Chapter XI, Section A.)*

11. **B**

Corner Office	Office A	Office B	Office C
2	3	2	1

Let's call the four offices "Corner Office," "Office A," "Office B," and "Office C." You have two choices (Cristen and Johnny) for the Corner Office. After that, you have three choices for Office A, two for Office B, and one for Office C. Therefore, you have (2)(3)(2)(1) = 12 ways of assigning the four offices with Cristen or Johnny occupying the corner office. *(See Chapter XI, Section A.)*

12. **B** Half of the students signed up for soccer, so that's $\frac{1}{2}(180) = 90$ students. One-third of the students signed up for baseball, so that's $\frac{1}{3}(180) = 60$ students. The $180 - (90 + 60) = 180 - 150 = 30$ remaining students signed up for table tennis or volleyball. Of the 30 remaining students, twice as many signed up for volleyball as signed up for table tennis. Let x be the number of students who signed up for table tennis and $2x$ be the number of students who signed up for volleyball, so $x + 2x = 30$, $3x = 30$, and $x = 10$. *(See Chapter XI, Section B.)*

13. **C** If 25% of the 40 chorus members must be boys, there must be a total of $0.25(40) = 10$ boys selected. In the first round, because 80% of the 30 students were girls, 20% of the 30 students were boys and 20% of 30 is $0.20(30) = 6$. Because ten boys are needed and six were already selected in the first round, in the second round the number of boys selected must be $10 - 6 = 4$. *(See Chapter XI, Section A.)*

14. **D** From 500 to 600, the digit 5 is used 100 times as the hundreds digit, 10 times as the tens digit, and 10 times as the units digit. The number of times the digit 5 would appear is $100 + 10 + 10 = 120$. *(See Chapter XI, Section A.)*

15. **C** If x is number of students in Mr. Cohen's class and y is the number of pieces of chocolate in the box, then $2x + 25 = y$ and $3x + 5 = y$ or $2x + 25 = 3x + 5$ and $x = 20$. The number of students in Mr. Cohen's class is 20. *(See Chapter XI, Section B.)*

16. **C** Because the value of the kth term is $5k - 1$, solve $5k - 1 > 100$ and you have $5k > 101$ or $k > 20.2$. You know that k has to be an integer and the smallest integer greater than 20.2 is 21, so $k = 21$ and $5k - 1 = 104$, which is the smallest term greater than 100. *(See Chapter XI, Section A.)*

17. **E**

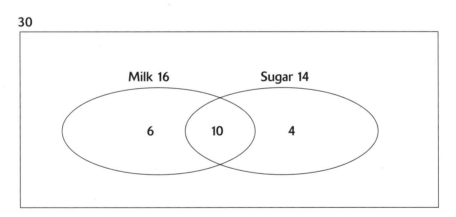

Use a Venn diagram to help you see that there are $16 - 10 = 6$ cups with only milk added and $14 - 10 = 4$ cups with only sugar added. Because there are $6 + 10 + 4 = 20$ cups of coffee with milk, sugar, or both, the number of cups of coffee with neither milk nor sugar is $30 - 20 = 10$. *(See Chapter X, Section B.)*

18. **D** Because you're charged $2 for each quarter-mile, the charge for each mile is $4(\$2) = \$8$ and the charge for n miles would be $8n$. The total charge, in dollars, is $10 + 8n$. *(See Chapter X, Section B.)*

19. **D** Because you're trying to find an exponent, express each side as a power with the same base and then set the exponents equal. Since $3^n + 3^n + 3^n = 3(3^n) = (3^1)(3^n) = 3^{n+1}$ and since $9^6 = (3^2)^6 = 3^{12}$, you know that $3^{n+1} = 3^{12}$ and $n + 1 = 12$ or $n = 11$. *(See Chapter XI, Section B.)*

20. B Because it takes 12 hours for one machine to print 600 copies, it would take 24 hours for one machine to print 1,200 copies. If three machines worked together to print 1,200 copies, it would take $\frac{24}{3} = 8$ hours.

You could also use an inverse proportion. The more machines you use, the less time it would require to print 1,200 copies.

Number of Machines	Hours	Number of Copies
1	24	1,200
3	x	1,200

Because the number of copies is the same, you have $(1)(24) = 3x$ or $x = 8$ hours. *(See Chapter X, Section B.)*

21. C

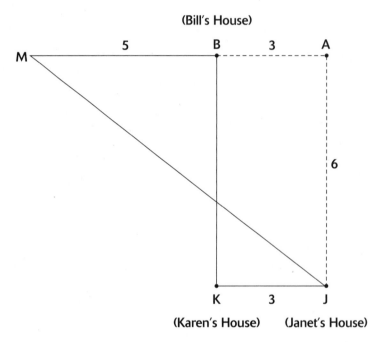

In the accompanying diagram of Mary's trip, if you extend $\overline{MB}$ to A and draw $\overline{AJ}$, $\triangle MAJ$ is a right triangle and quadrilateral $BAJK$ is a rectangle with $BA = KJ = 3$ and $BK = AJ = 6$. Because $AM = 8$, $(AM)^2 + (AJ)^2 = (MJ)^2$ or $8^2 + 6^2 = (MJ)^2$ and $MJ = 10$. *(See Chapter X, Section B.)*

22. D Because $m\angle BDE + 100° = 180°$, $m\angle BDE = 80°$. You know that the sum of the measures of the three angles of a triangle is $180°$. Therefore, $80 + 40 + m\angle BED = 180°$ or $m\angle BED = 60°$. Because $m\angle BED + x = 180°$, you have $60 + x = 180$, or $x = 120°$. *(See Chapter XI, Section C.)*

23. D

(1) Because $y = 2x + 1$, substitute $2x + 1$ for y in $2x - y$ and you have $2x - (2x + 1)$, which is equivalent to -1. Sufficient.

(2) Because $2y - 4x = 2$, divide both sides of the equation by 2, and you have $y - 2x = 1$, which is equivalent to $y = 2x + 1$. Substituting $2x + 1$ for y in $2x - y$, you have $2x - (2x + 1)$ or -1. Sufficient.

Each statement alone is sufficient. *(See Chapter XII, Section B.)*

24. **D**

(1) Because the perimeter of the square *ABCD* is 12, the length of once of its sides is 3. Therefore, the area of *ABCD* is $(3)^2$ or 9. Sufficient.

(2)

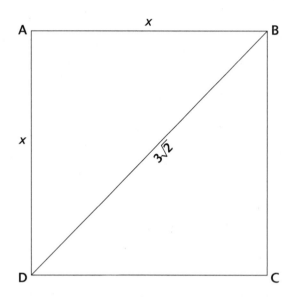

ABCD is a square. Therefore, $AB = BC = DC = AD$. $\triangle ABD$ is an isosceles right triangle. Using the Pythagorean theorem, you have $x^2 + x^2 = \left(3\sqrt{2}\right)^2$, which is equivalent to $2x^2 = 18$ or $x = \pm3$. Because x represents the length of a side of a square, $x = 3$. (You could also use a 45°-45° right-triangle relationship to find x.) The area of *ABCD* is 3^2 or 9. Sufficient.

Each statement alone is sufficient. *(See Chapter XII, Section C.)*

25. **C**

(1) Because n is divisible by 6, n is a multiple of 6, and $n = 6, 12, 18, 24, \ldots$ Therefore, n may or may not be divisible by 12. Not sufficient.

(2) Because n is divisible by 4, n is a multiple of 4, and $n = 4, 8, 12, 16, \ldots$ Therefore, n may or may not be divisible by 12. Not sufficient.

Taking statements (1) and (2) together, you know that n is a multiple of 4 and 6. The lowest common multiple of 4 and 6 is 12, and $n = 12, 24, 36, \ldots$ Thus, n is divisible by 12. Both statements together are sufficient. *(See Chapter XI, Section A.)*

26. B

(1) Two chords perpendicular to each other does not necessarily imply that one of the chords is a diameter. See the figure. Not sufficient.

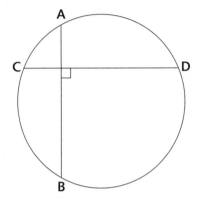

(2) Because the radius is 4 and $\overline{AB} = 8$, $\overline{AB}$ is twice the length of the radius. Thus, $\overline{AB}$ is a diameter of the circle. Statement (2) alone is sufficient. *(See Chapter XII, Section C.)*

27. A

(1) Because the sum of $a_1 + a_2 + a_3 + \ldots + a_{20}$ is 100, the mean of the set is $\frac{\text{sum}}{n} = \frac{100}{20}$ or 5. Sufficient.

(2) Knowing the standard deviation alone cannot determine the mean. Not sufficient.

Statement (1) alone is sufficient. *(See Chapter XII, Section A.)*

28. D

(1) If the lengths of the sides of a triangle satisfy the Pythagorean theorem, then the triangle is a right triangle. For this case, $10^2 + 24^2 = 26^2$, and then $\triangle ABC$ is a right triangle. Sufficient.

(2) Because $m\angle A + m\angle C = 90°$, $m\angle B = 180° - (m\angle A + m\angle C) = 90°$. Therefore, $\angle B$ is a right angle and $\triangle ABC$ is a right triangle. Sufficient.

Each statement alone is sufficient. *(See Chapter XII, Section C.)*

29. B To find the average of all four tests, you must have the total grade for the four tests.

(1) Does not provide enough information to find the grade for the fourth test. Not sufficient.

(2) The grade for the fourth test was a 92. Because the average of the first three tests was 84, the total grade for the first three tests was 3×84 or 252. Therefore, the total grade for all four tests was $252 + 92$ or 344, and the average was $\frac{344}{4}$ or 86. Sufficient.

Statement (2) alone is sufficient. *(See Chapter XII, Section A.)*

30. **E**

(1) There are infinitely many ordered pairs (x, y) satisfying the equation $y = x^2$—for example $(0, 0)$, $(1, 1)$, $(2, 4)$, . . . Not sufficient to determine the value of x.

(2) There are infinitely many ordered pairs (x, y) satisfying the equation $y = x + 2$—for example $(0, 2)$, $(1, 3)$, $(2, 4)$, . . . Not sufficient to determine the value of x.

Taking statements (1) and (2) together, you have $x^2 = x + 2$, which is equivalent to $x^2 - x - 2 = 0$. Factoring, you have $(x - 2)(x + 1) = 0$ or $x = -1$ or 2. Not sufficient to determine the value of x. Both statements together are not sufficient. *(See Chapter XII, Section B.)*

31. **B** Notice that $3^{x+1} > 9$ can be written as $(3^x)(3) > 9$. Dividing both sides of the inequality by 3, you have $3^x > 3$.

(1) The statement $3^x > 1$ is not sufficient to determine if $3^x > 3$.

(2) Because $x < 1$, $3^x < 3$. Therefore, $(3^x)(3) < 9$. Therefore, $3^{x+1} < 9$ and $3^{x+1} > 9$ is false. Sufficient.

Statement (2) alone is sufficient. *(See Chapter XII, Section B.)*

32. **C**

(1) The equation $x^2 - y^2 = 9$ can be written as $(x + y)(x - y) = 9$. However, it's not sufficient information to determine the value of $x - y$.

(2) There are infinitely many ordered pairs satisfying the equation $x + y = 3$. There isn't sufficient information to determine the value of $x - y$.

Statements (1) and (2) together, you have $x + y = 3$ and $x^2 - y^2 = 9$. Because $x^2 - y^2 = 9$ is equivalent to $(x + y)(x - y) = 9$, $3(x - y) = 9$ or $x - y = 3$. Sufficient.

Both statements together are sufficient. *(See Chapter XII, Section B.)*

33. **C**

(1) If $a = 2$, then $y = 2x^2 + b$. Depending on the value of b, y may or may not have any real roots. For example, if $b = 0$, then $y = 2x^2$ and $x = 0$ is a root. However, if $b = 2$, then $y = 2x^2 + 2$. Setting $y = 0$, you have $2x^2 + 2 = 0$, which has no real roots. Not sufficient.

(2) If $b = -8$, then $y = ax^2 - 8$. Depending on the value of a, y may or may not have any real roots. For example, if $a = 1$, then $y = x^2 - 8$. Setting $y = 0$, you have $x^2 - 8 = 0$ and $x = \pm\sqrt{8}$ are roots. However, if $a = -1$, then $y = -x^2 - 8$. Setting $y = 0$, you have $-x^2 - 8 = 0$ or $x^2 + 8 = 0$, which has no real roots. Not sufficient.

Taking statements (1) and (2) together, you have $y = 2x^2 - 8$. Setting $y = 0$, you have $2x^2 - 8 = 0$, and $x = \pm 2$. Thus, there are two real roots. Both statements together are sufficient. *(See Chapter XII, Section B.)*

34. A

(1) A cube has six congruent faces. Because the total surface area is 24, the area of one face is $\frac{24}{6}$ or 4. The area of a face is S^2; therefore, $S^2 = 4$ or $S = 2$. The volume of the cube is $V = S^3$ or $V = 2^3 = 8$. Sufficient.

(2) The statement $1 < S < 3$ is not sufficient to determine the value of S, and thus not sufficient to determine the value of V.

Statement (1) alone is sufficient. *(See Chapter XII, Section C.)*

35. B

(1) Because $x = 3$, three balls have been removed from the urn. However, you don't know the colors of the three balls, so you don't know the colors of the remaining balls in the urn. Statement (1) is not sufficient to determine the probability of picking a red ball from the urn.

(2) There are 19 balls initially—7 red and 12 blue. After x balls are removed, the ratio of red balls to blue balls is 3 to 5. Therefore, the urn could have 3 red balls and 5 blue or 6 red balls and 10 blue balls. In either case, the probability of picking a red ball from the urn is the same, $\frac{3}{8}$ or $\frac{6}{16}$, which is equivalent to $\frac{3}{8}$. Sufficient.

Statement (2) alone is sufficient. *(See Chapter XII, Section A.)*

36. D

(1) Because $\frac{2}{3}x = 12$, $2x = 36$ or $x = 18$. Therefore, $n = (0.20)(0.50)(18) = 1.8$. Sufficient.

(2) Because $\frac{3}{2}x = 27$, $3x = 54$ or $x = 18$. Therefore, $n = (0.20)(0.50)(18) = 1.8$. Sufficient.

Each statement alone is sufficient. *(See Chapter XII, Section B.)*

37. C

(1) Because k is a multiple of 5, k could be 15, 20, or 25. Not sufficient information to determine the value of k.

(2) Because k is an even number, k could be 8, 20, or 52. Not sufficient information to determine the value of k.

Taking statements (1) and (2) together, you have k a multiple of 5 and an even number. Thus, k must be 20. Both statements together are sufficient. *(See Chapter X, Section B.)*

Section 4: Verbal

1. **E** The underlined portion contains an error in parallel structure: *their playing avant-garde pieces* is not parallel to *a warm richness of tone, and elegant phrasing.* The only choice with a parallel phrase is Choice E, *an avant-garde repertoire.* Choices B, C, and D all contain a clause rather than a phrase, so they aren't parallel. *(See Chapter IX.)*

2. **C** The sentence contains a pronoun-antecedent agreement error. The pronoun *Each* must take the singular form of the verb *has.* Only Choice C uses the correct form of the verb and has no other

grammatical error. Choices B and D have the pronoun-antecedent error (and Choice B is a sentence fragment). Choice E is incorrect because it changes the subject to *Scientists,* which then needs the plural form of the verb *have. (See Chapter IX.)*

3. **C** The sentence begins with an introductory participial phrase that must be followed by the word it modifies. The *demand* is not doing the *transporting;* therefore, Choice A is incorrect. The correct answer must begin with the *supertankers,* so you can eliminate choices B and E. Choice D misplaces the adverb clause *as the demand for fuel has declined.* Only Choice C is correct. *(See Chapter IX.)*

4. **E** As it is, the sentence is a run-on (too many main clauses joined by commas). Choice B incorrectly uses the semicolon because the second half of the sentence is not a main clause. Choice C uses inconsistent verb tenses. Choice D also incorrectly uses the semicolon because it begins with a subordinate clause, not a main clause. Choice E is properly structured and correctly punctuated. *(See Chapter IX.)*

5. **E** The sentence contains an error in parallelism: The series of phrases beginning with *memorizing . . . , studying . . . ,* must be followed by another phrase beginning with a present participle. Only Choice E, which begins with *working,* is parallel. *(See Chapter IX.)*

6. **C** The sentence begins with a participial phrase, *Encouraged by the government to develop alternative-energy vehicles.* This phrase must be followed by the word being modified—in this case, *major automobile companies.* Choice A incorrectly puts *an energy-efficient car* after the phrase, a position that suggests that the car is encouraged by the government. Choice B is not a complete sentence because there is no verb for the subject *companies.* Choice D incorrectly uses the passive voice in the main clause. Choice E uses the awkward phrasing, *Being encouraged by* and the vague pronoun *it. (See Chapter IX.)*

7. **E** This sentence contains a misplaced modifier: the *collection* isn't a *photographer.* Choices B and D make the same error. Choice C lacks subject-verb agreement and awkwardly coordinates the two clauses rather than subordinating one as should logically be done. *(See Chapter IX.)*

8. **D** The sentence contains a pronoun-antecedent error: the plural pronoun *them* can't refer to the singular noun *wall.* Choices B and C also contain this error. Choice E has a subject-verb agreement error: *which originates* refers to the *appendages. (See Chapter IX.)*

9. **A** The sentence is grammatically correct as it is written. None of the other choices is idiomatically correct. *(See Chapter IX.)*

10. **D** The sentence contains a correlative conjunction that requires a parallel conjunction: *not only* needs *but also.* Choice B is awkward and wordy. Choice C is a sentence fragment. Choice E is awkwardly phrased. *(See Chapter IX.)*

11. **C** The sentence contains a subject-verb agreement error: The plural subject *capitalists* doesn't agree with the verb *is.* Choice B uses unparallel verbs, *resist* and *are putting, and lacks a conjunction between the two verbs.* Choice D has the awkward wording *consider the appeal of clean energy* before the verb *are putting.* Choice E awkwardly uses the passive voice. *(See Chapter IX.)*

12. **A** The sentence correctly uses the noun clause *That increased income from advertisements was necessary to defray the losses incurred by the magazine's decline in readership* as the subject of the verb *became.* None of the other constructions is grammatically correct. *(See Chapter IX.)*

13. **C** The sentence contains a subject-verb agreement error: The singular subject *increase* doesn't agree with the plural form of the verb *have.* It also has a misplaced modifier: *particularly in the coal sector,* which should be placed as closely as possible to the subject it modifies, *increase.* Choice B corrects the misplaced modifier but doesn't correct the agreement error. Choice D incorrectly uses the participle *being* as a verb. Choice E doesn't correct either of the original errors. *(See Chapter IX.)*

14. **B** The sentence is a fragment: The subject *Seaming Sisters* has no verb. Choice B corrects the error using the verb *has been.* Choice C is not parallel and needlessly inserts a subordinating conjunction. Choice D is a sentence fragment. Choice E is punctuated incorrectly: A semicolon should not be used to connect a subordinate clause to a main clause. *(See Chapter IX.)*

15. **B** The primary purpose of the passage is to give a brief history of the role of communication technology in the networking industry. It doesn't deal with new products, so Choice A is incorrect. It doesn't contrast network marketing to Internet sales (Choice C); in fact, it points out how they work together. Rather than qualify the generalization (Choice D), the passage supports it, and it certainly doesn't dispel the idea that network marketing is a competitive force (Choice E). *(See Chapter VII, Section A.)*

16. **D** The entire last paragraph of the passage suggests the advantages of targeting a specific consumer using communication technology. Choice A is incorrect because it implies a negative relationship between communication technology and consumers. Choices B, C, and E are off the topic. *(See Chapter VII, Section B.)*

17. **E** The author would agree that evolving technology has increased network sales. Although the fax is mentioned in the passage, it did not revolutionize the industry (Choice A). Choices B and C are off topic. The author does not discuss international sales, so Choice D is incorrect. *(See Chapter VII, Section B.)*

18. **D** To answer this question correctly, you must look through the passage and locate each of the characteristics mentioned in the choices. Each of the choices except Choice D has at least one characteristic that is not discussed in the passage. *(See Chapter VII, Section B.)*

19. **B** The passage points out that bacterial infections are caused by toxins transmitted through the cell wall. If this wall could be made impermeable, no toxins would be released. Choice A is an incorrect interpretation of the information in the passage. Choice C refers to millimeters rather than micrometers. Choice D is a misinterpretation of the information in the passage. Choice E is incorrect because the bacteria have no discernible nucleus. *(See Chapter VII, Section C.)*

20. **E** Choice A, B, C, and D can all be supported by evidence from the passage. Choice E can't be supported because no mention is made of proto-organisms with well-formed nuclei and discrete internal structures. *(See Chapter VII, Section B.)*

21. **E** The passage gives a brief overview of the classification of bacteria from Antonie van Leeuwenhoek's first discovery of bacteria, which he originally thought were animals (misconception), to the current classification of bacteria as prokaryotes. Choice A is too specific (no primeval times), and the passage doesn't mention mutations. Choice B is incorrect because the passage doesn't ridicule anyone. Choice C, while touched upon in the passage, is not the main purpose. Choice D is inaccurate. *(See Chapter VII, Section A.)*

22. **B** According to the passage, the statement *there is nothing temporary in his dramas* refers specifically to Shakespeare, not to other poets or to the time period. The end of the sentence, *truly did he dwell amidst the elements constituting man in every age and clime,* explains that his works are universal and people of every age can relate to them. Choices A and C are off topic. Choice D is not supported by the passage. Choice E is true, but wrong because the question asks only about the reference to Shakespeare, not to "poets." *(See Chapter VII, Section B.)*

23. **D** The author uses these men to contrast with Shakespeare. Because the author has made the point that Shakespeare transcends his time period, these men, in contrast, are closely linked to the time periods in which they lived. Choice A is inaccurate because it only refers to Milton. Choice B is the opposite of what is stated in the passage. Choice C is contradicted by the passage. Choice E is not supported by the passage. *(See Chapter VII, Section B.)*

24. **A** The author states that the government limits "the total amount of air or water pollution that may be emitted by issuing an equivalent number of allowances." Thus, the allowances are essentially the amount of pollution permitted. All the other choices reflect an inaccurate reading of the passage. *(See Chapter VII, Section B.)*

25. **C** At the end of the passage, the author lists the reasons it is important for a company to become "carbon neutral." He mentions good public relations and accountability. He does say compliance is voluntary rather than mandated by the government. *(See Chapter VII, Section C.)*

26. **D** The author's position throughout the passage has been supportive of activities that will lessen the negative impact on the environment. He would not agree with Choice A or Choice C. No evidence in the passage supports Choice B. Choice E is unrealistic. *(See Chapter VII, Section D.)*

27. **A** The author's argument would be most weakened by Choice A, which is counter to his position. Choice B is too vague to weaken his argument. Choices C, D, and E, while tangentially related, are not opposed to his position. *(See Chapter VII, Section B.)*

28. **C** The author's attitude has been supportive of reducing the impact of pollution throughout the passage. Thus, he would be appreciative of their efforts. *(See Chapter VII, Section F.)*

29. **C** The conclusion in the argument is that *Wind energy will become the international power source of the 21st century.* For this statement to be a logical conclusion, it must be based on the assumption that countries are seeking new sources of power that don't depend on fossil fuels. Choice C correctly states this assumption. Choice A is an example of a true statement, but it is not an assumption that leads to the conclusion at the end of the passage. Choices B, D, and E are also true, but wrong; they are off topic in that they present information relevant to wind turbines but not relevant to the conclusion. *(See Chapter VIII, Section D.)*

30. **E** The best answer that would weaken the conclusion must present evidence that wind energy is not going to become an international power source. Only Choice E presents negative information that weakens the case for wind energy. Choice C strengthens the conclusion; choices A, B, and D are merely statements about the characteristics of wind turbines. *(See Chapter VIII, Section D.)*

31. **D** Wellco's decision is based on its understanding that getting its advertisements out to as many people as possible and doing so as economically as possible is the best choice. Choice D supports this understanding. All the other choices are true statements, but they don't directly support the decision to go with a company that publishes multiple magazines. *(See Chapter VIII, Section D.)*

32. **C** If it were true that it is more cost-effective to target a specific audience in a specialty magazine than to simply get the word out to as many people as possible, then Wellco's decision would be weakened. None of the other choices directly weakens Wellco's decision. *(See Chapter VIII, Section D.)*

33. **D** The car manufacturer concludes that the fire extinguishers that deploy during accidents will reduce the number of deaths and injuries from all car fires; however, Choice D weakens this conclusion by pointing out that most injuries from car fires are the result of poor maintenance rather than accidents. All the other choices are off topic because they do not directly address the conclusion. *(See Chapter VIII, Section B.)*

34. **D** The missing information needed to complete the sentence logically must explain why the retailer would invest money to create an opulent setting. Choice D gives a reasonable explanation for expenditure. Choice A is incorrect because no indication is given that a discount price is available. Choice B incorrectly links bargain-hunting middle-income consumers to the setting, an illogical connection. Choices C and E are true statements that don't logically complete the sentence. *(See Chapter VIII, Section F.)*

35. **C** The passage indicates that heat loss is directly proportional to the area and thermal conductivity of a wall and inversely proportional to its thickness. Thus, a nonconductive, thick wall in a small room will be the most energy-efficient structure. *(See Chapter VIII, Section D.)*

36. **C** A physician would be more likely to prescribe a drug that costs the patient less (Choice A) and that the patient is more likely to take on schedule (Choice B). The data confirming the efficacy of Drug M would also lead physician to prescribe it (Choice D). In addition, the physician would make more money prescribing Drug M (Choice E). However, the side effect of increased pain upon injection would occur three times a year with Drug M as opposed to once a year with Drug P; this is the only reason that a physician would not prescribe Drug M. *(See Chapter VIII, Section D.)*

37. **E** The scientists who faced this dilemma in physics needed a theory that would account for both large and small parts of the universe. Super-string theory does this. Choice A would do nothing to resolve the dilemma. Choice B is true, but the wrong answer to the question because it is off topic. Choice C is again off topic. Choice D doesn't make much sense and only applies to quantum mechanics. *(See Chapter VIII, Section D)*

38. **A** Choice A best explains the discrepancy because, logically, babies with digestive disorders will not gain as much weight as healthy babies. Choice B is off topic as are choices D and E. Choice C is true but does not explain the discrepancy. *(See Chapter VIII, Section E.)*

39. **E** The school nurse concludes that the school's program has contributed to the decline in flu reports; however, the passage suggests the parents are making the reports. Their diagnosis may or may not be accurate. Thus, if parents have received additional information regarding flu versus cold, they may be making more accurate diagnoses. Choices A and B are irrelevant. Choice C is marginally related but is not the best answer. Choice D might account for fewer illnesses in general rather than specifically flu. *(See Chapter VIII, Section C.)*

40. **D** In order to convince the medical authorities, evidence must be given that the outcome is worth the effort and cost of screening. If the children's conditions will improve with early intervention, then the effort is worthwhile. Choices A, B, and E, while true, are not reasons to include VCFS in routine screening. Choice C is a fact, but it is not as persuasive as the point made in Choice D. *(See Chapter VIII, Section D.)*

41. **D** There are several ways to account for the discrepancy: It is important to note that fewer families don't mean fewer DVDs. Fewer families may be renting more DVDs per family. Choices A and C would, thus, explain the discrepancy. Choice B can account for the discrepancy; some families may not have responded honestly to the survey, because they were unwilling to appear unpopular. Choice E suggests that families with young children may be renting more DVDs for their children as more titles become available. Choice D presents an irrelevant scenario: The purchase of DVDs does not account for the discrepancy. *(See Chapter VIII, Section E.)*

Scoring Worksheets

Analytical Writing Assessment Scaled Score and Approximate Percentile	
Analytical Writing Assessment Scaled Score	**Approximate Percentile**
6	90
5	60
4	24
3	10
2	3
1	2
0	0

Quantitative		
	Number Correct	**Number Incorrect**
Problem solving (22 questions)		
Data sufficiency (15 questions)		
Total		

Quantitative subtotal (number correct) = _____

What Your Quantitative Score Means				
	Excellent	**Above Average**	**Average**	**Below Average**
Problem solving	18–22	15–17	9–14	0–8
Data sufficiency	12–15	9–11	6–8	0–5

Verbal		
	Number Correct	**Number Incorrect**
Sentence correction (14 questions)		
Reading comprehension (14 questions)		
Critical reasoning (13 questions)		
Total		

Verbal subtotal (number correct) = _____

What Your Verbal Score Means				
	Excellent	**Above Average**	**Average**	**Below Average**
Sentence correction	12–14	9–11	6–8	0–5
Reading comprehension	13–14	11–12	7–10	0–6
Critical reasoning	11–13	7–10	5–6	0–4

Quantitative subtotal + Verbal subtotal = Total score

_____ + _____ = _____

Note: Use your total score to locate your approximate percentile ranking in the following chart.

Total Score and Approximate Percentile Ranking		
Total Score (Quantitative and Verbal)	**800-Point Scale**	**Approximate Percentile**
64–78	710–800	91–99
53–63	660–700	81–90
45–52	610–650	71–80
37–44	580–600	61–70
32–36	550–570	51–60
26–31	510–540	41–50
22–25	470–500	31–40
18–21	430–460	21–30
7–17	380–420	11–20
0–6	200–370	0–10

II. Two-Month Cram Plan

	Two-Month Cram Plan		
	Analytical Writing and Verbal	**Integrated Reasoning**	**Quantitative**

8 weeks before the test	**Study Time:** 4½ hours
	❑ Take the **Diagnostic Test** and review answer explanations.
	   ❑ Compare your essay to the rubric in Chapter V and the samples in Chapter I, and target areas to improve.
	   ❑ Based on your errors on the Diagnostic Test, identify difficult topics and their corresponding chapters. These chapters are your targeted chapters.		

7 weeks before the test	**Study Time:** 1 to 2 hours
	❑ **Analysis of an Argument:** Chapter V
	   ❑ Read Sections A–B.
	   ❑ Write 1 practice essay from Section C. Compare your essay to the rubric in Section B.
	   ❑ If this is a targeted chapter, write 2 additional essays from Section C.
		Study Time: 20 minutes
		❑ **Integrated Reasoning:** Chapter VI
		❑ Read Section A1.
			Study Time: 1 to 2½ hours (depending on your Diagnostic Test results)
			❑ **Reviewing Math Concepts:** Chapter X
			   ❑ Read Sections A1–A2.

6 weeks before the test	**Study Time:** 1 to 2½ hours (depending on your Diagnostic Test results)
	❑ **Reading Comprehension:** Chapter VII
	   ❑ Read the chapter.
	   ❑ Do practice questions 1–10.
		Study Time: 20 minutes
		❑ **Integrated Reasoning:** Chapter VI
		   ❑ Read Section B1.
			Study Time: 1 to 2½ hours (depending on your Diagnostic Test results)
			❑ **Reviewing Math Concepts:** Chapter X
			   ❑ Read Section A3.
			❑ **Solving Word Problems:** Chapter X
			   ❑ Read Section B.

5 weeks before the test	**Study Time:** 1 hour
	❑ **Critical Reasoning:** Chapter VIII
	   ❑ Read Sections A–D.
	   ❑ Do practice questions for each section.
		Study Time: 20 minutes
		❑ **Integrated Reasoning:** Chapter VI
		   ❑ Read Section C1.
			Study Time: 2 hours
			❑ **Problem Solving:** Chapter XI
			   ❑ Do the practice problems in Sections A–B.

4 weeks before the test	**Study Time:** 1 hour
	❑ **Critical Reasoning:** Chapter VIII
	   ❑ Read Sections E–F.
	   ❑ Do practice questions for each section.
	   ❑ If this is a targeted chapter, do the 10 additional practice questions at the end of the chapter.
		Study Time: 20 minutes
		❑ **Integrated Reasoning:** Chapter VI
		   ❑ Read Section D1.
			Study Time: 1½ to 2 hours
			❑ **Problem Solving:** Chapter XI
			   ❑ Do the practice problems in Section C.
			❑ **Data Sufficiency:** Chapter XII
			   ❑ Do the practice problems in Section A.

continued

	Analytical Writing and Verbal	Integrated Reasoning	Quantitative

3 weeks before the test	**Study Time:** 1 hour
	 ❑ **Sentence Correction:** Chapter IX
	  ❑ Read Sections A–B.
	  ❑ Do practice questions for each section.
	  ❑ If this is a targeted chapter, do the 6 additional practice questions at the end of the chapter.
		Study Time: 20 minutes
		 ❑ **Integrated Reasoning:** Chapter VI
		  ❑ Do practice questions 1–3, Section A2.
		  ❑ Check against solutions provided.
			Study Time: 1½ to 2 hours
			 ❑ **Data Sufficiency:** Chapter XII
			  ❑ Do the practice problems in Sections B–C.

2 weeks before the test	**Study Time:** 4½ hours ❑ Take the **Practice Test** and review answer explanations. ❑ Based on your errors on the Practice Test, identify difficult topics and their corresponding chapters. Target these chapters for extra review.		

7 days before the test	**Study Time:** 1 hour
	 ❑ Based on the **Practice Test,** review targeted chapters.
	 ❑ **Analysis of an Argument:** Chapter V
	  ❑ Reread chapter.
	  ❑ If this is a targeted chapter, write 1 more essay.
		Study Time: 20 minutes
		 ❑ **Integrated Reasoning:** Chapter VI
		  ❑ Do practice questions 1–2, Section B2.
		  ❑ Check against solutions provided.
			Study Time: 1 hour
			 ❑ **Reviewing Math Concepts:** Chapter X
			  ❑ Reread Section A.

6 days before the test	**Study Time:** 1 hour
	 ❑ **Reading Comprehension:** Chapter VII
	  ❑ Reread the chapter.
	  ❑ If this is a targeted chapter, redo practice questions 1–10.
		Study Time: 20 minutes
		 ❑ **Integrated Reasoning:** Chapter VI
		  ❑ Do practice questions 1–4, Section C2.
		  ❑ Check against solutions provided.
			Study Time: 1 hour
			 ❑ **Solving Word Problems:** Chapter X
			  ❑ Reread Section B.

5 days before the test	**Study Time:** 1 to 1½ hours
	 ❑ **Critical Reasoning:** Chapter VIII
	  ❑ Reread chapter.
	  ❑ If this is a targeted chapter, do the additional 10 practice questions at end of chapter.
		Study Time: 20 minutes
		 ❑ **Integrated Reasoning:** Chapter VI
		  ❑ Do practice question 1, Section D2.
		  ❑ Check against solution provided.
			Study Time: 1 to 1½ hours
			 ❑ **Problem Solving:** Chapter XI
			  ❑ Review Sections A–B.

4 days before the test	**Study Time:** 1 hour
	 ❑ **Sentence Correction:** Chapter IX
	  ❑ Reread chapter.
	  ❑ If this is a targeted chapter, do the additional 6 practice questions at end of chapter.
		Study Time: 20 minutes
		 ❑ **Integrated Reasoning:** Chapter VI
		  ❑ Do practice questions 4–6, Section A2.
		  ❑ Check against solutions provided.
			Study Time: 1 hour
			 ❑ **Problem Solving:** Chapter XI
			  ❑ Review Section C.
			 ❑ **Data Sufficiency:** Chapter XII
			  ❑ Review Section A.

	Analytical Writing and Verbal	Integrated Reasoning	Quantitative

3 days before the test	**Study Time:** 1 hour
	❑ **Analysis of an Argument:** Chapter V
	  ❑ Review chapter.
	  ❑ If this is a targeted chapter, write 1 more essay.
		Study Time: 20 minutes
		❑ **Integrated Reasoning:** Chapter VI
		  ❑ Do practice questions 5–8, Section B2.
		  ❑ Check against solutions provided.
			Study Time: 1 hour
			❑ **Data Sufficiency:** Chapter XII
			  ❑ Review Sections B–C.

2 days before the test	**Study Time:** 1 hour
	❑ Review Chapters VII, VIII, and IX.
	❑ Redo all practice questions for targeted chapters.
		Study Time: 30 minutes
		❑ **Integrated Reasoning:** Chapter VI
		  ❑ Do practice questions 5–8, Section C2, and practice question 2, Section D2.
		  ❑ Check against solutions provided.
			Study Time: 1 hour
			❑ Redo questions that you answered incorrectly on the **Practice Test** and check the answer explanations.

1 day before the test	❑ Relax. . . . You're well prepared for the test. ❑ Have confidence in your ability to do well.		

Morning of the test	**Reminders:**
	❑ Have a good breakfast.
	❑ Take the following items with you on test day:
	  ❑ Your admission ticket and photo ID
	  ❑ A watch
	❑ Try to go outside for a few minutes and walk around before the test.
	❑ Most important: Stay calm and confident during the test. Take deep, slow breaths if you feel at all nervous. You can do it!		

III. One-Month Cram Plan

	Analytical Writing and Verbal	Integrated Reasoning	Quantitative

4 weeks before the test	**Study Time:** 4½ hours
	❏ Take the **Diagnostic Test** and review answer explanations.
	    ❏ Compare your essay to the rubric in Chapter V and the samples in Chapter I, and target areas to improve.
	    ❏ Based on your errors on the Diagnostic Test, identify difficult topics and their corresponding chapters. These chapters are your targeted chapters.		

3 weeks before the test	**Study Time:** 1 to 2 hours (depending on your Diagnostic Test results)
	❏ **Analysis of an Argument:** Chapter V
	    ❏ Read Sections A–B.
	    ❏ Write 1 practice essay from Section C. Compare your essay to the rubric in Section B.
	    ❏ If this is a targeted chapter, write 2 additional essays from Section C.
		Study Time: 40 minutes
		❏ **Integrated Reasoning:** Chapter VI
		    ❏ Read Section A1.
		    ❏ Do practice questions 1–3, Section A2.
		    ❏ Check against solutions provided.
			Study Time: 2 to 3½ hours (depending on your Diagnostic Test results)
			❏ **Reviewing Math Concepts:** Chapter X
			    ❏ Read Sections A–B.
			    ❏ Do practice problems.

2 weeks before the test	**Study Time:** 3 to 4 hours
	❏ **Reading Comprehension:** Chapter VII
	    ❏ Read the chapter.
	    ❏ Do practice questions 1–10.
	❏ **Critical Reasoning:** Chapter VIII
	    ❏ Read Sections A–F.
	    ❏ Do practice questions for each section.
	    ❏ If this is a targeted chapter, do the 10 additional practice questions at the end of the chapter.
	❏ **Sentence Correction:** Chapter IX
	    ❏ Read Sections A–B.
	    ❏ Do practice questions for each section.
	    ❏ If this is a targeted chapter, do the 6 additional practice questions at the end of the chapter.
		Study Time: 40 minutes
		❏ **Integrated Reasoning:** Chapter VI
		    ❏ Read section B1.
		    ❏ Do practice questions 1–2, Section B2.
		    ❏ Check against solutions provided.
			Study Time: 6 hours
			❏ **Problem Solving:** Chapter XI
			    ❏ Read Sections A–C.
			    ❏ Do practice problems.
			❏ **Data Sufficiency:** Chapter XII
			    ❏ Read Sections A–C.
			    ❏ Do practice problems.

continued

	Analytical Writing and Verbal	Integrated Reasoning	Quantitative
7 days before the test	**Study Time:** 4½ hours ❏ Take the **Practice Test** and review answer explanations. 　❏ Based on your errors on the Practice Test, identify difficult topics and their corresponding chapters. Target these chapters for extra review.		
6 days before the test	**Study Time:** 1 hour ❏ Based on the **Practice Test,** review targeted chapters. ❏ **Analysis of an Argument:** Chapter V 　❏ Reread chapter. 　❏ If this is a targeted chapter, write at least 1 more essay.	**Study Time:** 40 minutes ❏ **Integrated Reasoning:** Chapter VI 　❏ Read section C1. 　❏ Do practice questions 1–4, Section C2. 　❏ Check against solutions provided.	**Study Time:** 1 hour ❏ **Reviewing Math Concepts:** Chapter X 　❏ Reread Section A.
5 days before the test	**Study Time:** 1 hour ❏ **Reading Comprehension:** Chapter VII 　❏ Reread the chapter. 　❏ If this is a targeted chapter, redo practice questions 1–10.	**Study Time:** 40 minutes ❏ **Integrated Reasoning:** Chapter VI 　❏ Read Section D1. 　❏ Do practice question 1, Section D2. 　❏ Check against solution provided.	**Study Time:** 1 hour ❏ **Solving Word Problems:** Chapter X 　❏ Reread Section B.
4 days before the test	**Study Time:** 1 hour ❏ **Critical Reasoning:** Chapter VIII 　❏ Reread chapter. 　❏ If this is a targeted chapter, do the 10 additional practice questions at end of chapter.	**Study Time:** 20 minutes ❏ **Integrated Reasoning:** Chapter VI 　❏ Do practice questions 4–6, Section A2. 　❏ Check against solutions provided.	**Study Time:** 1 hour ❏ **Problem Solving:** Chapter XI 　❏ Review Sections A–C.
3 days before the test	**Study Time:** 1 hour ❏ **Sentence Correction:** Chapter IX 　❏ Reread chapter. 　❏ If this is a targeted chapter, do the 6 additional practice questions at end of chapter.	**Study Time:** 20 minutes ❏ **Integrated Reasoning:** Chapter VI 　❏ Do practice questions 3–4, Section B2. 　❏ Check against solutions provided.	**Study Time:** 1 hour ❏ **Data Sufficiency:** Chapter XII 　❏ Review Sections A–C.
2 days before the test	**Study Time:** 1 hour ❏ Review Chapters VII, VIII, and IX. ❏ Redo all practice questions for targeted chapters.	**Study Time:** 30 minutes ❏ **Integrated Reasoning:** Chapter VI 　❏ Work practice questions 5–8, Section C2 and practice question 2, Section D2. 　❏ Check against solutions provided.	**Study Time:** 1 hour ❏ Redo questions that you answered incorrectly on the **Practice Test** and check the answer explanations.

	Analytical Writing and Verbal	Integrated Reasoning	Quantitative
1 day before the test	❑ Relax. . . . You're well prepared for the test. ❑ Have confidence in your ability to do well.		

Morning of the test	**Reminders:**
	❑ Have a good breakfast.
	❑ Take the following items with you on test day:
	    ❑ Your admission ticket and photo ID
	    ❑ A watch
	❑ Try to go outside for a few minutes and walk around before the test.
	❑ Most important: Stay calm and confident during the test. Take deep, slow breaths if you feel at all nervous. You can do it!		

IV. One-Week Cram Plan

One-Week Cram Plan		
	Analytical Writing and Verbal	**Integrated Reasoning**	**Quantitative**

7 days before the test	**Study Time:** 4½ hours
	❑ Take the **Diagnostic Test** and review answer explanations.
	   ❑ Compare your essay to the rubric in Chapter V and the samples in Chapter I, and target areas to improve.
	   ❑ Based on your errors on the Diagnostic Test, identify difficult topics and their corresponding chapters. These chapters are your targeted chapters.		

6 days before the test	**Study Time:** 1 to 2½ hours (depending on your Diagnostic Test results)
	❑ **Analysis of an Argument:** Chapter V
	   ❑ Read Sections A–B.
	   ❑ Write 1 practice essay from Section C. Compare your essay to the rubric in Section B.
	   ❑ If this is a targeted chapter, write 2 additional essays from Section C.
		Study Time: 40 minutes
		❑ **Integrated Reasoning:** Chapter VI
		   ❑ Read Section A1.
		   ❑ Do practice questions 1–3, Section A2.
		   ❑ Check against solutions provided.
			Study Time: 2 to 3½ hours (depending on your Diagnostic Test results)
			❑ **Reviewing Math Concepts:** Chapter X
			   ❑ Read Section A.
			   ❑ Review formulas and key concepts.

5 days before the test	**Study Time:** 2 to 3½ hours (depending on your Diagnostic Test results)
	❑ **Reading Comprehension:** Chapter VII
	   ❑ Read the chapter.
	   ❑ Do practice questions 1–10.
	❑ **Critical Reasoning:** Chapter VIII
	   ❑ Read Sections A–F.
	   ❑ Do practice questions for each section.
	   ❑ If this is a targeted chapter, do the 10 additional practice questions at the end of the chapter.
		Study Time: 40 minutes
		❑ **Integrated Reasoning:** Chapter VI
		   ❑ Read Section B1.
		   ❑ Do practice questions 1–2, Section B2.
		   ❑ Check against solutions provided.
			Study Time: 2 to 3½ hours (depending on your Diagnostic Test results)
			❑ **Solving Word Problems:** Chapter X
			   ❑ Read Section B.
			   ❑ Do practice problems.

continued

	Analytical Writing and Verbal	Integrated Reasoning	Quantitative

4 days before the test	**Study Time:** 1½ to 2 hours
	❏ **Sentence Correction:** Chapter IX
	  ❏ Read Sections A–B.
	  ❏ Do practice questions for each section.
	  ❏ If this is a targeted chapter, do the 6 additional practice questions at the end of the chapter.
		Study Time: 40 minutes
		❏ **Integrated Reasoning:** Chapter VI
		  ❏ Read Section C1.
		  ❏ Do practice questions 1–4, Section C2.
		  ❏ Check against solutions provided.
			Study Time: 2 to 3 hours
			❏ **Problem Solving:** Chapter XI
			  ❏ Read Sections A–C.
			  ❏ Do practice problems.

3 days before the test	**Study Time:** 4½ hours ❏ Take the **Practice Test** and review answer explanations. ❏ Based on your errors on the Practice Test, identify difficult topics and their corresponding chapters. Target these chapters for extra review.		

2 days before the test	**Study Time:** 1 to 2 hours
	❏ Based on the **Practice Test,** review targeted chapters.
	❏ **Analysis of an Argument:** Chapter V
	  ❏ Reread chapter.
	  ❏ If this is a targeted chapter, write at least 1 more essay.
		Study Time: 40 minutes
		❏ **Integrated Reasoning:** Chapter VI
		  ❏ Read Section D1.
		  ❏ Do practice question 1, Section D2.
		  ❏ Check against solution provided.
			Study Time: 2 to 3 hours
			❏ **Data Sufficiency:** Chapter XII
			  ❏ Read Sections A–C.
			  ❏ Do practice problems.

1 day before the test	**Study Time:** 1½ to 2 hours
	❏ **Reading Comprehension:** Chapter VII
	  ❏ Reread the chapter.
	  ❏ If this is a targeted chapter, redo practice questions 1–10.
	❏ **Critical Reasoning:** Chapter VIII
	  ❏ Reread chapter.
	  ❏ If this is a targeted chapter, do the 10 additional practice questions at the end of the chapter.
	❏ **Sentence Correction:** Chapter IX
	  ❏ Reread chapter.
	  ❏ If this is a targeted chapter, do the 6 additional practice questions at the end of the chapter.
		Study Time: 45 minutes
		❏ **Integrated Reasoning:** Chapter VI
		  ❏ Do practice questions 4–6, Section A2; practice questions 3–4, Section B2; practice questions 5–8, Section C2; and practice question 2, Section D2.
		  ❏ Check against solutions provided.
			Study Time: 1½ to 2 hours
			❏ Redo questions that you answered incorrectly on the **Practice Test** and check the answer explanations.

Morning of the test	**Reminders:**
	❏ Have a good breakfast.
	❏ Take the following items with you on test day:
	  ❏ Your admission ticket and photo ID
	  ❏ A watch
	❏ Try to go outside for a few minutes and walk around before the test.
	❏ Most important: Stay calm and confident during the test. Take deep, slow breaths if you feel at all nervous. You can do it!		

V. Analysis of an Argument

The Analytical Writing section of the GMAT is an Analysis of an Argument essay. This section is designed to measure your ability to think critically and to express yourself articulately. You're presented with an argument to analyze by evaluating the reasoning, evidence, and conclusion. The argument may be on any topic. You don't need any specific knowledge of the topic to answer the question.

You're given 30 minutes to complete the essay response to the prompt. Your task is to examine the argument critically, pointing out the strengths and the weaknesses of the argument's reasoning and conclusions. You should indicate flaws in the argument, baseless or false assumptions, alternative explanations, and missing information that is necessary for a sound conclusion. You can offer counterarguments, evidence that would strengthen the persuasiveness of the argument, and other feasible conclusions. Your analysis must be presented in correct essay form using the conventions of standard written English.

Here is a sample Analysis of an Argument prompt:

> The following appeared in a local Chamber of Commerce report.
>
> "Last year, Ketti's Cat Grooming Salon moved from Main Street to Park Place. Because business has increased 20 percent since the move, relocating was a good decision. This conclusion is also supported by the fact that, in Ketti's old location, two other businesses, a tailor shop and a shoe-repair shop, have opened and closed."
>
> Discuss the logic of this argument. In your discussion, be sure to analyze how well reasoned you think it is and evaluate the use of evidence in the argument. For example, you may need to consider what faulty or questionable assumptions underlie the thinking and what alternative explanations or counterexamples might weaken the conclusion. In your response, you may want to discuss what sort of evidence would strengthen or refute the argument, what changes in the argument would make it more logically sound, and what information would help you more accurately evaluate its conclusion.

A. Approach to the Essay

1. Thinking

Take about two minutes to read the argument carefully, thinking about the conclusion or conclusions that are embedded in the argument. The final conclusion is usually at the end of the argument, but other conclusions may appear in the middle.

As you read, ask yourself the following questions:

- Do I follow the argument's reasoning?
- Do I feel it has appropriate evidence?
- Is the conclusion logical?

As you brainstorm, jot down ideas on your note boards as the ideas occur to you. Don't worry about order or organization—just get all your thoughts down in these first two minutes.

2. Analysis

Take about four minutes to analyze the argument. Use your note boards to jot down your answers to the following questions. They'll form the basis for your essay.

- What are the underlying assumptions of the argument?
- What are the key features of the argument?
- What constitutes proof or evidence in this argument? Identify the evidence used to prove the argument.
- What are the weaknesses in the assumptions of the argument? Are there unwarranted leaps from an assumption to an unverified conclusion?
- What is the conclusion? Is there enough information to logically support the conclusion in this argument? What additional evidence would be needed to make the conclusion sound?
- Are there counterarguments to the conclusion that could be alternate explanations for the results?

As you analyze the argument, look for the following flaws in reasoning.

a. Faulty Underlying Assumptions

An assumption is an unstated *premise* (the reason given in support of the conclusion) that must connect the stated premises and the conclusion. Assumptions must be based on logical evidence. For example, if an argument states that Sam bought a new house in Florida (premise), you might assume he lives in Florida (conclusion). The assumption that if Sam buys a house, he will live in it is based on the premise, but it could be a faulty assumption, because the fact that Sam purchased a house does not necessarily mean he lives in it.

Here are some examples of faulty underlying assumptions:

- **An assumption that nothing has changed in the time period of the situation.** For example:

  The following appeared in a teacher's association bulletin.

  "In the last school in which Principal Studious worked, she was known as a very tough administrator. The teachers disliked and resented her. Very often she called teachers into her office and berated them for chronic lateness, lazy work habits, and sloppy record-keeping. When she arrives at her new position at Midrange High School next September, she will again create a hostile work environment."

  Analysis: The argument makes several faulty assumptions:

  - The reports about the principal from the first school are accurate.
  - The problem lies with the principal and not with the teachers. (Perhaps, the teachers *were* guilty of chronic lateness, lazy work habits, and sloppy record-keeping.)
  - The principal's actions in her former school will mirror her actions in her new position. (What happened in the past will always happen the same way in the future.)

- **An assumption that one action mutually excludes another action.** For example:

  The following appeared in a memorandum from a company's marketing department.

  "Sales of a sweetened cereal product that traditionally makes a hefty profit have decreased. Some company officials argue that the composition of the cereal needs to be updated to reflect the growing health-consciousness of consumers. However, new packaging of other breakfast products has resulted in increased sales. All that the company has to do is update the packaging of the sweetened cereal product and sales will increase."

Analysis: The argument makes several faulty assumptions:

- The only reason for declining sales is outdated packaging.
- If the company updates the packaging, no change will be needed in the product itself. (One action excludes another action.)
- Increased sales of the other breakfast product can be solely attributed to the new packaging.

- **An assumption that what applies to one person must necessarily apply to all people.** For example:

The following appeared in a flyer sent out by a bottled-water delivery company.

"In an effort to lose weight, David gave up drinking all diet beverages. David lost 8 pounds in 2 months. All people who want to lose weight should give up diet drinks, and they will lose 1 pound each week."

Analysis: This argument makes several faulty assumptions:

- All dieters who mirror David's practice will experience the same weight loss. (What applies to one must apply to all.)
- The elimination of diet soda actually contributed to David's weight loss.
- All other dietary factors in David's eating habits did not contribute to his weight loss.
- All of David's other experiences (exercise, emotional stress) did not contribute to his weight loss.

- **An assumption that one cause necessarily and consistently produces the same effect.** For example:

The following appeared in a local newspaper endorsing the reelection of Candidate North for the position of state senator.

"Vote for North, and you will be voting for a woman who has been a positive force for economic recovery in our state. In the past four years that she has held office, all state employees have received wage increases, two major industries have decreased their air and water pollution, and traffic congestion on the interstate highway has decreased by 23 percent. In a recent telephone poll, most state residents who were called responded that they felt optimistic that the state economy would continue to flourish under four more years of North's tenure. To continue this positive growth, don't vote for South; he'll surely lead the state in the wrong direction."

Analysis: This argument makes several faulty assumptions:

- North was responsible for wage increases and decreases in pollution and traffic congestion.
- The telephone calls were a random sample rather than a poll of identified North supporters.
- Candidate South does not support the same causes as North.
- Four more years of Candidate North's tenure will continue the economic growth.

b. Weak, Inappropriate, or Misleading Information

The conclusions in an argument may rely on information that is ambiguous, irrelevant, or misleading. Here are some examples of unreliable information that should make you question the validity of a conclusion:

- **Drawing an illogical analogy between two unlike situations.** For example:

The following appeared in promotional literature for a billboard company.

"Beth's Baby Furniture Outlet installed a large billboard on the side of the turnpike exit. Sales of baby furniture increased 14 percent in the next fiscal quarter. Dr. Mary Chen, a local dentist, would like to

69

increase her dental practice. All she has to do is install an advertising billboard on the side of the turnpike and her patient load will increase substantially."

Analysis: This argument draws an illogical analogy: People choose their dentist the same way they choose a baby furniture store. This argument also draws questionable conclusions:

- A direct correlation exists between the billboard and the increased sales.
- No other factors (such as another store closing, a new line of furniture, a favorable write-up in the press, or a new road) are present to explain the increase.
- In order to increase her patient load, all Dr. Chen needs to do is to advertise.

- **Employing vague or undefined terms in the argument.** For example:

The following appeared in an advertisement for a new gym.

"Jungle Gym has a fabulous new fitness program, terrific equipment, and great trainers. As a special promotion, we are offering the following guarantee: Join the gym today, and by three months from now, you'll be physically fit and satisfied with your body image."

Analysis: The claim in the argument is faulty because the terms are left undefined:

- How is physical fitness defined? Is it the same for all people? How will it be measured at the end of three months?
- What constitutes satisfaction? How is it measured?
- What is body image? If a client wants to look like a body builder or a movie star to satisfy his or her ideal body image, will the gym guarantee results?
- What is the guarantee? What will the unsatisfied client get?

- **Using an unreliable survey.** For example:

The following appeared in a local newspaper column on education.

"A survey of children in Western Elementary School indicated that English was their favorite subject, and science, their least favorite subject. Teachers who want their students to be happy should include more English than science in their curriculum."

Analysis: This argument employs an unreliable survey of elementary school students.

- No indication is given of how many students were included in the survey—3? 12? 141? How old are the students? What grades are they in?
- No indication is given about how the survey was conducted or how the questions were phrased. (Did the English teacher give the survey, or was it given by an outsider?)
- No specific information is factored in: Who teaches English, and who teaches science? The classroom teacher? A specialist? When is each subject taught? Where? How?
- The conclusion is questionable: Should the goals of the teacher be predicated on students' preferences?

- **Misleading statistical evidence that uses a small sample to generalize about a larger one.** For example:

The following appeared in a local newspaper.

"Last month, 12 female college basketball players went to the governor's office to protest cuts in the state's budget for intercollegiate women's sports. Among all the colleges and universities in the state, there are 24,000 female athletes. Because the other female athletes didn't go to the protest, most female athletes obviously don't care about funds for athletics. Therefore, the governor doesn't need to change the budget allocations."

Analysis: This argument contains misleading statistical evidence that uses a small sample to generalize about a larger one:

- The argument assumes that the number of athletes who appear in the governor's office is equal to the number of athletes who care about the budget cuts.

- No evidence is given about how the 12 athletes were chosen. Perhaps they were elected as delegates to state the position of the group as a whole to the governor.

- The argument disregards the unfeasibility of 24,000 athletes being able to appear at the governor's office at one time on one day.

- The argument concludes that the governor doesn't need to change budget allocations based on this one incident.

c. Drawing Unwarranted Conclusions

Always try to identify the conclusion at the end of the argument and/or conclusions within the argument and evaluate the validity of the evidence. The conclusion will often be introduced by the word *therefore*. Here are some examples of conclusions that rest on unjustified evidence:

- **Leaping from assumption to conclusion without adequate evidence.** For example:

  The following appeared in the health column of a local newspaper.

  "Several people who returned from a trip to the island of Papanuay developed flu-like symptoms two weeks after their return. To prevent an epidemic of influenza, public health officials immediately shut down all air and water traffic to the island. This action will end any threat of a flu epidemic."

  Analysis: The argument presents several inadequately supported conclusions:

  - The people who got the flu contracted it on the island. Who are they? Did they know each other prior to the trip? Are they related to one another? Do they work for the same company? Attend the same school? Share an activity?

  - The infected people haven't already spread the virus to all those with whom they have come into contact.

  - The virus with "flu-like" symptoms actually is the influenza virus and is contagious. (No mention is made of medical testing.)

  - A threat of epidemic exists.

- **Basing a conclusion on any of the reasoning flaws outlined above.** For example, a conclusion based on vague or misleading statistics:

  The following statement appeared in a memorandum distributed to high school teachers.

  "Guidance counselors took a poll of their students last week and found that 44 percent of the students are failing math. Therefore, it is obvious our math courses are too hard, and we have to simplify the math curriculum."

  Analysis: The conclusion is flawed because it is based on a vague or misleading statistic, and it makes unwarranted leaps:

  - How many students took the poll? How were the questions worded?

  - How were the students who took the poll selected? Did all the guidance counselors participate?

  - What other factors might explain the students' difficulties with math?

3. Planning and Organizing

When you feel satisfied that your analysis is complete, take four minutes to use your analysis to plan your response. After the argument is presented, the prompt is usually phrased as follows:

> Discuss the logic of this argument. In your discussion, be sure to analyze how well reasoned you think it is and evaluate the use of evidence in the argument. For example, you may need to consider what faulty or questionable assumptions underlie the thinking and what alternative explanations or counterexamples might weaken the conclusion. In your response, you may want to discuss what sort of evidence would strengthen or refute the argument, what changes in the argument would make it more logically sound, and what information would help you more accurately evaluate its conclusion.

Before you begin writing, recheck your analysis to be sure you've done a thorough job. Use the prompt as a guide for your response. If you break it down into its components, you'll find just what you have to do:

- Discuss the logic of the argument.
- Analyze how well reasoned it is.
- Evaluate the use of evidence in the argument.
- Consider faulty and questionable assumptions.
- Offer alternative explanations.
- Give counterexamples.
- Discuss what evidence would strengthen or refute the argument.
- Explain changes in the argument that would make it more logically sound.

Here is an example of an Analysis of an Argument question followed by a sample outline:

> The following appeared in a report of a local board of education.
>
> "The board of education of Brilliance High School has looked at projected college majors of most graduating seniors and has found that the most popular major is technology and the least popular is music. Because this indicates that students do not have an interest in music, the board has decided to eliminate the music program from the curriculum and require all students to take technology courses instead. This same action was recently taken in a neighboring district, and the district won national awards in technology. The board expects the school to win awards next year."
>
> Discuss the logic of this argument. In your discussion, be sure to analyze how well reasoned you think it is and evaluate the use of evidence in the argument. For example, you may need to consider what faulty or questionable assumptions underlie the thinking and what alternative explanations or counterexamples might weaken the conclusion. In your response, you may want to discuss what sort of evidence would strengthen or refute the argument, what changes in the argument would make it more logically sound, and what information would help you more accurately evaluate its conclusion.

I. **Introduction:** The argument is flawed for several reasons.

   A. The function of a school board is to provide an educational experience for all its students, not to win awards.

   B. The board's actions may not be in the best educational interest of all its students.

   C. The board is basing its decision on questionable evidence and analogy (to the other school's experience).

II. **Questionable Evidence**

    A. **Faulty conclusion:** The number of music majors indicates the number of students interested in music.

    B. **Unwarranted assumption:** College major indicates strong interest in a field (may or may not be true).

    C. **Vague terms:** "Most popular" and "least popular."

III. **Alternative Explanations**

    A. Music may be a strong interest, but careers are limited.

    B. More students major in technology because this field is broader and easier to enter than music.

    C. Some students go into technology to make money to allow them more leisure time to enjoy hobbies and artistic pursuits (such as music).

IV. **Invalid Assumptions**

    A. The student body of Brilliance High School is comparable to that of the neighboring school.

    B. Winning technology awards is an important goal of a school board.

    C. Students will win awards when the curriculum is changed. (This assumes that all variables in the two schools are the same.)

    D. Nurturing music talent, even of a few students, is not a worthy goal.

V. **Conclusion:** The school board's argument is faulty in that it does not consider the importance of education in the arts and places unwarranted emphasis on winning awards.

4. Writing

You'll need about 18 minutes to write the essay. Because the analytical essay is both a critical-thinking assessment and a writing assessment, you need to express your ideas as effectively as possible. Be aware of the conventions of standard written English as you write. You won't have much time for revision, so concentrate on clear, concise sentences without awkwardness, redundancies, or clichés.

a. Develop Your Examples

In the topic sentence of each of your body paragraphs, state the point that you'll develop and then explain how the point relates to the argument. Follow with an explication of your analysis so the reader understands the flaws in the reasoning and conclusions of the argument. Try to give specific details by offering alternative explanations, pointing out illogical assumptions and unwarranted conclusions, and indicating critical information that is missing from or misinterpreted in the argument.

Remember: In the Analysis of an Argument essay, your own feelings and opinions on the situation presented in the argument are not relevant.

b. Organize Coherently

As you develop your examples, be sure to use transitional phrases. Transitional words link ideas and indicate the relationship of ideas within a sentence, a paragraph, or a passage. They are essential tools for a writer who wants to achieve a clear and logical flow of ideas.

Transitional words are the key to coherence, and essay raters are trained to spot them. Use transitional words within the paragraph as well, to help your ideas flow logically.

The following table offers examples of transitional words.

Important Transitional Words	
Words Used to Indicate an Example	**Words Used to Show a Result**
For example	Accordingly
For instance	Consequently
Specifically	Hence
	Therefore
Words Used to Indicate a Reason	**Words Used to Indicate More Information**
As	Besides
Because	Furthermore
Due to	In addition
Since	Moreover
Words Used to Contrast	**Words Used to Show Similarity**
Although	Again
But	Also
Despite	Another
However	Equally
In contrast	In the same way
Nevertheless	Likewise
On the other hand	Similarly
Still	Too
Whereas	
While	
Yet	
Words Used to Establish Time Relationships	**Words Used for Emphasis**
After	Assuredly
At last	At the same time
At this point	Clearly
Before	Indeed
During	Once
Later	Then
Next	Then again
Recently	To be sure
Soon	Without doubt
Until	

Here is a sample paragraph from an Analysis of an Argument question using transitional words and phrases. This paragraph is part of a response to the example regarding the board of education for Brilliance High School.

> **It is clear** from the faulty logic of the decision that the board of education is putting prestige over education. **While it is true that** meeting the needs of the majority of students is an important goal, a curriculum must not disregard the needs of the minority. **Moreover,** the board shows a blatant disregard for the development of the appreciation of music in the students of Brilliance High. **Instead of** fostering a liberal education and a love for the arts, the revised curriculum will limit students' options. **Indeed,** as technology becomes the focal point of education in the school, some students will graduate without ever hearing a symphony or playing a trombone.

c. Use Active Verbs

To make your writing lively rather than flat, avoid state-of-being verbs (forms of the verb *to be*) and weak passive sentences.

> **Weak:** There are many weak and inaccurate generalizations in the argument.
>
> **Strong:** The argument suffers from inaccuracies and weak generalizations.

d. Avoid Qualifying Phrases

Avoid phrases like *I believe* and *I think* because they weaken your position. An opinion is always more forceful and convincing if it is presented without such qualifying phrases as *I think* or *In my opinion.* Your writing will be crisper and more effective if you state your position directly and vigorously.

> **Weak:** I believe that that there are alternate explanations that could produce the same results.
>
> **Strong: Several alternate explanations could cause these same effects.**

e. Avoid Clichés

Clichés are overworked phrases that your reader has seen in hundreds of essays. Because these expressions are so prevalent, they have lost their freshness and meaning. Use of clichés suggests that you don't really have anything new to say. If you find yourself resorting to such stock phrases as "You can't tell a book by its cover," simply restate the idea in a straightforward manner: "People will often surprise you."

> **Weak:** The argument just beats around the bush.
>
> **Strong:** The generalizations in the argument weaken the probability of the stated outcome.

f. Use Sentence Variety

Most writers have a tendency to write simple sentences that follow the subject-verb pattern. The result is an essay that sounds flat and unsophisticated rather than lively and polished.

As you work on the practice essays at the end of this chapter, be conscious of your sentence structure. Try to incorporate as many of the sentence variety strategies in this section as you can. The more you practice these techniques, the more natural they'll become for you.

- **Combine simple sentences into compound or complex sentences.**

  Instead of: It is important to recognize the vague and ambiguous terms in the argument. They are that "many young people like to shop in small stores" and that "most shopping in small towns is done online." The terms *many* and *most* are vague.

  Write: Because the argument is flawed by the use of such vague terms as many in "many young people like to shop in small stores" and most in "most shopping in small towns is done online," the conclusion is weak.

- **Start a sentence with an adverb.**

  Instead of: The argument doesn't indicate at the end that the weather could have been a factor in the reduced revenue.

  Write: Clearly, the argument fails to acknowledge that the weather could have been a factor in the reduced revenue.

- **Combine sentences to clarify relationships.**

  Instead of: The demographics may reflect a shift in buying patterns. You can't assume more people will shop online.

  Write: Even if the demographics do reflect a shift in buying patterns, you can't necessarily assume that more people will shop online.

g. Employ Rhetorical Strategies

For the Analysis of the Argument essay, you want to demonstrate clarity, conciseness, and insightfulness. To accomplish that goal, present your ideas as persuasively as possible. Using the following words and phrases will help you accomplish that goal:

- **Relationship phrases:**

  "Although it might initially appear that . . ."

  "A closer examination reveals . . ."

  "Some serious concerns that have been omitted and must be addressed are . . ."

  "Most conspicuously, the argument fails to . . ."

  "In what appears to be an illogical leap, the argument . . ."

- **Effective verbs:**

  Negative: dismisses, disregards, fails, hinders, ignores, impedes, omits, subordinates, or undermines

  Positive: advances, cultivates, encourages, evinces, facilitates, fosters, or promotes

- **Effective adjectives:**

  Positive: cogent, coherent, convincing, incisive, key, lucid, primary, rational, sound, trenchant, or well reasoned

  Negative: ambiguous, dubious, inapt, inconclusive, irrelevant, problematic, questionable, tangential, unconvincing, or vague

5. Proofread

Leave about two minutes to proofread your essay. Because you won't have time to write a second draft, just try to fix the most obvious errors:

- **Revise any unclear sentences.**
- **Clarify ambiguous phrases.**
- **Remove wordy expressions.**
- **Correct grammatical mistakes.**
- **Check for typos.** Typos are the mark of a sloppy writer and create a negative impression on essay raters.

Remember: Don't try to change your essay dramatically. You're writing under time constraints, and you may end up making the paper seem disjointed and incoherent if you try to change too much.

B. GMAT Scoring

Your Analytical Writing Assessment (AWA) (Analysis of an Argument) will be scored twice: once by a trained rater (a human being) and once by an E-rater (a computerized essay-scoring program). If there is a discrepancy of more than one point between the two scores, a trained rater (a human being) determines the final score.

GMAT essay raters use a six-point rubric. The highest score an essay can receive is a 6 and the lowest is a 1. A 0 is given only to an essay that is completely off topic, is not written in English, merely repeats the prompt, or is a random series of characters.

The following rubric outlines what you need to do in order to receive each score. Use this rubric to assess your own practice essays. Better yet, ask an English professor or English graduate student to grade your essays using this rubric.

Rubric: Analysis of an Argument		
6	**5**	**4**
Presents an outstanding critique of the argument.	Presents a solid critique of the argument.	Presents an adequate critique of the argument.
Clearly identifies and thoroughly analyzes the key components of the argument.	Identifies and explains the key components of the argument.	Identifies the key components of the argument.
Insightfully develops an analysis and uses transitions effectively to show relationships between ideas.	Effectively develops an analysis and supports it with logically presented and connected ideas.	Develops a satisfactory analysis and indicates some connections between ideas.
Shows evidence of an effective organizational plan.	Shows evidence of a clear organizational plan.	Shows evidence of an organizational plan.
Demonstrates outstanding control of language, including apt vocabulary and sentence variety.	Demonstrates good control of language, including apt vocabulary and sentence variety.	Demonstrates competent control of language, including satisfactory vocabulary and some sentence variety.
Demonstrates superior control of standard written English with few, if any, grammatical errors.	Demonstrates control of standard written English with few grammatical errors.	Demonstrates competency in standard written English, but makes some grammatical errors.

continued

3	2	1
Presents an inadequate critique of the argument.	Presents a very weak analysis of the argument.	Presents a seriously flawed analysis of the argument.
Shows only partial understanding of the key components of the argument.	Shows little understanding of the key components of the argument.	Shows no understanding of the key components of the argument.
Develops irrelevant ideas or misinterprets the argument.	Poorly develops vague ideas that may or may not be related to the argument.	Provides no logical analysis.
Shows little evidence of an organizational plan.	Shows minimal evidence of an organizational plan.	Shows no evidence of an organizational plan.
Demonstrates little control of language, uses basic vocabulary, and lacks sentence variety.	Demonstrates very little control of language, and uses vocabulary that is imprecise, inappropriate, or incoherent.	Is seriously flawed in the use of language including weak and inappropriate vocabulary and poor sentence structure.
Demonstrates poor control over the elements of standard written English, and makes frequent grammatical errors.	Demonstrates near incompetence in the use of standard written English, and makes serious and frequent grammatical errors.	Demonstrates complete incompetence in the use of standard written English, and makes grammatical errors that are so egregious and so numerous that they impede understanding.

C. Sample Argument Questions

Practice writing several of the following Analysis of an Argument essays in the 30 minutes allotted for the task. After you finish, compare your essays to the rubric and to the sample graded essays in Chapter I. Next, take a few additional minutes to revise your essays—add details, correct errors, and look for places to improve vocabulary and sentence variety. Reread your revised essay to make sure you know what an effective finished product should look like. Then aim for that target on your test day.

- The following appeared in a report presented to the stockholders in the Excellent Manufacturing Company.

  "The Excellent Manufacturing Company has determined that its employees have low morale. To boost morale, the company has decided to offer its employees every other Friday off in July and August. The Superior Manufacturing Company, in a neighboring community, implemented this plan, and productivity increased by 16 percent. In addition, Superior Manufacturing found that, when the employees had two Fridays off each month, they had better attendance in September and October than they had in those months in the previous year. The Excellent Manufacturing Company predicts improved morale, productivity, and attendance as a result of the new Fridays-off plan."

  Discuss the logic of this argument. In your discussion, be sure to analyze how well reasoned you think it is and evaluate the use of evidence in the argument. For example, you may need to consider what faulty or questionable assumptions underlie the thinking and what alternative explanations or counterexamples might weaken the conclusion. In your response, you may want to discuss what sort of evidence would strengthen or refute the argument, what changes in the argument would make it more logically sound, and what information would help you more accurately evaluate its conclusion.

- The following appeared in an advertisement in a health and fitness magazine.

  "Comfy Sneakers have a cushioned inner lining and an angled sole. According to the manufacturer, an angled sole allows runners to maintain proper body position, run more efficiently, and burn more calories as they run. People who want to lose weight should purchase Comfy Sneakers."

Discuss the logic of this argument. In your discussion, be sure to analyze how well reasoned you think it is and evaluate the use of evidence in the argument. For example, you may need to consider what faulty or questionable assumptions underlie the thinking and what alternative explanations or counterexamples might weaken the conclusion. In your response, you may want to discuss what sort of evidence would strengthen or refute the argument, what changes in the argument would make it more logically sound, and what information would help you more accurately evaluate its conclusion.

- The following appeared in a newspaper editorial.

"Rap music with lyrics advocating violence has become increasingly popular among teenagers. In fact, a survey of teens found that 53 percent choose to listen to rap music. Recently, there has been an upsurge of violent incidents in the local high school. High school officials are not concerned about this upswing because they have made no effort to limit teenagers' access to rap music."

Discuss the logic of this argument. In your discussion, be sure to analyze how well reasoned you think it is and evaluate the use of evidence in the argument. For example, you may need to consider what faulty or questionable assumptions underlie the thinking and what alternative explanations or counterexamples might weaken the conclusion. In your response, you may want to discuss what sort of evidence would strengthen or refute the argument, what changes in the argument would make it more logically sound, and what information would help you more accurately evaluate its conclusion.

- The following information appeared in a handout from the owner of a local newspaper to his sales manager.

"Responses to a survey in last month's issue indicate that townspeople want to read more human-interest stories about local residents. If we cut out news about local sports teams and add more human-interest stories, we will increase our circulation and sell more newspapers."

Discuss the logic of this argument. In your discussion, be sure to analyze how well reasoned you think it is and evaluate the use of evidence in the argument. For example, you may need to consider what faulty or questionable assumptions underlie the thinking and what alternative explanations or counterexamples might weaken the conclusion. In your response, you may want to discuss what sort of evidence would strengthen or refute the argument, what changes in the argument would make it more logically sound, and what information would help you more accurately evaluate its conclusion.

- The following is a memorandum from the human relations committee of the Zippy Company.

"Research shows that people who exercise have fewer heart attacks and require fewer hospitalizations. Experts say swimming is an excellent form of exercise for people of all ages. To cut down on healthcare costs and to improve employee attendance, the Zippy Company should take away half of the employee parking lot and build a swimming pool in that space."

Discuss the logic of this argument. In your discussion, be sure to analyze how well reasoned you think it is and evaluate the use of evidence in the argument. For example, you may need to consider what faulty or questionable assumptions underlie the thinking and what alternative explanations or counterexamples might weaken the conclusion. In your response, you may want to discuss what sort of evidence would strengthen or refute the argument, what changes in the argument would make it more logically sound, and what information would help you more accurately evaluate its conclusion.

- The following is a report of the Short Hills High School basketball coach to his booster club.

"The members of Short Hills High School basketball team are, for the most part, average height. Treetop High School, on the other hand, has two boys on the team who are over 6'11" tall. There is no way Short Hills will be able to beat Treetop this year."

Discuss the logic of this argument. In your discussion, be sure to analyze how well reasoned you think it is and evaluate the use of evidence in the argument. For example, you may need to consider what faulty or questionable assumptions underlie the thinking and what alternative explanations or counterexamples might weaken the conclusion. In your response, you may want to discuss what sort of evidence would strengthen or refute the argument, what changes in the argument would make it more logically sound, and what information would help you more accurately evaluate its conclusion.

VI. Integrated Reasoning Questions

The revision to the GMAT format in June 2012 includes a 30-minute section called Integrated Reasoning. The goal of the section is to assess your ability to organize data, to read charts and graphs, and to analyze material from a variety of sources to draw conclusions. The section replaces one of the writing exercises in the previous version of the exam and is scored separately from the verbal and quantitative sections.

The Integrated Reasoning section is interactive in ways the remainder of the test is not, and capitalizes on the technology available. You may need to sort data in spreadsheets or make calculations with the help of an on-screen calculator. The types of questions go beyond the standard multiple choice, asking you to make judgments about the truth of statements based on the given information, to choose the correct completion of a statement, to determine values of two variables and integrate both into your answer, and to determine whether certain conclusions can reasonably be drawn from the information presented.

The Integrated Reasoning questions do not directly test your knowledge of business or business terminology, but may present scenarios that you would encounter in business or in business school. You can expect to see information presented in charts and graphs, as well as memos or simulated e-mails. The ability to understand those visual representations of data, to draw information from those different types of communication, and to incorporate that information into a decision are the primary skills the section aims to test.

Although the Integrated Reasoning section is not meant to be a math test, there is a certain amount of mathematical knowledge that is required. Familiarity with different styles of graphs and their appropriate uses, careful reading of scales and legends, and an acquaintance with simple spreadsheets will be essential. In addition, you'll need fundamental statistical concepts like mean, median, range, and outlier as well as a grasp of basic probability. You'll be expected to understand scatter plots, correlation, and regression lines. You'll need a familiarity with concepts like the slope of a line as a rate of change. You'll be asked to think about situations in which two related quantities are unknown, and that may demand some simple algebra.

It is important to remember, however, that the Integrated Reasoning is not a math section. The temptation to undertake long or complex calculations or algebraic manipulations should not only be avoided, but should be a sign to you that you're approaching the question the wrong way. A simple calculator will be provided, but nothing more sophisticated than the arithmetic of calculating a mean or finding a percent should be required.

You will have 30 minutes to complete the Integrated Reasoning section, which will include 10 questions. (To keep the length of the test at 3 hours and 30 minutes as it was in the past, one of the writing assessments will be eliminated.) Questions will be presented in groups, and each group will be preceded by the presentation of data, graphs, or other information on which the questions are based. Each section of presentation and questions will have one of four formats.

- **Table Analysis** will present data in a spreadsheet-like format. This data table can be sorted by clicking on the column headings. The table will be followed by three statements, and you will be asked to decide if each statement is true or false based on the information in the table.

- **Graphic Interpretation** will present a graph, followed by one or two sentences in which key words or phrases must be filled in to make the statement true. You'll be asked to choose the correct completion from a drop-down menu.

- **Multi-Source Reasoning** will, not surprisingly, present you with two or three sources of information. These may be text (a memo, e-mail, or article) or graphic and will be arranged on separate tabs so that you can click back and forth among them. Once you've had a chance to review all the information, you'll be presented with three statements that might be inferred from the information. Your task will be to decide if the information supports the conclusions. Each Multi-Source Reasoning data set also will have a standard multiple-choice question with answer choices A through E.
- **Two-Part Analysis** will describe a situation in which two values are unknown. (Expect the values to be somehow related. This isn't meant to just be two problems in one.) You'll be shown a list of possible values, including the two you're seeking. You must indicate the value of each by marking the appropriate spot in the chart.

The best preparation for any test is to practice, so review examples of each of the question formats. Along the way, you'll be able to focus in on any math or stats involved in the question, and strategies for tackling each type.

A. Table Analysis

The principal thing to remember for the table analysis is that the table can be sorted. That means that the questions will expect you to sort it. Take a moment to think about the kinds of questions that would make you want to sort the data. Maximum values, minimum values, ranges, and medians are obvious things to ask about. Remember, too, that this is about integrating information, so don't expect to be asked just for the median of a single column. You're more likely to be asked to compare the median of one column with the median of another.

1. Example

The table below contains information on commuting times and the changes in commuting times for several counties in a state, from 2008 to 2010.

Counties	Average Commute Time, 2010 (Minutes)	Change, 2009–2010 (Minutes)	Percentage Change, 2009–2010	Change, 2008–2009 (Minutes)	Percentage Change, 2008–2009
A	32.2	−2.4	−7	5.1	17
B	31.5	5.5	21	7.3	39
C	30.8	1.2	4	3	11
D	29.2	1.2	4	2.9	12
E	28.8	0.7	2	3.6	15
F	28.7	−0.8	−3	3.8	15
G	27.5	−2.4	−8	5	20
H	27	0.9	3	1.7	7
I	26	2	8	3.7	18
J	26	0.3	1	0.7	3
K	25.7	1	4	3.1	14
L	24.2	−1.5	−6	3	13

Counties	Average Commute Time, 2010 (Minutes)	Change, 2009–2010 (Minutes)	Percentage Change, 2009–2010	Change, 2008–2009 (Minutes)	Percentage Change, 2008–2009
M	23.7	−1.5	−6	2.8	13
N	22.6	0.8	4	3.6	20
O	20.1	−0.9	−4	3.1	17

Consider each of the following statements. For each statement, indicate whether the statement is true or false, based on the information provided in the table.

True	False	
		1. The largest change from 2008 to 2009 and the largest change from 2009 to 2010 both occurred in the same county.
		2. The county with the median commute time in 2010 had one of the three smallest changes in commuting time from 2008 to 2009.
		3. Two counties with the same change from 2008 to 2009 were both among the five longest commuting times in 2010.

For the first question, you'll want to sort the table first on the column that represents the change from 2008 to 2009, and see which county had the largest change.

Counties	Average Commute Time (Minutes), 2010	Change (Minutes), 2009–2010	Percentage Change, 2009–2010	Change (Minutes), 2008–2009	Percentage Change, 2008–2009
J	26	0.3	1	0.7	3
H	27	0.9	3	1.7	7
C	30.8	1.2	4	3	11
D	29.2	1.2	4	2.9	12
L	24.2	−1.5	−6	3	13
M	23.7	−1.5	−6	2.8	13
K	25.7	1	4	3.1	14
E	28.8	0.7	2	3.6	15
F	28.7	−0.8	−3	3.8	15
A	32.2	−2.4	−7	5.1	17
O	20.1	−0.9	−4	3.1	17
I	26	2	8	3.7	18
G	27.5	−2.4	−8	5	20
N	22.6	0.8	4	3.6	20
B	31.5	5.5	21	7.3	39

The largest change is 7.3 minutes for county B. Next, sort on the column for change from 2009 to 2010 and see if county B again has the largest change.

Counties	Average Commute Time (Minutes), 2010	Change (Minutes), 2009–2010	Percentage Change, 2009–2010	Change (Minutes), 2008–2009	Percentage Change, 2008–2009
A	32.2	−2.40	−7	5.1	17
G	27.5	−2.40	−8	5	20
L	24.2	−1.50	−6	3	13
M	23.7	−1.50	−6	2.8	13
O	20.1	−0.90	−4	3.1	17
F	28.7	−0.80	−3	3.8	15
J	26	0.30	1	0.7	3
E	28.8	0.70	2	3.6	15
N	22.6	0.80	4	3.6	20
H	27	0.90	3	1.7	7
K	25.7	1.00	4	3.1	14
C	30.8	1.20	4	3	11
D	29.2	1.20	4	2.9	12
I	26	2.00	8	3.7	18
B	31.5	5.50	21	7.3	39

It does, with 5.5 minutes, so the first question is true.

To attack the second question, you first need to determine which county had the median commuting time in 2010, so sort the table on average commute time in 2010, and look for the middle value. There are 15 counties listed, so the median value will be the eighth, when you have them in order.

Counties	Average Commute Time (Minutes), 2010	Change (Minutes), 2009–2010	Percentage Change, 2009–2010	Change (Minutes), 2008–2009	Percentage Change, 2008–2009
A	32.2	−2.4	−7	5.1	17
B	31.5	5.5	21	7.3	39
C	30.8	1.2	4	3	11
D	29.2	1.2	4	2.9	12
E	28.8	0.7	2	3.6	15
F	28.7	−0.8	−3	3.8	15
G	27.5	−2.4	−8	5	20
H	27	0.9	3	1.7	7

Counties	Average Commute Time (Minutes), 2010	Change (Minutes), 2009–2010	Percentage Change, 2009–2010	Change (Minutes), 2008–2009	Percentage Change, 2008–2009
I	26	2	8	3.7	18
J	26	0.3	1	0.7	3
K	25.7	1	4	3.1	14
L	24.2	−1.5	−6	3	13
M	23.7	−1.5	−6	2.8	13
N	22.6	0.8	4	3.6	20
O	20.1	−0.9	−4	3.1	17

The county with the median commuting time in 2010 is county H with 27 minutes. Then sort on the change from 2008 to 2009 and see if county H is among the three smallest changes.

Counties	Average Commute Time (Minutes), 2010	Change (Minutes), 2009–2010	Percentage Change, 2009–2010	Change (Minutes), 2008–2009	Percentage Change, 2008–2009
J	26	0.3	1	0.7	3
H	27	0.9	3	1.7	7
M	23.7	−1.5	−6	2.8	13
D	29.2	1.2	4	2.9	12
C	30.8	1.2	4	3	11
L	24.2	−1.5	−6	3	13
K	25.7	1	4	3.1	14
O	20.1	−0.9	−4	3.1	17
E	28.8	0.7	2	3.6	15
N	22.6	0.8	4	3.6	20
I	26	2	8	3.7	18
F	28.7	−0.8	−3	3.8	15
G	27.5	−2.4	−8	5	20
A	32.2	−2.4	−7	5.1	17
B	31.5	5.5	21	7.3	39

With a 1.7 minute change, county H is the second smallest change, so question 2 is true.

If you're still sorted on the change from 2008 to 2009, you can see that there are three pairs of counties with equal changes: C and L with 3 minutes, K and O with 3.1 minutes, and E and N with 3.6 minutes.

Counties	Average Commute Time (Minutes), 2010	Change (Minutes), 2009–2010	Percentage Change, 2009–2010	Change (Minutes), 2008–2009	Percentage Change, 2008–2009
J	26	0.3	1	0.7	3
H	27	0.9	3	1.7	7
M	23.7	−1.5	−6	2.8	13
D	29.2	1.2	4	2.9	12
C	30.8	1.2	4	3	11
L	24.2	−1.5	−6	3	13
K	25.7	1	4	3.1	14
O	20.1	−0.9	−4	3.1	17
E	28.8	0.7	2	3.6	15
N	22.6	0.8	4	3.6	20
I	26	2	8	3.7	18
F	28.7	−0.8	−3	3.8	15
G	27.5	−2.4	−8	5	20
A	32.2	−2.4	−7	5.1	17
B	31.5	5.5	21	7.3	39

This may make the third question seem confusing, but if you sort on commuting time in 2010, you can see that the five longest commuting times belong to counties A, B, C, D, and E, so none of those pairs are in the top five.

Counties	Average Commute Time (Minutes), 2010	Change (Minutes), 2009–2010	Percentage Change, 2009–2010	Change (Minutes), 2008–2009	Percentage Change, 2008–2009
A	32.2	−2.4	−7	5.1	17
B	31.5	5.5	21	7.3	39
C	30.8	1.2	4	3	11
D	29.2	1.2	4	2.9	12
E	28.8	0.7	2	3.6	15
F	28.7	−0.8	−3	3.8	15
G	27.5	−2.4	−8	5	20
H	27	0.9	3	1.7	7
I	26	2	8	3.7	18
J	26	0.3	1	0.7	3

Counties	Average Commute Time (Minutes), 2010	Change (Minutes), 2009–2010	Percentage Change, 2009–2010	Change (Minutes), 2008–2009	Percentage Change, 2008–2009
K	25.7	1	4	3.1	14
L	24.2	−1.5	−6	3	13
M	23.7	−1.5	−6	2.8	13
N	22.6	0.8	4	3.6	20
O	20.1	−0.9	−4	3.1	17

The third question is false.

Here are some things to remember for the Table Analysis section:

- The median of a set of data is the middle value when the data are ordered. If you have an even number of values, average the two in the middle. Sort the column before finding the median.
- The mean is found by adding all the values and dividing by the number of values. Use the calculator to help with the computation.
- The range is the difference between the largest and smallest value.
- Percent change is found by dividing the change by the original value and changing it to a percent. The calculator will be helpful for this.

2. Practice

The table below shows the waist measurement (in inches), the weight (in pounds), and the body fat percentage for 20 adult subjects.

	Waist (in)	Weight (lb)	Body Fat %
A	32	175	6
B	33	159	6
C	32	168	9
D	33	188	10
E	33	160	10
F	34	146	10
G	34	159	12
H	38	200	15
I	40	240	20
J	36	181	21
K	35	173	21
L	39	196	22
M	36	175	22
N	38	187	25
O	41	215	27

(continued)

	Waist (in)	Weight (lb)	Body Fat %
P	44	219	28
Q	38	188	30
R	40	192	31
S	41	205	32
T	44	246	38

Consider each of the following statements. For each statement, indicate whether the statement is true or false, based on the information provided in the table.

True	False	
		1. The subject with the highest weight also has the highest percentage of body fat.
		2. The subjects with the median body fat percentage have weights within a 5-pound range.
		3. The 25 percent of subjects with the lightest weights all had body fat percentages below 10 percent.

The table below represents mean scores of a national mathematics assessment, the percent of students deemed proficient, and the percent of students receiving a free lunch, for each state in the United States.

State	Mean Score	Percent Proficient	Percent Free Lunch
Alabama	229	23	55
Alaska	237	32	44
Arizona	232	27	52
Arkansas	238	32	57
California	230	25	53
Colorado	240	35	40
Connecticut	243	37	31
Delaware	242	36	39
Florida	242	34	48
Georgia	235	28	52
Hawaii	234	29	42
Idaho	241	35	44
Illinois	237	31	44
Indiana	245	40	41
Iowa	243	38	34
Kansas	248	42	41
Kentucky	235	27	53
Louisiana	230	22	70
Maine	242	36	36
Maryland	240	32	34
Massachusetts	252	47	27
Michigan	238	32	38

State	Mean Score	Percent Proficient	Percent Free Lunch
Minnesota	247	41	30
Mississippi	228	20	69
Missouri	239	33	42
Montana	244	39	38
Nebraska	238	33	39
Nevada	232	27	45
New Hampshire	249	44	19
New Jersey	249	42	29
New Mexico	228	22	67
New York	243	37	49
North Carolina	242	35	48
North Dakota	245	41	32
Ohio	245	39	37
Oklahoma	237	30	55
Oregon	236	31	44
Pennsylvania	244	40	35
Rhode Island	236	31	40
South Carolina	237	31	53
South Dakota	241	37	36
Tennessee	233	26	49
Texas	242	35	55
Utah	239	35	37
Vermont	246	42	31
Virginia	244	35	30
Washington	243	37	39
West Virginia	236	30	50
Wisconsin	244	40	34
Wyoming	244	40	36

Consider each of the following statements. For each statement, indicate whether the statement is true or false, based on the information provided in the table.

True	False	
		4. The states with the lowest mean score on the assessment also had the largest percentage of students eligible for a free lunch.
		5. All states with mean scores of 244 or better had proficiency rates at or above the median proficiency rate.
		6. The state with the lowest percentage of students eligible for a free lunch also had the largest percentage of students proficient.

Answers

1. **True** Sort the table on weight and you find the highest weight is 246 pounds. Sort on body fat, and you find the highest body fat percentage is 38 percent, which aligns with 246 pounds.

2. **False** Sort the table on body fat and find the median, the average of the tenth and eleventh values. Both values are 21, so the median is 21. These two subjects have weights of 173 and 181 pounds, a range of 8 pounds.

3. **False** Sort the table on weight. Twenty-five percent of the sample is five subjects. Examine the body fat percentages for the five lightest subjects and you see that only two of them have body fat percentages below 10 percent.

4. **False** Sort on mean score. The lowest mean score was 228 in Mississippi and New Mexico. Sort on percent eligible for a free lunch. While Mississippi and New Mexico ranked second and third, Louisiana had the highest percentage.

5. **True** Sort on proficiency rate to find the median, the average of the twenty-fifth and twenty-sixth values. The median proficiency rate is 35 percent. Sort again on mean score and note that Ohio, Virginia, and Montana have mean scores of 39 percent, 35 percent, and 39 percent.

6. **False** Sort on the percentage eligible for a free lunch. New Hampshire has the least with 19 percent and Massachusetts is second, with 27 percent. New Hampshire's students achieved a 44 percent proficiency rating, second to Massachusetts's, with 47 percent.

B. Graphic Interpretation

You can expect these questions to test your ability to draw information from a graph and to assess your basic statistical knowledge as well as your familiarity with fundamental concepts of linear algebra. You may see a scatter plot showing the relationship between two variables, or a bar graph showing the frequency with which certain values were recorded. You may be presented with a circle graph that divides a whole into parts, or a line graph showing the change in a quantity over time. The types of questions you may be asked will depend on the type of graph presented.

With a scatter plot, and possibly a regression line, you can expect questions about the relationship between the variables, and the regression line as representing that relationship. You may be asked about deviations from the pattern—outliers—and about linear algebra concepts like slope, intercepts, and the equations of lines.

Bar graphs or circle graphs provide more opportunities to ask questions about probabilities, the chance that a particular value will occur. Line graphs, because they present change over time, suggest questions about rate of change, or slope.

1. Examples

Questions 1–3 refer to the following graph, which shows the number of power boat registrations, in thousands, and the number of manatee killed in Florida from 1983 to 2001. The line is the regression line for the points.

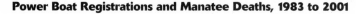

Power Boat Registrations and Manatee Deaths, 1983 to 2001

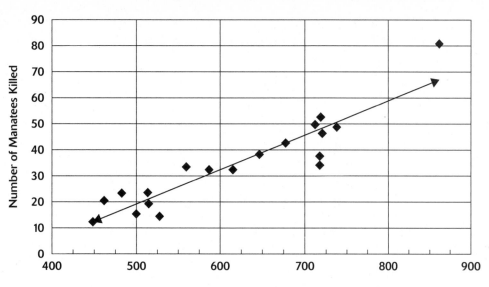

Number of Power Boat Registrations (in thousands)

Power Boat Registrations and Manatee Deaths, 1983 to 2001

Use the choices provided to fill in the blanks in each of the following statements based on the information given by the graph.

---

1. There is _____ (a weak positive, a weak negative, a strong positive, a strong negative, no) correlation between the number of power boats registered and the number of manatee killed.

This question is testing your understanding of correlation. If the scatter plot shows a generally linear pattern there is a correlation. If the slope of the line is positive, that is, if the line rises from left to right, there is a positive correlation. If the line has a negative slope and falls from left to right, there is a negative correlation. The closer the points fit to a line, the stronger the correlation. In this case, the points fit closely to a line with a positive slope, so there is a strong positive correlation.

---

2. The regression line predicts _____ (35, 38, 45, 50, 60) manatee deaths when there are 800,000 power boat registrations.

This question just asks you to find the coordinates of a point on the regression line. It's a prediction because there is no point in the scatter plot for 800,000 power boat registrations, but the point (800, 60) on the regression line tells you that the pattern of the data suggests that if there were 800,000 power boat registrations, you could expect approximately 60 manatee deaths.

Questions 3–4 refer to the following graph, which shows the results of an administration of a standardized test, broken down by gender.

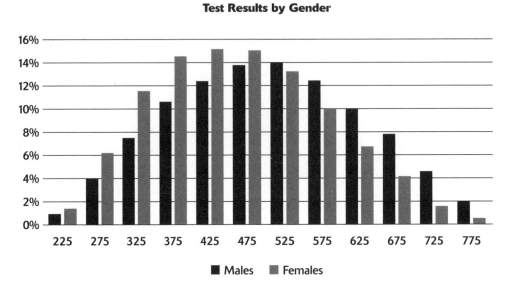

Use the choices provided to fill in the blanks in each of the following statements based on the information given by the graph.

3. Approximately _____ (1%, 4%, 5%, 7%, 12%, 13%) of men earned scores under 300.

Scores under 300 would be scores of 225 or 275. Add the percents for these, being careful to take the percents for the men and only the men. Approximately 1 percent + 4 percent = 5 percent of men earned those scores.

4. The probability that a female test-taker, selected at random, will have a score of 575 is approximately _____ (5%, 10%, 20%, 25%, 50%).

This question asks you to use relative frequency as an estimate of probability. The graph indicates that 10 percent of the female test-takers earned a score of 575, so the probability of randomly selecting a female test-taker with that score is 10 percent.

Here are some things to remember for the Graphical Interpretation section:

- Correlation talks about whether two variables are related. A perfect correlation would show up as a scatter plot that made a perfect line. The closer to that perfect line, the stronger the correlation. If both variables increase, there is a positive correlation. If one increases as the other decreases, there is a negative correlation.

- Slope is a rate of change. It compares the vertical movement to the horizontal movement. slope $= \dfrac{\text{rise}}{\text{run}} = \dfrac{\text{change in } y}{\text{change in } x}$. A line with a positive slope rises from left to right, but a line with a negative slope falls from left to right. A line with a zero slope is horizontal. The steeper the line, the farther from zero its slope is.
- An outlier is a data point that doesn't fit the pattern.
- The probability of an event can be estimated by its relative frequency.

2. Practice

Questions 1–2 refer to the following graph, which shows results of research on marijuana as a gateway drug. Each data point represents the report from one country with the percent of people reporting having tried marijuana and the percent reporting use of other drugs.

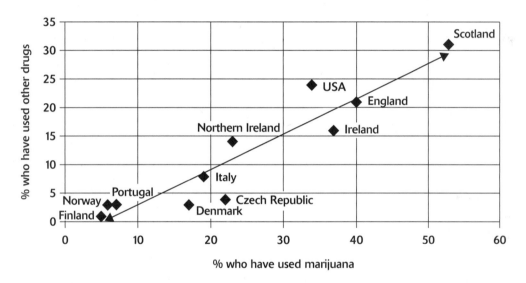

Use the choices provided to fill in the blanks in each of the following statements based on the information given by the graph.

1. The line of best fit suggests that in a country where 50 percent of the population has used marijuana, approximately _____ (4%, 14%, 21%, 28%, 50%) of the population will have used other drugs.

2. If the data from the USA were not included the slope of the line would be _____ (significantly steeper, slightly steeper, unchanged, slightly flatter, significantly flatter).

Questions 3–4 refer to the following graph, which shows the recorded annual rainfall in inches for a county in Southern California from 1980 to 2001. The dotted line represents average rainfall over the period.

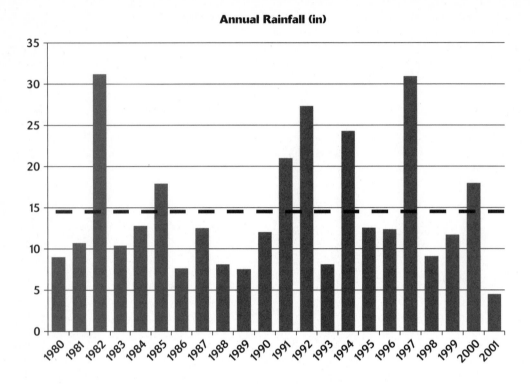

Annual Rainfall (in)

Use the choices provided to fill in the blanks in each of the following statements based on the information given by the graph.

3. The county reported above average rainfall in approximately _____ (3%, 15%, 20%, 32%, 45%) of the years represented in the graph.

4. The three-year period with the largest average rainfall was _____ (1980–1982, 1983–1985, 1987–1989, 1990–1992, 1995–1997).

Answers

1. **28%** The line of best fit suggests that in a country where 50 percent of the population has used marijuana, approximately 28 percent of the population will have used other drugs. Tracing up from 50 on the horizontal axis, you encounter the trend line at the point (50, 28).

2. **Slightly flatter** If the data from the USA were not included, the slope of the line would be <u>slightly flatter</u>. The position of the USA data point above the line pulls upward, so eliminating it would allow the line to drop. The point is not dramatically deviant from the line, however, so the effect would be small.

3. **32%** The county reported above average rainfall in approximately <u>32 percent</u> of the years represented in the graph. There are seven years—1982, 1985, 1991, 1992, 1994, 1997 and 2000—when rainfall was above average. Seven of the 22 years shown represents approximately 32 percent.

4. **1990–1992** The three-year period with the largest average rainfall was <u>1990 through 1992</u>. Use the onscreen calculator to average the rainfall for each three-year period. In 1980 to 1982, the average was about 17 inches of rain. From 1983 to 1985, between 13 and 14 inches. Average rainfall from 1987 to 1989 was only slightly over 9 inches. The average for 1990 to 1992 exceeded 20 inches, with 1995 to 1997 coming in second with between 18 and 19 inches. (Visual clues may help you rule out 1987 to 1989, the lowest of the group, and possibly 1983 through 1985, the second lowest.)

C. Multi-Source Reasoning

The multi-source reasoning questions will provide you with three sources of information. These may be text, for example, one or more e-mails, an excerpt from an article, or a memo. They may be numeric or graphical, including various sorts of graphs. Then you'll be asked if certain inferences are supported by the information in these sources. You can expect each statement to combine information from more than one source.

1. Examples

Questions 1–4 refer to the following e-mails and graph.

E-mail from Director of Public Affairs to Head of R&D

What's our public stance on carbon emissions? I'm seeing press releases from major corporations. One electronics house recorded a reduction in CO_2 levels of more than 30 percent, as compared to levels in 2000, with a five-year plan that targeted just 5 percent reductions. A big delivery house announced goals of reducing CO_2 emissions by 20 percent of 2005 levels by 2020 and improving the fuel efficiency of its fleet with electric vehicles and hybrid vehicles. What are we doing? We need to be seen as innovators.

E-mail from Head of R& D to Director of Public Affairs

The research seems to say that greenhouse gases are still a problem and will continue to be for the foreseeable future. We do see companies, including our competitors, patting themselves on the back for what they've done or are planning to do, but the science shows carbon emissions still increasing. We are doing the standard things: reducing energy usage both by team awareness and by strategic equipment replacement, improving fuel efficiency in our own vehicle fleet, and encouraging smart commuting. But if you want to go for something that might get more attention, there's a study telling us that companies adopting cloud computing show 40 to 50 percent power savings, with resultant reduction in carbon emissions. We're already doing some document management, but we could make a push to move to cloud computing in a big way. It would reduce our costs, including infrastructure costs, and position us as forward thinking.

The graph below shows worldwide carbon emissions, in millions of tons, from 1965 to 2008.

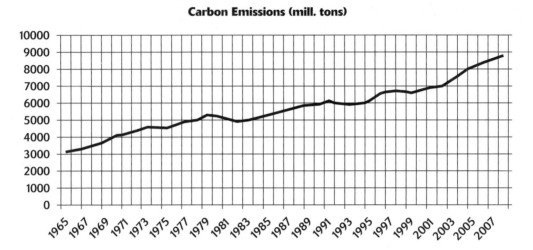

Carbon Emissions (mill. tons)

Consider each of the following questions. Does the information in the three sources support the inference as stated?

Yes	No	Inference
		1. The contention that greenhouse gases are a concern is exaggerated because the rate of growth of CO_2 emissions has slowed markedly since 2002.
		2. Because the company is already working on increasing the fuel efficiency of its vehicle fleet, it can expect to see similar 20 percent reductions in carbon emissions.
		3. Cloud computing can reduce CO_2 emissions to 1975 levels.

    4. If companies worldwide imitated the delivery company, by 2020, the worldwide carbon emissions would be reduced to levels approximately equal to those in

        A. 2007.
        B. 2006.
        C. 2005.
        D. 2004.
        E. 2003.

In the first question, the reference is to the head of R&D's statement that "The research seems to say that greenhouse gases are still a problem and will continue to be for the foreseeable future." The graph shows the level of emissions, so the slope of the graph would represent the rate of growth. In the years following 2002, the graph is still increasing, and until 2007, the slope is significantly larger than pre-2002. This inference is not supported by the information.

The second question combines the director's observation about a company's planned 20 percent reduction, which involved greater vehicle efficiency as well as other action, with the head of R&D's mentioning that the company was already making moves toward fuel efficiency. There is nothing in either source, however, to suggest that the plans are parallel or can be expected to produce similar results. This inference is not supported.

For the third question, consider the claim made for cloud computing: "40 to 50 percent power savings, with resultant reduction in carbon emissions." The reference to "1975 levels" refers to the graph and the fact that the level of emissions in 1975 was about half of the level in 2008. But the claim is not for a 50 percent reduction in emissions, but a 50 percent power saving. The inference cannot be supported.

The final question will also require a little calculation. Don't forget that you have a calculator available. If companies worldwide imitated the delivery company—that is, reducing CO_2 emissions by 20 percent of 2005 levels, a big "if"—then a worldwide reduction in emissions of 20 percent of the 2005 level of approximately 8 billion tons, or a reduction of about 1.6 million tons, from the 2008 level of approximately 8.7 billion tons, would bring the level to about 7 billion tons, the level in 2003. The correct answer is E.

Here are some things to remember for the Multiple-Source Reasoning section:

- Use all your sources but only your sources. Don't include information from other sources or make assumptions.
- You don't have to give a reason for your decision, but if you can't point to information in the sources that supports a yes, you probably want to say no.

2. Practice

Questions 1–4 refer to the following e-mails and graph.

E-mail from Human Resources Officer to Policy Consultant

The concern about U.S. unemployment figures extends beyond simply the percent of the population unemployed. It is the trend over the last 10 to 12 years that is shocking. In 2000, the unemployment rate in the United States was lower than that in the European Union, lower than that in the United Kingdom, lower even than Japan. In the fourth quarter of 2001, the United States passed Japan, and with the steep climb that began in 2008, now shows unemployment numbers comparable to those of the European Union.

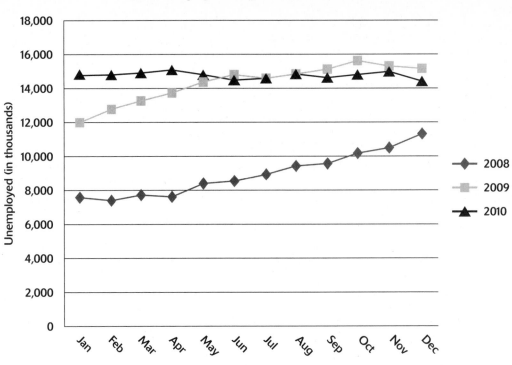

U.S. Unemployment by Month, 2008 - 2010

E-mail from Policy Consultant to Human Resources Office

In February 2009, Congress passed the American Recovery and Reinvestment Act, commonly referred to as "the stimulus." Some would point to the fact that unemployment continued to climb after February 2009 as evidence that the stimulus was ineffective; however, a lag of several months between the passage of legislation and the roll out of programs is to be expected. The nearly level unemployment numbers in the second half of 2009 and 2010, compared to the steep climb in the previous 18 months, suggest that the stimulus did have some positive effect. Hopefully, the jobs bill passed in August 2010, aimed at saving government jobs, will also have a positive effect.

Consider each of the following statements. Does the information in the three sources support the inference as stated?

Yes	No	Inference
		1. If the pattern of increase seen in late 2008 and early 2009 had continued, the unemployment rate in the United States would have significantly surpassed that of the European Union.
		2. While the U.S. employment rate has climbed, the unemployment rate in Japan has been unchanged since 2000.
		3. If the leveling of the unemployment rate in the second half of 2009 was a result of the stimulus bill of February 2009, then the dip in unemployment at the end of 2010 may be the result of the jobs bill of August 2010.

4. In the early 2000s, the United States unemployment rate was

    A. the highest among developed nations.
    B. the lowest among developed nations.
    C. higher than the unemployment rate in the European Union.
    D. lower than the unemployment rate in the United Kingdom.
    E. higher than the U.S. unemployment rate in 2009.

Questions 5–8 refer to the following e-mails.

E-mail from Market Analyst to Director

Have you seen the figures on the number of people without health insurance? From one year to the next, we saw an increase in the number of people without health insurance in all income groups, including those making more than $75,000 per year. As you might expect, the greatest percentage of the uninsured were unemployed, with only slightly lower numbers for those working part time, but the greatest increase in uninsured, surprisingly, was among those working full time. We've always assumed that people in that group want a premium package, but are we pricing ourselves out of the market in this economy? Should we be marketing a healthcare basics package to this group?

E-mail from Director to Market Analyst

Generally, the people in that upper income category are also on the upper end of the age spectrum. When we look at the data by age group, we see increases in the number of uninsured in almost every age category. Only young people 18 to 24 years of age saw a slight decline in the number of uninsured. Among children under 18 and adults 35 to 64 years old, there were slight increases, and those 25 to 34 years of age had the largest increase. That last category may be where many of those high income respondents are. Of course, the number uninsured for senior citizens, 65 and older, was less than one-tenth that of any other group, thanks to Medicare. We're already marketing Medicare supplemental plans. Others in the 25-to-64 range are probably getting healthcare through their employers. Is the increase in the unemployment figures the real reason for the decline in insurance, or is there something else we've neglected?

E-mail from Market Analyst to Director

There is one aspect that jumps out of the survey and perhaps we need to find a way to address it. Those identifying as being of Hispanic origin showed over 30 percent uninsured, nearly double the rate for blacks and Asians, and almost triple that of non-Hispanic whites. I know that the unemployment rates for Hispanics are high, but the unemployment number for African Americans is equally high, if not higher. I don't think the inability to obtain insurance through an employer can totally explain this. Should we look at the way we market ourselves in the Hispanic community?

Consider each of the following statements. Does the information in the three sources support the inference as stated?

Yes	No	Inference
		5. The number of people who do not have health insurance is increasing because people can no longer afford health insurance.
		6. The Director believes that increasing unemployment is responsible for the rise in the number of uninsured.

Yes	No	Inference
		7. The increase in the number of uninsured people is due in part to senior citizens who do not have Medicare.

8. The reason that the Hispanic population has the highest percentage of uninsured is

    A.   they have the highest unemployment rate.

    B.   they have the lowest income.

    C.   they lack the educational background necessary for employment.

    D.   they lack the language skills necessary for employment.

    E.   not explained by this data.

Answers

1. **Yes** The first e-mail tells you that the United States now has "unemployment numbers comparable to those of the European Union" and the graph shows that while current rates are basically flat, late 2008 and early 2009 saw the rate climbing sharply.

2. **No** You are told that U.S. employment was once below that of Japan, but has passed Japan; however, you do not have any information about changes, if any, in Japan's unemployment numbers.

3. **Yes** The e-mail suggests that the effects of legislation do not manifest in the unemployment numbers until several months after passage. The graph shows a decline in unemployment in late 2010. While you cannot be certain, it is reasonable to think that the dip might be caused by the jobs bill of August 2010.

4. **D** According to the e-mail, the U.S. unemployment rate in the early 2000s was lower than the rate in the European Union, the United Kingdom, and Japan. It clearly was not the highest among developed nations, and there is no evidence to support the claim that it was the lowest among developed nations. Because the U.S. unemployment rate climbed significantly in 2008 and 2009, you can conclude that the U.S. numbers were significantly lower in the early 2000s.

5. **No** Increases in the number of uninsured were seen in most age groups and at all income levels, but the reasons for those increases are not clear.

6. **Yes** The Director's e-mail includes the observation that people are "probably getting healthcare through their employers" and a question about whether anything other than rising unemployment is contributing to the increase in the number of uninsured.

7. **No** You are told that the rate of uninsured persons in the 65+ age category is a small fraction of that in other age groups, and that the dramatic difference is due to Medicare. Nothing in the e-mails speaks of seniors not having Medicare.

8. **E** The Hispanic population has the highest percentage of uninsured, but this is not attributed directly to unemployment, income, education, or language.

D. Two-Part Analysis

Because you're looking for two distinct but related values, one of two things is going to happen here. Either you're going to have to find one value first, and use that information to determine the other value, or you're going to have to solve what mathematics calls a system of equations: two equations that both contain the same two variables. Remember, however, that this is not a math section, so you're not going to be expected to do a lot of algebra. You'll see the possible solutions, so if you can get a general sense of the relationship of the two quantities, you may be able to guess and test your way through this.

1. Example

Orders placed with a certain company receive a discount, calculated as a percent of the cost of the order, but are also subject to a sales tax, calculated as a percent of the discounted amount. An order for $10,000 in goods, pre-discount, had a final invoice of $9,858. An order for $8,000 in goods, pre-discount, had a final invoice of $7,886.40.

In the table below, identify the discount rate given by the company, and the rate of sales tax applied.

Discount Rate	Tax Rate	
		2%
		4%
		6%
		7%
		8.5%
		12%

You could try to tackle this algebraically, using variables for the discount rate and the tax rate, but the results could be more complicated than you really want to face.

$$10,000\left(1-\frac{x}{100}\right)\left(1+\frac{y}{100}\right)=9,858$$

$$8,000\left(1-\frac{x}{100}\right)\left(1+\frac{y}{100}\right)=7,886.40$$

Instead, gather what insight you can from the problem and then look to the answer options. The $10,000 order ended up costing $9,858, so you're looking at a net reduction of about 1.5 percent, and because it's a *reduction,* you know the discount exceeds the tax. Experience will give you a sense of possible tax rates and you can see that the discount, while larger, is not dramatically larger. Then it's time to look at the possible answers. Trying them with the calculator will show you there was a discount of 7% and a tax rate of 6%.

Here are some things to remember for the Two-Part Analysis section:

- Algebra may be helpful, but it's not a math test.
- Deduce the general relationship of the two quantities.
- Eliminate impossible choices.
- Test the remaining answers.
- Don't forget you have the use of a calculator.

2. Practice

Directions: Use the given information to determine the values of both variables. Mark the appropriate box in the table to indicate the values.

1. A total investment of $100,000 is divided between two instruments. The amount invested in the lower yield stock fund is three times that invested at the higher-yield real estate account. The combined return on the investments for the year is $7,200, with the better return exceeding the smaller by $1,200. Find the rate on each investment.

Real Estate Account	Stock Fund	
		1.2%
		1.3%
		4%
		5.6%
		7.2%
		16.8%

2. Arthur's Auto Parts and Carl's Car Repair both have standing monthly orders with the same supplier for belts, at $4 each, and hoses, at $10 each. Arthur's standard shipment is 1,000 belts and 500 hoses, while Carl's larger enterprise receives 2,500 belts and 2,000 hoses. Recently, the supplier raised prices. Arthur's total monthly invoice increased 6.3 percent, but Carl's total invoice increased 7 percent. Find the percent increase in the cost of the belt and the cost of the hose.

Belt	Hose	
		2.1%
		2.8%
		4.5%
		6.4%
		7.9%
		9.1%

Answers

1. The $100,000 is divided with one quarter, or $25,000, in the real estate account and three-quarters, or $75,000, in the stock fund. You know the sum and the difference of the returns on the investments. To approach it algebraically, call the rates x and y, and you have $25{,}000x + 75{,}000y = 7{,}200$ and $25{,}000x - 75{,}000y = 1{,}200$. Add the equations.

$$
\begin{array}{l}
25{,}000x + 75{,}000y = 7{,}200 \\
\underline{25{,}000x - 75{,}000y = 1{,}200} \\
50{,}000x \qquad\quad = 8{,}400
\end{array}
$$

Divide 8,400 by 50,000 to get a rate of 16.8 percent. An investment of $25,000 at 16.8 percent would earn $4,200, so the $75,000 investment would have to earn $3,000. To do that, it would have to be invested at a rate of 4 percent.

To approach the problem without algebra, recognize that a return of $7,200 on a total investment of $100,000 represents a 7.2 percent return. Because one investment earns less than the other, try one greater than 7.2 percent and one less than 7.2 percent.

Real Estate Account	Stock Fund	
		1.2%
		1.3%
	X	4%
		5.6%
		7.2%
X		16.8%

2. Arthur's original shipment was $1000 \times \$4 + 500 \times \$10 = \$9{,}000$. It increased 6.3 percent to $9,567. Carl's order was $2{,}500 \times \$4 + 2{,}000 \times \$10 = \$30{,}000$, and increase 7 percent to $32,100. Call the percent increase in the cost of a belt x and the percent increase in the price of a hose y. The new prices are $4(1 + x)$ and $10(1 + y)$, so the increases are $4x$ and $10y$.

Solve:
$$
\begin{array}{l}
1{,}000(4x) + 500(10y) = 567 \\
2{,}500(4x) + 2{,}000(10y) = 2{,}100
\end{array}
$$

or
$$
\begin{array}{l}
4{,}000x + 5{,}000y = 567 \\
10{,}000x + 20{,}000y = 2{,}100
\end{array}
$$

By multiplying the top equation by 4 and subtracting.

$$16,000x + 20,000y = 2,268$$
$$\underline{10,000x + 20,000y = 2,100}$$
$$6,000x = 168$$
$$x = 0.028$$
$$10,000(0.028) + 20,000y = 2,100$$
$$20,000y = 2,100 - 280$$
$$y = 0.091$$

The belt increased 2.8 percent and the hose increased by 9.1 percent.

Belt	Hose	
		2.1%
X		2.8%
		4.5%
		6.4%
		7.9%
	X	9.1%

VII. Reading Comprehension

The critical reading passages on the GMAT are taken from several different content areas: the social sciences, the physical or biological sciences, economics, marketing, and human resources. The passages are fairly short (about 300 to 400 words), and each passage is followed by a set of about two to eight questions. Most of the questions fit into the following categories:

- Main purpose or central idea
- Supporting idea
- Inference
- Application
- Structure
- Style and tone

To successfully complete the GMAT critical reading passages, keep in mind the following strategies:

- **Always read actively.** Focus on what the author is trying to tell you. Think as you read—don't allow your mind to drift. Have a mental dialogue with the text.

- **If you're confused by a sentence or a paragraph, don't reread.** The sentence or paragraph may become clearer as you read, or there may not be any questions about that part of the passage. If you have to reread, do so as you answer the questions.

- **Stay interested in the passage.** Link the passage in your mind to a familiar topic. This strategy will help you stay focused.

- **Take notes on note boards as you read.** These notes don't have to be extensive—just jot down the main idea of each paragraph or plot a cause-and-effect relationship.

- **Watch for keywords and phrases that indicate a shift or transition in the passage.** A passage may appear to present a position that the author supports; then the author may begin a sentence with *but* or *however* and negate the previous position.

- **Don't allow your personal feelings or your own knowledge about the topic to influence your answers.** Always go back to what is stated in or implied by the text for support for your answer.

- **Always read *all* the choices before you select an answer.** Use process of elimination as you read the choices. If you're sure an answer is wrong, eliminate it. After you've read all the choices, look again only at the choices that you haven't eliminated, and evaluate their accuracy. Don't be fooled by an answer that makes a correct statement but doesn't answer the specific question. A statement may be true based on the information in the passage, but it may still be the wrong answer because it doesn't answer the question you're being asked.

- **Don't second-guess questions that appear to be too easy.** The test is constructed with a range of questions, and, especially at the beginning, an answer may simply be accessible.

- **Be on the lookout for *except* questions.** For *except* questions, four of the answers will be right. In these questions, you're looking for the *wrong* answer.

- **Take your time on the first few questions.** Because the GMAT is adaptive, it adjusts to your level of ability. You want to be sure to get the first few questions right so the computer will keep increasing the level of difficulty. Difficult questions are worth more than easy ones.

A. Main Purpose or Central Idea Questions

Main purpose questions ask you to determine the author's purpose in writing the passage. In other words, why did the author write this piece? What was he trying to accomplish? To answer these questions, you must think about the passage as a whole. Is the author trying to argue a position? Describe a situation? Propose a new approach? Prove or disprove a theory?

Sometimes, within a passage an author will have more than one purpose, but for this question, you're only looking for the *main* purpose. Be sure to discriminate between the main point of the essay and the auxiliary evidence.

Central idea questions may be posed in several ways:

- What is the main idea of the passage?
- With which of the following statements would the author most likely agree?
- What is the best title for the passage?
- This passage is primarily concerned with. . . .

To answer this central idea question, ask yourself: If I had to sum up the gist of this passage in one sentence, what would I say? It's often helpful to think about this question as you read the passage, and jot down the main idea on your note boards.

Try to follow the author's logic as you read, and be alert for the thesis of the passage. If you're having difficulty finding the main idea of the passage, quickly reread the first sentence in each paragraph; most of these sentences will relate to the central idea of the passage.

EXAMPLE:

> Many bacteria are unable to move from place to place. They have, however, a vibrating movement known as the *Brownian motion,* which is purely physical. Some other kinds of bacteria are endowed with powers of locomotion. Motion is produced by means of fine, threadlike projections of protoplasm known as *cilia,* which are developed on the outer surface of the cell. By means of the rapid vibration of these organs, the cell is propelled through the medium. Nearly all bacteria belonging to a group known as cocci are immotile, while the bacilli, or rod-shaped bacteria, may or may not be. The cilia on a bacterium are so delicate that it requires special treatment to demonstrate their presence.

The main idea of the passage is that

A. all bacteria are incapable of movement although some can vibrate in place.
B. bacteria are able to travel through a variety of media by means of their cilia, strong whiplike tails.
C. bacteria can move by means of the threadlike projections of protoplasm called cilia.
D. bacteria were originally categorized as animals, but because of their inability to move, they have been reclassified as plants.
E. although some bacteria are incapable of movement, others have mechanisms that allow them to travel through a medium.

Choice A is inaccurate because the passage states, "other kinds of bacteria are endowed with powers of locomotion." Choice B is also inaccurate because the passage does not state that cilia are strong tails. Choice C, while true, is a detail, not the main idea of the passage. Choice D is not supported by the information included in the passage. Choice E is correct because it is the larger topic that is supported by the details in the passage.

B. Supporting Idea Questions

To answer supporting idea questions, you must first distinguish between main and subordinate ideas. You may be asked about a specific piece of information and how it's used in the passage. You may be asked to assess the value of information that's given as evidence to support the main idea, or why the author included a particular piece of information.

Consider the detail in light of the author's purpose. If he's trying to support a theory, the detail may be evidence. On the other hand, he may be using it to refute the ideas of another. Also, consider why the author chose this particular piece of information to use: Why is it effective or ineffective?

EXAMPLE:

In every society, even the most primitive, some form of musical expression exists. From the percussive sounds of prehistoric man beating on a hollow log to the magnificent symphonies of Beethoven, music satisfies a need for artistic expression in human society. The universal appeal of musical expression suggests that it is linked to our psychological makeup. We use music to express feelings of love, despair, fear, hope, and splendor; yet, at the same time, music can engender these same feelings in us. In recent research, the influence of music on human psychological states has revealed the power of sound to create or alter mood. Music has even been used to reduce pain in chronic sufferers. Was William Congreve prophetic then, when he said, "Music soothes the savage breast"?

The author uses the example of William Congreve to

A. contrast with Beethoven's belief that music is artistic rather than mathematical.
B. substantiate the claim of psychologists that music can cure psychotic episodes.
C. link the primitive forms of music to the magnificent symphonies of the 17th century.
D. predict changes in the forms of music that foreshadow modern syncopation.
E. support his position that music has mood-altering properties.

The author uses William Congreve to *support* his position; thus, you can eliminate choices A, C, and D. This narrows your choices to B and E. He doesn't discuss the claim that music can cure psychotic episodes, but he does propound the mood-altering characteristics of music. Choice E is the best answer.

C. Inference Questions

These questions ask you to *infer,* or draw conclusions, from evidence implied but not directly stated in the passage. You must be able to follow the author's logic as he presents his information and infer the intended meaning from what is suggested.

Although the answer will not be directly stated in the passage, always use textual evidence to support your choice. Be careful not to allow your own opinions to influence your answer to the question.

EXAMPLE:

> Undoubtedly, if we could know the history of primitive loom work in America prior to the coming of the white man, we would find an extended distribution of weaving, but all early textiles have been lost owing to the destructability of the material and the lack of climatic and other conditions suitable for their preservation—conditions such as are present in the hot desert lands of the Southwest and the coastal region of Peru. However, so many impressions of weavings have been found on early pottery as to assure us that beautiful work of this kind was made in the eastern, middle, and southern United States. Currently, in western British Columbia, indigenous tribes practice four interesting types of weaving.

Which of the following statements can be inferred from the passage?

- **A.** Peruvian weavers implemented a preservation technique that allowed their weaving to endure for hundreds of years.
- **B.** The climate in the eastern United States is too moist to be conducive to the preservation of textiles.
- **C.** Weavers of British Columbian tribes were able to create fabrics that involved intricate patterns found nowhere else.
- **D.** The invention of the loom made remarkable changes in the methods used by pre-Columbian tribes to weave ceremonial robes.
- **E.** Considering the climate of the desert in the Southwest, it is noteworthy that any relics of tribal weaving exist today.

Choice A, while it may be true, isn't supported by any evidence in the passage. Choice C also isn't supported by evidence; all the passage indicates is that there are currently weavers in British Columbia. Choice D takes a detail mentioned in the passage, the loom, and carries the implication too far; the passage doesn't state that the loom made dramatic changes or that pre-Columbian tribes wove ceremonial robes. Choice E contradicts the evidence in the passage that a hot, dry climate is conducive to preservation of fabric. Choice B is correct because the passage implies that textiles from tribes in the east didn't survive because the climate wasn't hot and dry; you can infer that the climate was too moist to prevent the textiles from deteriorating.

D. Application Questions

Application questions require you to extrapolate—that is, to use critical thinking to go beyond what is directly stated in the passage. You must draw conclusions from what you read and apply them to new or parallel situations. You may be asked how the author would continue his discussion or argument, or you may be asked which of the choices is most similar to the situation in the passage. In all cases, your understanding of the passage is only half the answer. It is critical that you be able to *apply* your understanding to something new.

Be on the lookout for choices that make correct, logical statements, but aren't parallel to the existing example. Don't be distracted if the parallel situation is very different from the one in the passage; for example, a passage about the movement of electrons might be parallel to a choice about dance movements rather than a choice about protons.

Among the choices, you'll find some that contradict the point of the passage; eliminate these quickly and move on. Also, be alert for choices that make assumptions not supported by the passage; eliminate these.

Here is a sample application question:

The Tunguska explosion was a powerful explosion that occurred in Central Siberia in 1908 near the Tunguska River. At the time, the bizarre and catastrophic nature of the blast engendered apocalyptic visions among the superstitious inhabitants of that remote region. Herds of reindeer within a few miles of the blast were instantaneously incinerated; nomads were thrown from their tents miles away; all vegetation within a 2,000-square-mile radius was destroyed. When observers finally arrived at the site several months later, they found not a huge crater as they had predicted, but thousands of trees knocked outward from the blast center. Today, most scientists attribute the blast to an air burst from a comet or a meteor exploding several miles above the surface of the Earth. Had this blast occurred above a densely populated metropolitan area, it would have decimated a city the size of Chicago.

Which of the following is most similar to the effect of the blast on the trees?

    A.   Falling debris from an imploded building that crashes inward toward the center of the site
    B.   A random pattern of falling blocks from a 2-foot tower that is knocked over
    C.   The spokelike arrangement of pick-up sticks when a tightly held bunch is released
    D.   The parallel linear lines formed by iron filings when a U-shaped magnet is drawn through them
    E.   A V-shaped crater excavated from the earth by a bulldozer blade

Information in the passage indicates that the trees were knocked outward from the center of the blast. The pattern that is most similar to this is Choice C, pick-up sticks that fall in a spokelike pattern.

E. Structure Questions

The author of the passage clearly had some sense of organization as he wrote the passage. As you read, try to determine the pattern of ideas.

Here are some common structures utilized by GMAT passages:

- Thesis or theory followed by supporting examples
- Arguments for and against a specific issue, with or without a solution
- A cause-and-effect sequence demonstrating how one aspect is a result of another
- A comparison of several ideas, pointing out similarities and differences among the views
- A chronological survey with relevant commentary

Keywords can help you determine the structural pattern of a passage. As you read, pay particular attention to *signal words,* introductory or transitional words that establish relationships within the passage.

Here are words that signal a contrast or contradiction:

- despite
- however
- in spite of

- although
- even though
- nevertheless
- but
- yet
- rather than
- instead

Here are words that signal ideas that are similar:

- in addition
- and
- moreover
- furthermore
- for example
- likewise

Here are words that signal a cause-and-effect relationship:

- because
- thus
- as a result
- therefore
- consequently
- hence
- since

EXAMPLE:

Before the Civil War had ended, however, the transformation of the United States from a nation of farmers and small-scale manufacturers to a highly organized industrial state had begun. Probably the single, most important influence was the war itself. Those four years of bitter conflict illustrate, perhaps more graphically than any similar event in history, the power that military operations may exercise in stimulating all the productive forces of a people. In thickly settled nations, with few dormant resources and with practically no areas of unoccupied land, a long war usually produces industrial disorganization and financial exhaustion. The Napoleonic Wars had this effect in Europe; in particular, they caused a period of social and industrial distress in England. The few years immediately following Waterloo marked a period when starving mobs rioted in the streets of London, setting fire to the houses of the aristocracy and stoning the Prince Regent whenever he dared to show his head in public, when cotton spindles ceased to turn, when collieries closed down, when jails and workhouses were overflowing with a wretched proletariat, and when gaunt and homeless women and children crowded the country highways.

The author uses the example of the Napoleonic Wars in Europe to

A. provide a contrast between the effect of these wars on the European economy and the effect of the Civil War on U.S. industry.

B. point out similar patterns of wartime industrial organization among the nations of Europe during the reign of Napoleon.

C. connect the wartime disorganization of industry in France during the 19th century with the rise of anti-monarchical feelings in Regency England.

D. argue that the consequences of war on a nation with few resources is always cataclysmic.

E. use a historical example to point out the cyclical nature of the rise and fall of empires.

The example of the Napoleonic Wars is used in the passage to contrast with the effect of the Civil War on industrialization in the U.S. The passage indicates that the Civil War stimulated the industrial segment of the economy, while, in Europe, war had the opposite effect. The best answer is Choice A.

F. Style and Tone Questions

Some questions on the GMAT ask you to consider the *tone* of a line or of the whole passage. Other questions ask about the author's *attitude* toward someone or something. Be sure you know whose attitude you're looking for and toward whom or what. There may be questions that test your understanding of *rhetoric,* the art of using language to accomplish your purpose.

As you read, consider where you might find this passage: Would it be in a textbook? In a personal response? In a defense? In a scientific journal? Some questions will ask you to discern the intended audience for this piece or in what type of publication it would most likely be found.

In addition, you should be able to recognize literal versus metaphorical language. *Literal language* is meant to be taken at face value; it denotes what it means. *Metaphorical language* is not meant to be taken literally. For example, the statement "My pockets are empty" may *literally* denote that there is nothing in the pouches in my pants or skirt; metaphorically, it may mean that I'm broke or poor.

Here are key tone/attitude words used on the GMAT, along with their definitions:

- **Indignant:** Angry at unfairness or injustice
- **Objective:** Neutral, impartial
- **Subjective:** Based on personal opinion
- **Detached:** Neutral, not emotionally or personally involved
- **Equivocal:** Deliberately vague or misleading
- **Ambivalent:** Having mixed feelings, seeing both sides of an issue
- **Cynical:** Pessimistic, expecting the worst from others
- **Skeptical, incredulous, dubious:** Disbelieving, doubtful

EXAMPLE:

For over 80 years formerly indigenous wolves have been missing from the southwestern United States and Mexico. Hunted to near extinction, the so-called Mexican wolves dwindled to a handful before efforts were made to bring back the species. Nurturing the few remaining animals, the U.S. Fish & Wildlife Service employed state-of-the-art breeding techniques to restore the population. When efforts were started to reintroduce the wolves, local ranchers protested vigorously. The wolves, they argued, are a natural predator of livestock. Some states have refused to allow the wolves to be released on their lands, arguing that the cost to farmers and ranchers is too great. As the 21st century begins, the future of the Mexican wolf remains uncertain.

The tone of the passage suggests that the author's attitude toward the reintroduction of the wolves is

A.   indignant, because his sympathy clearly lies with the efforts to save this endangered species.
B.   cynical, because he does not believe that any effort to save this endangered species has a chance to be successful.
C.   hostile, because he has no patience with the efforts of human beings to interfere with the natural world.
D.   ambivalent, because he acknowledges that both sides in this issue have valid positions.
E.   incredulous, because he can't accept the fact that any person would object to the reintroduction of an indigenous species.

The author of this passage presents both sides of the issue with fairly neutral language. Although he appears to sympathize with the plight of the wolves, he also understands the position of the ranchers. Choice A doesn't take into account his understanding of the ranchers' position. Choice B is inaccurate because he doesn't speculate about the likelihood of success of the venture. Choice C is incorrect because he doesn't appear to be impatient with the efforts. Choice E is incorrect because he clearly understands the position of the ranchers. Choice D is the right answer because the author is ambivalent: He presents both sides of the issue and understands that each has a valid position.

Practice

Directions (1–10): These questions are based on the content of the accompanying passages. Carefully read each passage in this section and answer the questions that follow each passage. Answer the questions based on the content of the passages—both what is stated and what is implied in the passages.

Passage 1

Nature is crammed with devices to protect and maintain the organism against the stress of the environment. Any structural feature that is useful because of its construction is a structural adaptation; when such adaptations are given, the mechanist has, for the most part, a relatively easy task in his interpretation. He has a far more difficult knot to disentangle in the case of the so-called functional adaptations, where the organism modifies its activities (and often also its structure) in response to changed conditions. The nature of these phenomena may be illustrated by a few examples so chosen as to form a progressive series. If a spot on the skin is rubbed for some time, the first result is a direct and obviously mechanical one: The skin is worn away. But if the rubbing is continued long enough, and is not too severe, an indirect effect is produced that is precisely the opposite of the initial direct one: The skin is replaced and becomes thicker than before, and a callus is produced that protects the spot from further injury. The healing of a wound involves a similar action. Again, remove one kidney or one lung and the remaining one will, in time, enlarge to assume, as far as it is able, the functions of both. Finally, it has been found in certain cases, including animals as highly organized as salamanders, that if the egg is separated into two parts at an early period of development each part develops into a perfect embryo animal of half the usual size, and a pair of twins results. In each of these cases, the astonishing fact is that a mechanical injury sets up in the organism a complicated adaptive response in the form of operations, which, in the end, counteract the initial mechanical effect. It is no doubt true that somewhat similar self-adjustments or responses may be said to take place in certain nonliving mechanical systems, such as the spinning top or the gyroscope, but those that occur in the living body are of such general occurrence, of such complexity and variety, and of so designlike a quality, that they may fairly be regarded as among the most characteristic of the vital activities. It is precisely this characteristic of many vital phenomena that renders their accurate analysis so difficult and complex a task.

1. Which of the following is the main idea of the passage?

   A. The question of man's place in nature is one of the most momentous with which natural science has to deal, and it has occupied the attention of thinking men in every age.
   B. When matter is reduced to its lowest terms—life—it seems to have its root in chemical change.
   C. Scientific investigation can do no more than push forward the limits of knowledge.
   D. Organic adaptations often run counter to direct or obvious initial mechanical conditions.
   E. The greatest task of the biologist is to study the organism from the historical point of view, considering it as the product of a continuous process of evolution.

2. The difficult knot refers to

   A. structures in organisms that resist scientists' efforts to understand their purpose.
   B. the behavioral modification in an organism in response to altered conditions.
   C. the division of labor within a cell that allows differentiation into diverse organs.
   D. mechanical adjustments that irregularly occur in nonliving systems.
   E. issues that biologists face when attempting to find morphological evidence to support evolutionary processes.

3. All of the following are examples of the phenomena of organ modification *except:*

   A. If the leg of a lobster is amputated, the wound not only heals, but a new leg is regenerated in place of that which has been lost.
   B. A climbing plant will grow tendrils to sustain itself against the action of gravity or the wind.
   C. Humpback whales travel to cold waters for feeding; they go to warmer waters to give birth.
   D. Grasshoppers that feed on rye grass, a hard grass, have larger heads with greater chewing power than those that feed on softer grasses.
   E. Stems of wheat plants grown without support are stronger and less flexible that those grown with supports.

4. It can be inferred from the passage that the author believes the adaptive response in organisms

    A. is regular and predictable in both plants and animals.
    B. relies on simple duplicative processes within each organism.
    C. is counterproductive to healing and cell regeneration.
    D. is frequent, complex, and varied.
    E. is very different from nonliving mechanisms that self-correct.

5. Which of the following best describes the organization of the passage?

    A. The historical background of a research method is chronicled.
    B. Two divergent theories are compared and contrasted.
    C. An assertion is supported by several illustrations.
    D. The limitations of a methodology are revealed.
    E. A particular case is presented as an exception to a general rule.

Passage 2

Once found, archeological deposits must be carefully examined and meticulously recorded. Their form, content, and function may be difficult to interpret. Precise determinations of site boundaries, artifact type and style, feature function, and site condition almost always require extensive testing and verification. Historic archeological resources, such as building foundations or associated features of standing structures such as cisterns, mill races, or garden paths, moreover, are not always recognized or adequately treated. Methods used by archeologists to collect and analyze data further contribute to the special status of archeological resources. In order to accurately analyze archeological data, archeologists must carefully record the positions of all artifacts and deposits encountered during excavations. This physical relationship between excavated materials and their exact location is called "archeological context." Artifacts and other deposits located within their archeological context are said to have "integrity." Integrity is lost when archeological resources are disturbed or removed without careful context documentation.

Excavation is the primary method archeologists use to recover information. Although some excavations only uncover, sample, and rebury archeological deposits, all excavations permanently alter the context of archeological resources to some degree. This places archeologists in a unique position—the excavations necessary to recover archeological resources always affect the data they collect.

Archeologists have responded to this paradox by working to preserve archeological resources in place whenever possible. When excavation is necessary, extraordinarily rigorous methods are used to recover, record, and analyze data within the context of their discovery. In order to preserve as much of the context as possible, archeologists generally strive to collect relatively small samples from sites that can be preserved. Total recovery of archeological resources from a locale usually occurs only when all other alternatives for preservation are exhausted.

Such practices preserve the all-important contextual record and permit future study. This is important because archeological resources are significant not just for what they have already revealed, but for what they can tell us about past lifeways at some later date when more sophisticated techniques and analytic methods are available. By preserving archeological resources in place and keeping careful records of what has been recovered, archeologists work to assure that our past, indeed, has a future.

6. The author is primarily concerned with

   A. advocating a substantial change in the methodology of archeology.
   B. explaining a traditional approach to recording data.
   C. delineating the importance of archeological context.
   D. challenging the approach of researchers who collect samples too small to classify.
   E. urging the preservation of historical sites by limiting access of the public.

7. It can be inferred from the passage that the author would support regulations that

   A. open previously restricted sites to amateur archeologists who would provide much needed assistance.
   B. limit the artifacts that can be extracted from any particular archeological site.
   C. apply more analytical methods to the classification of items recovered from prehistoric sites.
   D. require archeologists to have more integrity than other scientists.
   E. increase the number of sites available to archeological expeditions.

8. The author's attitude toward the total recovery of archeological resources from a given locale is

   A. qualified disagreement.
   B. mocking disrespect.
   C. total agreement.
   D. irate indignation.
   E. curious skepticism.

9. Which of the following would an archeologist consider of primary importance in a historical site?

   A. Uncovering and removing every relic from a given area
   B. Carefully noting and recording the position of a garden path
   C. Finding deposits of a valuable mineral previously thought to be exhausted
   D. Allowing interested spectators to get close enough to a site to appreciate the beauty of recovered pottery
   E. Permanently dismantling an ancient cistern to reveal water-collection methods of prehistoric tribes

10. In the third paragraph, the author refers to which of the following as a paradox?

    A. Items once thought old and worthless have become valuable as antiques.
    B. A modern society that prides itself on its forward-thinking attitude prizes remnants of the past.
    C. Objects that are no longer used reveal much about the people who originally used them.
    D. Researchers find that, by excavating the past, they can learn lessons that will help in the future.
    E. The data that are carefully collected by the archeologist are often modified by the process of collection.

Answers

1. **D** The author introduces the concept of mechanical adaptation and points out the "astonishing fact [is] that a mechanical injury sets up in the organism a complicated adaptive response in the form of operations, which, in the end, counteract the initial mechanical effect." This is his main idea. He doesn't mention choices A, B, or E. Choice C is true, but it is not his main point. *(See Section A.)*

2. **B** The answer is in the third sentence: "difficult knot to disentangle in the case of the so-called functional adaptations, where the organism modifies its activities (and often also its structure) in response to changed conditions." All the other choices are not supported by the content of the passage. *(See Section B.)*

3. **C** Choices A, B, D, and E are examples of mechanical adaptation by an organism. Migratory patterns are not mechanical, but behavioral. *(See Section D.)*

4. **D** The passage suggests that the adaptive response is frequent, complex, and varied. It is not regular and predictable (Choice A) and not simple (Choice B). It is not counterproductive to healing (Choice C); in fact, it aids healing. It is similar to nonliving things like the gyroscope and the top, objects that self-correct (Choice E). *(See Section C.)*

5. **C** The author makes an assertion in the first sentence and then supports it using multiple examples. No historical background is included (Choice A). Choice B is incorrect because two divergent theories aren't presented. The limitations of a methodology aren't revealed (Choice D), and no exception is presented (Choice E). *(See Section E.)*

6. **C** The author emphasizes the importance of context, retaining the integrity of the site. He doesn't advocate a change (Choice A) or explain an approach (Choice B). He would disagree with Choice D. Although he would probably agree with Choice E, it is not his primary concern in this passage. *(See Section A.)*

7. **B** The author makes it clear that he favors removing as few artifacts as possible from a site. Choice A would be counter to his concerns. He might support choices C and E, but they aren't mentioned in the passage. Choice D misinterprets "integrity" as it is used in the passage. *(See Section C.)*

8. **A** The author would object to total removal of artifacts from a site except in cases "when all other alternatives for preservation are exhausted." That would fit the definition of "qualified disagreement." He is not mocking (Choice B) or irate (Choice D). He certainly wouldn't agree (Choice C) and does not indicate skepticism in the passage (Choice E). *(See Section F.)*

9. **B** The author mentions the importance of carefully noting characteristics of a site such as garden paths. Choice A would be the opposite of what he would advocate. Choices C and D aren't mentioned in the passage. He does mention a cistern (Choice E), but it is clear that he wouldn't want to permanently dismantle it. *(See Section B.)*

10. **E** The author refers to the paradox that arises when a scientist wants to preserve data intact but must disturb it in order to recover it. All the other choices can be construed as paradoxes, but they aren't discussed by the author in the passage. *(See Section B.)*

VIII. Critical Reasoning

The critical reasoning questions are designed to test your ability to analyze a situation and make carefully reasoned judgments about it. Each question consists of a situation, an argument, a dialogue, or an incomplete statement, followed by one or two questions. Each question is self-contained; you don't need to have any particular knowledge in order to answer correctly. You do need to be able to consider and evaluate the merits and weaknesses of a conclusion or an argument.

Here are some general strategies for answering the critical reasoning questions on the GMAT:

- Read the question before you read the problem, so you know what aspect of the situation to focus on.
- Read the information presented in the problem very carefully.
- Separate verifiable facts from information propounded as if it were factual.
- Be alert for conclusions that do not necessarily or logically follow from the information provided.
- Be sure you answer exactly what the question asks.
- Read all the choices before selecting the best answer.

A. Using Deductive Reasoning

Review Chapter V, which covers much of the critical thinking processes you'll need to answer the critical reasoning questions. Because you'll be tested on your perceptive reading and analysis of arguments in these questions, especially note:

- Faulty assumptions
- Weak, inappropriate, or misleading information
- Vague or irrelevant statistics
- Unwarranted conclusions
- Missing information

Most critical reasoning questions require you to use deductive reasoning to evaluate the logic of an argument, plan, discrepancy, or problem. In deductive reasoning, you're presented with a series of premises or declarative statements. From these premises, you should be able to draw a conclusion, providing the evidence that you've been given is true and the reasoning that you've used to reach it is sound. In the easy critical reasoning questions, you should have little problem following the logic of the argument. As the questions get more difficult, however, you may want to use the note board provided to map or diagram the argument.

If you can, plot the situation using letters to reduce it to simple logic.

EXAMPLE:

> Ralph started a company in Finleytown that washed windows in commercial buildings. His Sparkle View Company was very successful, and he was able to earn a substantial salary and retire at age 50. Ralph's cousin Pete sold his auto repair company in Maintown and opened a Sparkle View Company so that he, too, will be able to retire when he reaches 50.
>
> Which of the following is a faulty assumption upon which Pete bases his conclusion?
>
> **A.** Because Finleytown is a small city with a population of 60,000, while Maintown has 120,000 residents, more people will know Ralph and patronize his business.
>
> **B.** The commercial sector of Maintown is mostly comprised of office buildings, which have more windows than retail outlets do.
>
> **C.** Ralph had little experience in the window-washing business, but he took a community-college course in starting a small business, which helped him set up his company.
>
> **D.** The auto repair business provides an essential service, while window washing is more of a luxury than a necessity.
>
> **E.** The factors that led to Ralph's success will necessarily translate to the same success for Pete.

The correct answer is **E**. Pete's conclusion is based on his assumption that what transpired with Ralph's business will automatically transpire with his business. If you were to diagram this problem, you might come up with something like this:

A: Ralph starts window washing business.

B: Success.

C: Pete starts window washing business.

So:

A = B

A = C

Does C = B? Not necessarily.

The critical reasoning questions can be categorized by type. We cover the various types of critical reasoning questions in the following sections.

B. Plan Questions

These questions present you with a strategy, a proposal, or a possible plan. It's up to you to evaluate the strategy, proposal, or plan and decide whether it's logical, sound, or worthwhile. Ultimately, you may be asked whether the strategy, proposal, or plan should be implemented, revised, or rejected.

Here's how you should approach plan questions:

1. Read the question before you read the plan so you know exactly what you're evaluating.

2. Read the plan. As you read, assess the information provided about the plan: Is it logical? Will it work? Does it contain generalizations that don't necessarily reflect the evidence? What are its strengths and weaknesses?

3. Consider the motives of those presenting the plan. Do they have the qualifications to be experts? Are they unbiased, or do they have vested interests in the outcome of the plan?

4. Consider all five answer choices in light of the specific question. Use process of elimination and reject those choices that are either irrelevant or contradictory to the situation.

5. Reread the remaining choices, and select the best answer to fulfill the requirements of the question.

EXAMPLE:

> The Florida Department of Highways is concerned about high traffic volume on Greentree Road, an exit on the 75-mile marker on the Florida State Turnpike. The department's engineers have proposed the construction of a new exit on Palms Road at the 68-mile marker. The plan will cost $3.3 million but will, according to the official prospectus, alleviate the Greentree Road congestion and save taxpayers time and money.
>
> Which of the following, if true, casts the most doubt on the effectiveness of the plan as a solution to the traffic problem?
>
> A. The construction of a new exit will allow the Department of Highways to raise the tolls on the turnpike and create additional revenue.
>
> B. The land survey on Palms Road revealed underground springs that can be channeled into neighboring communities to provide much-needed well water.
>
> C. Several of the engineers assigned to this project have invested in the construction of a new shopping center to be built on Palms Road.
>
> D. The shopping mall on Greentree Road has released statistics that show an upswing in the number of shoppers this year as compared to the number for the past 10 years.
>
> E. A survey of drivers has indicated that many are in favor of construction of the new exit.

The correct answer is **D.** You're looking for the piece of information that "casts the most doubt on the effectiveness of the plan." Consider the basic assumption of those making the plan: that the traffic problem is one that can be alleviated by construction of an additional exit. Is there any information in the plan that states that traffic surveys have been done to determine the accuracy of this assumption? Because this information is not contained in the plan, you can't assume that it has been done. If the traffic has been caused by an increase in mall shoppers on Greentree Road, the new exit will not alleviate the problem. Choice D indicates that an upswing in the number of shoppers at the mall has been documented; because this increase (not the lack of turnpike exits) may be the cause of the traffic problem, this information "casts doubt on the effectiveness of the plan as a solution to the traffic problem." Choices A and B add information that isn't relevant to the issue at hand. Choice C offers a possible (though unethical) explanation for the push for a new exit. Choice E merely expresses opinion and doesn't address the issue.

C. Argument Questions

Argument questions fall into two categories: those that ask you which choice strengthens or weakens an argument, and those that ask you which answer choice is most similar to the original argument.

1. Strengthen or Weaken an Argument

These questions present you with an issue in dispute. Usually, both sides of the issue will offer supporting evidence of varying reliability. You must evaluate the sides of the argument, assess the quality of the evidence and the reliability of those offering opinions, and come to some conclusion. You may be asked which choice will best strengthen an argument, which choice will most weaken an argument, or which choice presents the wisest course of action.

Here is how you should approach these questions:

1. Read the question before you read the argument so you know exactly what you're evaluating.
2. Identify the sides of the argument, considering the strengths and weakness of each side. Is the evidence offered as proof *really* proof, or merely a restatement of opinion?
3. Assess the qualifications of those offering opinions: Are they impartial experts or those who have a vested interest in the outcome?
4. Are there cause-and-effect relationships in the argument based on faulty logic?
5. Find the conclusion. Don't necessarily assume that the conclusion is at the end of the argument. It could be in the beginning or in the middle.
6. Note flaws in the logic of the conclusion.
7. Consider all five answer choices. Use process of elimination to cross out those choices that are either irrelevant or contradictory to the situation.
8. Reread the remaining choices and select the best answer to fulfill the requirements of the question.

EXAMPLE:

Members of the Pit Bull Owners Association are concerned about the poor reputation that the breed has with the public because of a few incidents involving attacks on other dogs and children. They argue that pit bulls are loyal pets that make loving companions. The fault, they contend, lies with pit bull owners who specifically train their dogs to fight by mistreating them.

Which of the following, if true, would weaken the dog owners' position?

A. Pit bulls were originally bred in England for their drive and loyalty and were used on farms to eradicate vermin.
B. According to veterinary statistics, pit bulls have been involved in more dog attacks involving human injury than any other breed of dog.
C. Originally known as an ideal family pet and owned by such luminaries as Helen Keller, pit bulls were featured in magazines as "baby sitter" dogs.
D. For aficionados of the vicious "sport" of dog fighting, pit bulls are the perfect breed for their courage, fierce loyalty, and tenacity.
E. The myth that pit bulls are able to lock their jaws on their victims has done much to fuel the fear that pit bulls are far too dangerous to be acceptable house pets.

The correct answer is **B.** The position of the dog owners rests on the conclusion that the dogs don't deserve their bad reputation, but they're clearly biased in favor of the breed. Choice B is correct because it refutes their position using an authoritative source: Because more pit bulls are involved in human injury than any other breed, there must be some truth to the bad reputation. Choice A discusses the breed's use to kill vermin, but although this speaks to the breed's prowess in destroying pests, it doesn't necessarily carry over to human attacks. Choice C merely describes some interesting historical data. Choice D refers to the reasons pit bulls are chosen for dog fighting, but it doesn't address human attacks. Choice E refers to the bad reputation of the dogs but refutes one particular aspect as a myth.

2. Parallel Argument

These questions will present you with an issue in dispute. The answer choices consist of other arguments. The question after the argument asks you which of the arguments in the answer choices is most like the original argument, or it may ask which pattern of reasoning is most like the original. Your task is to understand the pattern of reasoning present in the problem, and then find the same pattern in the choices.

In answering parallel argument questions, follow these steps:

1. Read the problem carefully, and try to determine the pattern of the argument. If it helps you to clarify the pattern of the problem, plot it on your note board using A, B, C, and so on.
2. Read through the choices carefully, looking for the pattern of each problem.
3. Evaluate the similarity of the pattern of each of the five answer choices. Don't be misled by choices that deal with a similar topic but use a different thinking pattern. For example, if the problem deals with law enforcement, don't automatically assume that the correct answer will also deal with a law enforcement issue. It may be about a different topic entirely but use the same pattern of logic.
4. Use process of elimination to narrow your choices.
5. Find the closest pattern to the situation in the problem.

EXAMPLE:

> Company K discovered a way to manufacture plastic cups more inexpensively than traditional methods, but the cups can become toxic if heated to 100°F. Because the cups are clearly labeled for cold drinks, the company doesn't feel obligated to put a warning on the cups.
>
> The reasoning in the argument above is most similar to the reasoning in which of the following arguments?
>
> **A.** Company L has discovered a new way to manufacture tissues that will create a product that is both durable and germicidal. However, the costs of manufacturing will raise the cost of the product significantly. The company has decided to proceed with the new product and pass the increased costs on to the consumer.
> **B.** Company M has created a new fabric for children's ski hats that is less costly to manufacture than products currently on the market. However, in very warm weather, the hats give off an odor that causes nausea and vomiting in the wearer. Because the hats are specifically intended for cold-weather wear, Company M has decided to continue its manufacture without informing the public of the problem.

C.   Company N has found a way to bio-enhance tomato soup so that one serving provides all the daily nutritional needs of consumers. The new soup, however, has a distinctly bitter taste and smells like sauerkraut. Company N has decided to continue the production of the new product anyway and refrain from mentioning the unpleasant taste and odor.

D.   Executives of Company O have been informed by their product development department that the inside lining of their newest product, a lightweight thermos for keeping food hot or cold, has a tendency to separate from the outer cover when substances over 200°F are placed inside. Because the directions state that no substance over 180°F should be put in the thermos, the executives have decided further action is unnecessary.

E.   Company P designs bedroom slippers with a no-skid bottom. Recently, several consumers have complained that the no-skid material can become slippery when wet. Company officials have decided to investigate new materials that will maintain traction even when wet.

The correct answer is **B.** To answer a parallel argument question, you're looking for the repetition of a pattern. The pattern in the question is:

New product with low production cost + Unusual conditions that make the product dangerous (unexpected temperature) → Company takes no action and/or responsibility

If this question were presented to you on the GMAT, you would jot down the pattern on your note board. This would make it less likely that you'd be distracted by similar but wrong patterns in the choices.

Choice A deals only with cost of production rather than with the danger to the consumer; eliminate it because it isn't a parallel argument. Choice C seems to be parallel because the product has unpleasant effects, but no element of danger to the consumer is present so it isn't correct. Choice D is close, but the directions do warn the consumer of the potential danger so it isn't the best choice. Choice E isn't parallel because the company officials have decided to take action to protect the consumer. Choice B is the best answer: The new product has a low production cost, temperature adds an element of danger to the consumer, and the company has decided to take no action.

D. Conclusion Questions

These questions present you with one or more premises. Then a conclusion based upon these premises will be given, or you'll be asked to select the most logical conclusion based on the premises.

1. Select a Conclusion

In this type of question, you're presented with a situation based on a series of premises. Following the situation, the question asks something like: "Which of the following can best be logically concluded from the preceding premises?" or "If the statements above are true, which of the following conclusions can most logically be drawn?" If you look carefully at the questions, you'll see that they don't ask for the *only* possible conclusion, just the *best* conclusion out of the five presented, or the *most* logical conclusion, not the *only* logical conclusion. This means that you *could* come up with a better conclusion, but don't allow that to influence your answer. You can choose only from among the choices presented, so don't get distracted if your exact conclusion is not among the choices.

Here is how you should approach these questions:

1. Read the premises carefully so that you understand the basis upon which you'll draw your conclusion.
2. Think about a logical conclusion that can be drawn from the premises in the question.
3. Carefully read and evaluate the logic of each of the five choices.
4. Use process of elimination to narrow your choices.
5. From the remaining choices, find the conclusion that either best matches your conclusion or that is most logical based on the premises.

EXAMPLE:

> A study of female college students living in dormitories found that 35 percent of the students gained at least 8 pounds between their freshman year and their junior year. In contrast, young women who lived at home and went directly from high school to the workplace averaged a 1 pound weight gain in their first year of work.
>
> If the statements above are true, which of the following conclusions can most logically be drawn?
>
> **A.** College dorms and cafeterias provide a wide array of choices to students, ranging from healthy meals of vegetables, fruit, and protein to high-calorie snacks such as pizzas and shakes.
> **B.** Living away at college is more stressful than living at home, and stress leads to overeating.
> **C.** With no parental controls and nutritional guidance, freshman women are free to make unhealthy choices and indulge in more alcohol and high-calorie fast food.
> **D.** Studies have shown that more male freshman students than female freshman students gain weight in their first year of college.
> **E.** Young women who worry about weight gain in college are more likely to suffer from such eating disorders such as bulimia and anorexia.

The correct answer is **C.** First, examine the premises: Clearly, there is a factor in college life that predisposes young women to weight gain. Ask yourself: What is the most logical variable? Most likely, you'll come to the conclusion that women living in a dormitory are no longer under the control and guidance of their parents; this should lead you to conclude that parental control is an important factor. Now, examine the choices. You should be able to eliminate choices D and E rather quickly because they're off-topic; neither is directly relevant to the issue. Next, eliminate Choice B because it's a statement that may be true but that makes several assumptions that are not supported with the provided evidence; there are no statistics or facts given comparing stress in college to stress in the workplace, and no evidence is presented linking stress to overeating. You're left with choices A and C, both good possibilities, but Choice A does not consider that working women may face the same meal choices as college women. Thus, Choice C is the most logical conclusion because it factors in the key variable, living away from home.

2. Evaluate a Conclusion

In this type of question, you're presented with several premises followed by a conclusion. Your task is to evaluate the logic of the conclusion. Sometimes you're looking for the strengths of the conclusion; other times, the weakness. The question may be phrased in a variety of ways:

- Which of the following provides the best justification for the conclusion?
- Which of the following most weakens the conclusion?
- Which of the following is the most serious flaw in the conclusion?

Again, logical thinking is your best tool. Look for illogical assumptions, assumptions that are based on fallacious logic, or those based on no logic at all.

Here is how you should approach these questions:

1. Read the premises carefully so that you understand the basis upon which the conclusion is drawn.
2. Carefully consider the conclusion: Is it based on logic? Is it based on unwarranted assumptions? Is there enough information presented to draw this conclusion?
3. Carefully read and evaluate the logic of each of the five answer choices in light of the conclusion.
4. Use process of elimination to narrow your choices. Reject all irrelevant choices.
5. Find the answer that is most logical.

EXAMPLE:

A recent survey of students accepted to prestigious colleges revealed that students from Nevada were admitted with a mean high school grade point average (GPA) of 92.4. Students accepted from California averaged a 96.2 GPA. The father of a family living in California used this information to conclude that the family should move to Nevada so that his son, an excellent student, would have a better chance of getting into a prestigious college than if they remained in California.

Which of the following, if true, would most seriously weaken the family's conclusion?

A. The curriculum in Nevada has more requirements and is far more academically demanding than that in California.
B. Both California and Nevada use a system of weighting that gives more numerical weight to honors and AP courses.
C. The number of students enrolled in AP courses in most California high schools far exceeds the number enrolled in most Nevada high schools.
D. Many California students enter a tuition-free two-year or four-year program in the University of California system.
E. In an attempt to increase national diversity, many prestigious colleges make a concerted effort to admit students from all 50 states.

The correct answer is **A.** The father has based his conclusion on the assumption that his son will have a better chance of getting into a prestigious college if they live in Nevada because he won't need as high a GPA as he would when applying from California. In drawing this conclusion, the father assumes an equality of grading that may or may not be present between California and Nevada, and he also assumes that his son will find it easier to get a 92 in Nevada than to get a 96 in California. To get the correct answer, you're looking for the choice that most weakens the father's conclusion. You can eliminate Choice D because it isn't relevant to the conclusion. Choice C seems related because it deals with the number of students enrolled in what are usually the most demanding courses, but, because the population of California is far greater than that of Nevada, this piece of information actually becomes an irrelevant fact. Choice B also appears to be relevant but is not, because it states a condition that is the same in both states. Choice E is the tempting "distracter" because it *supports* the conclusion; if you forget that you're looking for the choice that *weakens* the conclusion, you may be distracted into choosing E. Choice A weakens the conclusion because it explains the discrepancy in GPA: It's harder to get a high average in Nevada than it is in California. Therefore, there is no logical reason for the father to think that his son will have an advantage applying from Nevada rather than California.

E. Discrepancy Questions

Some questions present you with a situation that seems inconsistent or paradoxical. Your task is to note the apparent discrepancy and conceive a logical explanation for the conflict. You may be given an unexpected outcome and asked which of the choices would best explain this result.

Follow these steps in answering a discrepancy question:

1. Read the situation carefully so that you understand the basic conflict or discrepancy.
2. Carefully consider the differences: Think about an explanation that could account for these results.
3. Read and evaluate the logic of each of the five answer choices in light of the discrepancy. Try to find a choice that can sensibly explain the paradoxical results.
4. Use process of elimination to narrow your choices. Reject choices that only offer a partial explanation, that offer irrelevant information, or that make the discrepancy even more inexplicable.
5. Find the answer that most logically accounts for the discrepancy.

EXAMPLE:

> A suburb of Scottsdale, Arizona, is a popular retirement area. Most of the communities have age requirements of 55 and older. Interestingly, many of the supermarkets in the area have noticed robust sales of sugared cereals and snacks popular with young children.
>
> Which of the following, if true, best accounts for the apparent discrepancy in the situation?
>
> **A.** Many senior citizens are on restricted diets and must limit their intake of high-cholesterol and high-carbohydrate products.
> **B.** Several communities have banded together to sponsor a food drive to raise money for a new cardiac-care unit in the local hospital.
> **C.** Many residents of retirement communities have grandchildren from out of state who visit them several times throughout the year.
> **D.** Supermarkets in Scottsdale have found that TV commercials advertising sweetened cereal and cartoon-character-affiliated snacks are very successful with children ages four to eight.
> **E.** Studies have found that increased sugar intake among elderly patients in assisted living facilities has resulted in an increase in the incidence of diabetes.

The correct answer is **C.** The increased sale of food popular with children is unexpected in a retirement community. Some logical explanation must account for this apparent discrepancy. Choice A deepens the discrepancy, so you can eliminate it. Choice B might account for increased food sales in general but not specifically children's snacks. Choice D would explain an increase in a community with a large population of young children, which is not the case here. Choice E offers information that is peripheral to the issue and would suggest that senior citizens should avoid sugared snacks. Only Choice C offers a logical explanation: If many grandchildren are visiting, a rise in sales of children's snacks makes sense.

F. Incomplete Information Questions

Incomplete information questions require you to reason and deduce missing information. One kind of question presents you with a situation and asks you which choice best completes the passage. Others ask you to consider what piece of information is missing from the passage: Does it need another premise or piece of evidence to make it logical?

1. Complete the Question

In these questions, the last sentence is left unfinished, and the sentence ends with a blank line. Your task is to complete the sentence with the most logical answer.

Here is how you should approach these questions:

1. Read the situation carefully so that you understand the premises and the conclusion (if there is one).
2. Think about what information would logically complete the meaning of the sentence and make the situation consistent.
3. Carefully read and evaluate the logic of each of the five choices.
4. Use process of elimination to narrow your choices.
5. Find the choice that best completes the unfinished sentence.

EXAMPLE:

> A high school guidance counselor recently gave all seniors a questionnaire about plagiarism. On the questionnaire, 40 percent of students reported that they had plagiarized on at least one paper. School officials believe the percentage may actually be higher because _____.
>
> **A.** some students who admitted to plagiarizing once may have plagiarized more frequently
> **B.** statistics taken from high schools across the nation indicate that 62 percent of high school students have cheated on tests
> **C.** some students who did not take the survey have never plagiarized
> **D.** some students who claimed not to have plagiarized may have not have been truthful
> **E.** some students who claimed to have plagiarized may not have been truthful

The correct answer is **D**. To complete this sentence, you must consider what factor would make the school officials believe that more students plagiarized than admitted to doing so on the questionnaire. Choice B should be the first answer you eliminate because it is not relevant. Cheating on tests is not the same as plagiarism. Next, eliminate Choice A because the frequency of plagiarism is not the issue at hand. You can eliminate Choice C as well, because students who did not take the survey and did not plagiarize would not affect the statistic in question. That leaves choices D and E; you must read carefully and use logic to know that Choice E can't be correct because, if students who admitted to plagiarism lied, the percentage would go down rather than up. Choice D is the correct answer because if students who denied engaging in plagiarism lied, then the percentage would rise.

2. Missing Information

In these questions, your task is to ascertain what information is needed to make the situation more logical. You'll be asked such questions as: The conclusion would be more reasonably drawn if which of the following were inserted into the argument as an additional premise? What additional piece of evidence is necessary before a sound conclusion may be drawn?

Here is how you should approach a missing information question:

1. Read the situation carefully so that you understand the premises and the conclusion (if there is one).
2. Think about what information is necessary before a reasonable conclusion can be drawn.
3. Carefully read and evaluate the logic of each of the five answer choices.
4. Use process of elimination to narrow your choices.
5. Find the choice that contains information that would best lead to a sound conclusion.

EXAMPLE:

> Corn Farmer 1: Last year was such a good year for us, and the outlook for this year was good, too. A weak Australian wheat crop last year led Chinese cattle growers to buy record amounts of our corn to feed their herds.
>
> Corn Farmer 2: I am in serious economic trouble because exports of corn are down significantly this year.
>
> Assuming that all the following are true, what piece of information is needed to make the above conversation logical?
>
> **A.** The price of corn per bushel rose 11 percent from last year to this year.
> **B.** New research has indicated that corn oil is a healthy alternative to peanut oil.
> **C.** A sudden increase in rainfall led to the end of a major drought in Australia.
> **D.** Chinese cattle ranchers have found that cattle fed a diet consisting solely of corn produce the same quality of beef as those fed a diet of wheat.
> **E.** The global economic crisis has had little impact on Chinese cattle ranchers.

The correct answer is **C.** The missing piece of information must explain the downturn in corn exports. Because Farmer 1 indicated that one reason for the upswing in corn exports was the poor wheat crop from Australia, a change in conditions that led to the poor crop would explain the change. Choice A seems to contradict the conversation, so you can eliminate it. Choice B might lead to an upswing in corn sales, so you can eliminate that also. Choices D and E would have little or no impact on the corn farmers. Choice C is correct because an increase in rainfall in Australia would lead to an improved wheat crop; because the poor wheat crop led to the increased corn sales in the first place, it is logical to assume that an improved wheat crop would lead to a diminished need for corn.

Practice

Directions (1–10): Analyze the situation in each question and select the answer that is the best response to the question.

1. Recently, efficiency experts at a discount megastore decided to increase the store's profits by reducing waste and increasing efficiency in the stores. The first action has been to require manufacturers of detergents to eliminate as much water as possible from their formulas and package their products in concentrated form. The store executives estimate that this plan will reduce the cost of packaging material, free up shelf space, and permit more dramatic displays of merchandise.

   Which of the following, if true, would most support the plan of the efficiency experts?

   A. The packaging industry has experienced such a sharp downturn in demand for polystyrene, a key ingredient used in molding plastic containers, that it has been forced to lay off 13 percent of employees in one factory alone.

   B. The water used in the manufacture of detergents and other cleaning products is purified at the same water-treatment plants that purify water used in soft drinks and juice boxes sold in public schools.

   C. Detergent manufacturers estimate that smaller containers will lower the wholesale price of laundry products by 7 percent next year and by 11 percent the following year.

   D. By increasing the number of hours that employees work and hiring fewer new employees, discount stores have been able to reduce payroll taxes and the cost of health benefits, a reduction that has saved the companies hundreds of thousands of dollars this year.

   E. By increasing the number of items on display shelves and the attractiveness of the presentations, discount stores hope to entice shoppers to spend more per shopping trip.

2. A brand of footwear claims to have created a new design to help consumers lose weight by burning fat and building muscle as the wearer walks. The manufacturer claims the inclined sole in the shoes will reduce foot and ankle injury while it doubles the fat-burning effects of walking in regular sneakers. It also claims that those who wear its shoes for 30 minutes of walking every day will increase their endurance and enhance the aerobic effects of exercise.

   Which of the following, if true, most seriously undermines the claims of the footwear designer?

   A. Clinical trials have shown that inclined soles tend to cause undue stress on the Achilles tendon, a potentially painful and debilitating injury.

   B. Studies show that 30 minutes of daily walking will increase muscle mass in the calf, creating a more efficient metabolic rate in the breakdown of body fat.

   C. It can be mathematically calculated that the angle of incline of the sole of the shoe is directly proportional to pronation of the metatarsal bones of the forefoot.

   D. Exercise, especially walking, has been shown to have significant health benefits, especially for the elderly, who tend to have a more sedentary lifestyle.

   E. The American Association of Medical Experts states that walking for 30 minutes every day has little impact on prevention of heart disease.

3. Many cruise lines advertise that their cruises are a good vacation choice for people who suffer from arthritis. Arthritis, which is often exacerbated by cold, damp climates, can be debilitating, and sufferers do not always get a chance to get away and travel comfortably. Cruise-line operators aver that they are especially skilled at dealing with passengers who have various disabilities. Cruise ships, they point out, are self-contained—everything a vacationer needs is onboard, from meals to entertainment to medical facilities.

BlueSea cruise line is a well-priced cruise operator with a good reputation for service. Why would a person with arthritis not to elect to go on a BlueSea cruise?

   A. All staterooms on BlueSea ships have bathrooms equipped with handrails and wide-opening shower doors.

   B. Crew members on BlueSea cruise line do their best to accommodate wheelchairs on the cruise tours.

   C. Travel agents often recommend BlueSea cruises for passengers seeking tours of Alaska at a reasonable price.

   D. The BlueSea fleet consists of small ships, all of which are especially built to travel along the west coast of northern Canada to the waterways of Alaska, the only route of this line.

   E. All BlueSea cruise ships are constructed with dining and entertainment facilities on the highest level and cabins on the lower four levels.

4. Many school districts have no difficulty filling English and social studies teaching positions. In the fields of science and math, however, they face a shortage of qualified applicants. Clearly, more college graduates with degrees in the sciences or mathematics are working for major corporations than are entering the field of education.

Assuming that all the following assertions are true, which most weakens the above conclusion?

   A. Although the economy is flagging, more college graduates are majoring in business and marketing than ever before.

   B. Proportionally, more women than men are applying to graduate programs in science and math.

   C. College graduates with degrees in math and science are being recruited by large companies, many of which are offering high salaries and signing bonuses.

   D. Citing the advantages of satisfying sense of self-worth, frequent vacations, and summers off, 54 percent of graduating science and math majors are seeking high school teaching positions.

   E. More science and math teachers are continuing their educations; indeed, many have received doctorates in their fields.

5. In a recent article in a nature magazine, the author finds that American parks are not as attractive as those in Italy. The article compares 25 parks in the United States to 25 parks in Italy and asserts that the Italian parks have more aesthetically pleasing arrangements of plants and trees and offer more visual stimulation.

    What is the most serious flaw in the author's presentation?

    A.   The author does not consider that many parks in Italy have existed for hundreds of years and have had time to develop mature plantings.
    B.   The author does not acknowledge that many Italian parks are located on former large, opulent estates and no expense was spared in their design and construction.
    C.   The criteria the author used for selecting the parks could be those that best support his primary contention.
    D.   The author does not recognize that many American parks, including Central Park in New York City and Mohican State Park in Ohio, have won awards for their scenic beauty.
    E.   Because of economic woes, the National Parks budget has been cut by 21 percent this year.

6. Carrot farmers in a particular region have been troubled by an insect invasion that has decimated their crops. A few farmers have employed the pesticide Bug-go, which destroys 100 percent of the pests, but it causes the carrots to be a pale gold color rather than orange. A few other farmers have used the pesticide Beagoner, which destroys about 60 percent of the insects, but does not affect the color of the carrots.

    Before the remaining farmers make an informed decision between Bug-go and Beagoner, they must ascertain the answers to all the following questions *except:*

    A.   Does the color of a carrot affect its taste or its nutritional value?
    B.   How much damage will the 40 percent of the insects unaffected by Beagoner cause?
    C.   Is the cost of using Beagoner the same as that of using Bug-go?
    D.   Will the public be willing to purchase carrots that are not orange?
    E.   Will the 40 percent of insects unaffected by Beagoner be destroyed by Bug-go?

7. Studies of the genetic makeup of cheetahs show that the animals have a dramatic lack of genetic diversity. Usually, animals that display this lack of genetic diversity are on the track to extinction. Yet, in areas in which human and nonhuman predators are not prevalent, the cheetah populations thrive.

    Given the bleak genetic outlook of the cheetah, which of the following would explain the thriving population?

    A.   Some zoologists have found that many cheetahs in captivity are infertile.
    B.   Genetic patterns in laboratory tests are often contraindicative of patterns exhibited in the wild.
    C.   Biologists who conduct genetic testing predict that recessive traits will appear more frequently with inbred species.
    D.   Farmers in Africa shoot cheetahs because they believe the animals are a threat to their livestock.
    E.   DNA analysis is the most accurate predictor of the genetic health of a species.

8. Many MBA programs are seeking to reverse the perception of their graduates as avaricious corporate drones, enriching their company's wealth without regard to moral or ethical laws. In response to this perception, 20 percent of graduates of one prestigious university have signed a voluntary pledge to put the needs of the greater good of humanity ahead of corporate gain. At another renowned institution, enrollment is up significantly in courses in business ethics. This new emphasis will put an end to corporate greed.

The argument rests on what assumption?

A. The ethics of business is a legitimate area of study in an MBA program.
B. In a weak economy, the need to increase earnings overshadows ethical responsibility.
C. A capitalistic society inevitably leads to social inequities that can't be reversed by legislation.
D. Voluntary commitment to social responsibility translates into concrete action.
E. The recent prominence of ethical considerations is a reaction to the post-Enron and post-Madoff climate.

9. The Lower Columbia River Estuary Partnership recently held a three-day conference on the river's health. New data collected by the U.S. Geological Survey and National Oceanic and Atmospheric Administration show concentrations of pesticides, industrial compounds, and flame retardants in the river. A proposal has been made to impose stringent restrictions on methods and practices of disposal of waste in residences, businesses, and farms. In order to prevent unwarranted restrictions, it is crucial to show that _____.

A. the proposed controls must be implemented without delay
B. a causal link exists between purportedly harmful substances and environmental damage
C. the most obvious offenders of the existing controls must be the most severely punished
D. the evidence pinpointing the source of pollutants is ambivalent
E. any existing damage to the Lower Columbia River is reversible

10. The town of Reading has a large lending library in the center of town. The neighboring town of Hicks, with which Reading has a reciprocal book-lending agreement, also has a centrally located library. More books are taken out per year in Reading than in Hicks. Therefore, the residents of Reading are more well-read than those of Hicks.

All the following statements weaken the conclusion *except:*

A. The population of Reading is twice the population of Hicks.
B. The library in Hicks is open three days a week while the library in Reading is open every day.
C. The library in Hicks has a full-time research assistant available to help schoolchildren with research projects.
D. The Reading library lends out more books per capita than any other library in the state.
E. The Reading library has a reading room with comfortable chairs and sofas.

Answers

1. **E** The increased number of items and the improved presentation will logically result in increased sales and increased profits. Choices A and B contain irrelevant information. Choice C may lower the wholesale price, but there is no necessary conclusion that this will result in more profit, especially if this lower price is passed on to consumers. The employee changes may increase profits, but not as a direct result of the new plan.

2. **A** If the inclined soles lead to more injuries, this will seriously undermine the manufacturer's claim. Choice C and D are irrelevant. Choice B supports walking as exercise but not necessarily in this brand of footwear. Choice E belittles the health advantages of walking.

3. **D** If arthritis is "exacerbated by cold, damp climates," a sufferer would not want to take a cruise to northern Canada and Alaska, regions with chilly, damp climates. Choices A and B would seem to support the claim. Choice C is irrelevant. Choice E doesn't factor in the fact that the ships are well equipped for passengers with disabilities so they must have elevators.

4. **D** The conclusion is that "more college graduates with degrees in the sciences or mathematics are working for major corporations than are entering the field of education." This conclusion is weakened by the information that 54 percent (more than half) of the math and science graduates are entering the field of education. Choice A and B are only marginally relevant. Choice C would strengthen the conclusion. Choice E is not directly relevant.

5. **C** All the choices might explain the greater beauty of the Italian parks, but Choice C *most seriously* weakens the credibility of the writer's conclusion.

6. **E** All the choices must be answered except the issue of the 40 percent of insects unaffected by Beagoner, because this question has already been answered in the argument: Bug-go kills 100 percent of pests.

7. **B** If the genetic tests indicate that the animals lack genetic diversity, yet the species has thrived, the only logical explanation of the discrepancy is that the tests are not accurate predictors of survival. Choices A, C, and D aren't relevant to the specific issue. Choice E yields the opposite results.

8. **D** The argument rests on the assumption that the altruistic intentions of the students will be realized in the real world. Choice A is marginally related but is not a direct assumption. Choice B contradicts the conclusion of the argument, as does Choice C. Choice E gives the reason for the new emphasis, but it is not an assumption that leads to the conclusion.

9. **B** Because the government would not want to impose unwarranted restrictions, it is essential to prove a causal link between the substances and the environmental damage before the controls are implemented. Choice A won't prevent the unnecessary restrictions. Choice C is more likely to support the enforcement of strict measures. Choice D is too vague to support the restrictions. Choice E doesn't affect the restrictions.

10. **D** The only choice that could support the conclusion is Choice D—the fact that Reading lends out more books *per capita* could be used as evidence that its citizens are more well read. Choices A and B might explain more books taken out, but not necessarily more *per capita.* Choices C and E aren't relevant to the conclusion.

IX. Sentence Correction

The sentence correction questions on the GMAT test your knowledge of standard written English, the English used by educated writers. These questions also test your editing skills. You don't have to identify parts of speech or parts of a sentence, and you won't encounter spelling mistakes. You have to distinguish between correct and incorrect grammatical constructions and make decisions about using language correctly and effectively. You have to correct sentences that are awkward and nonidiomatic—not phrased the way educated people speak and write.

On the CAT GMAT, you'll be presented with a sentence with an underlined portion; sometimes the whole sentence is underlined. Your task is to figure out whether the underlined part is correct or needs to be revised. If you think it's correct, you'll pick Choice A. (Choice A is always the same as the sentence in the question.) If something seems wrong, read choices B, C, D, and E to find the correct revision.

EXAMPLE:

Before making a presentation, each of the students <u>involved in the innovative research program was required to calculate both the costs and the potential profit to be gained from their invention.</u>

A. involved in the innovative research program calculated both the costs and the potential profit to be gained from their invention.
B. involved into the innovative research program calculated both the costs and the potential profit to be gained from his or her invention.
C. involving in the innovative research program calculated both the costs and the potential profit to be gained from their invention.
D. being involved in the innovative research program calculated both the costs and the potential profit to be gained from their invention.
E. involved in the innovative research program calculated both the costs and the potential profit to be gained from his or her invention.

The correct answer is E. You can eliminate Choice A because the sentence has a pronoun antecedent agreement error. The pronoun *each* is singular and must take the singular pronoun *his or her.* Choice B corrects the pronoun error, but has an idiom error, "involved into." Choices C and D both use the incorrect verb forms, *involving* and *being involved,* and don't correct the pronoun-antecedent error.

Here are some general strategies for answering the sentence correction questions on the GMAT:

- Read the entire sentence through to the end.
- Look carefully at the underlined portion.
- Check the most obvious errors first: subject-verb agreement, pronoun-antecedent agreement, tense, or awkward or non-idiomatic phrasing.
- Be sure the answer you select doesn't correct one error, only to make another error somewhere else.
- Trust your ears. If part of the sentence sounds wrong, it probably is wrong.

A. Punctuation

Because the sentence correction questions consist of fairly complex sentences, most of which have more than one clause, you need to know the rules of correct punctuation.

1. Commas

Commas are used for many purposes. We cover them in the following sections.

Warning: Beware of the *comma-splice error:* two main clauses joined by a comma.

> *Incorrect:* I entered the room quietly, all the students looked up.

Correct the comma splice by using the semicolon, adding a conjunction, or making one of the main clauses into a subordinate clause.

> *Correct:* I entered the room quietly; all the students looked up.
> *Correct:* I entered the room quietly, but all the students looked up.
> *Correct:* Even though I entered the room quietly, all the students looked up.

a. To Separate Items in a Series

Commas are used to separate items in a series.

> Michael is responsible for planning, scheduling, and editing. (words in a series)
> Michael is responsible for planning the media coverage, scheduling the games, and editing the game films. (phrases in a series)
> I told Johnny that the taxi arrived late, that the meeting was disappointing, and that the entire event was a disaster. (clauses in a series)

b. Before Conjunctions That Join Main Clauses

Use a comma before a conjunction (such as *and, or, for, nor, but,* or *yet*) that joins main clauses.

> The candidate has campaigned in favor of economic stability and continued growth, but he still urges patience from his constituents.

c. To Set Off Expressions That Interrupt the Sentence

Commas are used to set off expressions that interrupt the sentence. Parenthetical expressions are set off with commas.

> The members of Congress, I am sure, will vote in favor of the president's bail-out plan.
> Retail stores like Goodsmart, for example, have lowered prices in view of the economic hardships facing many customers.

Words used in direct address are set off in commas.

> Dr. Hoffman, your assistant is looking for you.

Introductory words are set off with commas.

> Well, there certainly are a lot of comma rules.

d. With Direct Quotations

Commas are used with a direct quotation.

> The supervisor announced, "All workers must take a furlough without pay next week."

e. To Set Off Appositives

Commas are used to set off an appositive. An *appositive* is a word or phrase that follows a noun or pronoun to explain or identify it.

> The economic recovery plan, a five-step program involving a partnership of government and industry, went into effect on Monday. (The appositive phrase is *a five-step program involving a partnership of government and industry.*)

Appositives can be restrictive or nonrestrictive. Nonrestrictive appositives are frequently set off from the remainder of the sentence with commas. This signals that the appositive is not essential to understanding the meaning of the sentence. Restrictive appositives, which are essential to understanding the meaning of a sentence, are not set off by commas.

> My brother, Richard, is an engineer. (nonrestrictive)

This sentence indicates that Richard is not essential to the meaning of the sentence; in other words, I have only one brother and his name is Richard.

> My brother Richard is an engineer. (restrictive)

This sentence indicates that Richard is essential to the meaning of the sentence; I have more than one brother, and Richard is the one who is the engineer.

f. With Nonrestrictive Clauses or Phrases

Commas are used with nonrestrictive clauses or phrases. A nonrestrictive clause or phrase is not essential to the meaning of the sentence.

> The book, the one on the left side of the shelf, is an interesting study of cellular biology. (The phrase *the one on the left side of the shelf* is nonrestrictive; it isn't essential to the meaning of the sentence.)

> The book that is on reserve is the one I need for my research. (The clause *that is on reserve* is restrictive; it is essential to the meaning of the sentence.)

g. To Set Off Geographical Names, Addresses, and Dates

Use commas to set off geographical names, addresses, and dates.

> Observers visited the branch office in Weston, Connecticut, last week.
>
> The presidential election will determine who lives at 1600 Pennsylvania Avenue, Washington, D.C.
>
> Ms. Gold met her two partners on August 6, 2007, in Omaha, Nebraska.

h. To Separate Two Adjectives

Use a comma to separate two adjectives when the word *and* can be inserted between them.

> The Coton de Tulear is a relatively rare breed of alert, friendly dogs.

Note: Do not use a comma if you would not use the word *and* between the adjectives.

> Sun Valley is an expensive winter resort. (You would not say "an expensive *and* winter resort.")

i. To Separate Contrasting Parts of a Sentence

Use a comma to separate contrasting parts of a sentence.

> The file on my desk marked "Urgent" is Jan's, not Jeff's.

j. After Introductory Phrases or Clauses

Use a comma after an *introductory adverb clause* that begins with a subordinating conjunction such as *after, although, as, because, before, if, since, though, until, unless, when, whenever, where,* or *while.*

> Until I save all the work I have done, please do not turn off the computer.

Use a comma after a *participial phrase.* A *participle* is a verb that functions like an adjective to modify a noun or pronoun.

> Raising her hand tentatively, Ella questioned the purpose of the new regulations. (The phrase *Raising her hand tentatively* is a participial phrase modifying Ella.)

Use a comma after an *infinitive phrase* (to + verb).

> To make a call on the iPhone, simply say the name of the person to whom you want to speak.

Use a comma after a long prepositional phrase or a series of prepositional phrases.

> In the middle of a long conversation, I lost service and found myself talking to no one.

2. Semicolons

The semicolon is used

- To join main clauses.
- Between main clauses connected by a conjunctive adverb or a connecting phrase.
- Between main clauses if there is a comma within one or both clauses or between items in a series if there are commas within the series.

a. To Join Main Clauses

Use the semicolon between closely related main clauses in a compound sentence when the main clauses are not connected by a conjunction.

Many airlines plan to install WiFi on all their planes; Eastern Airlines does not.

b. Connection between Main Clauses

The semicolon is used between main clauses connected by a conjunctive adverb or a connecting phrase.

Many airlines plan to install WiFi on all their planes; however, Eastern Airlines does not.

My computer has been causing many problems; in fact, it totally crashed last week.

Note: Use a semicolon before the connecting phrase and a comma after it.

Here are some common conjunctive adverbs:

- Besides
- Consequently
- Furthermore
- However
- Indeed
- Instead
- Moreover
- Nevertheless
- Therefore
- Yet

Here are some common connecting phrases:

- At the same time
- For example
- For instance
- In fact

- On the other hand
- That is

Note: Use the semicolon only when these phrases connect *main* clauses.

c. To Separate Main Clauses

The semicolon is used between main clauses if there is a comma within one or both clauses or between items in a series if there are commas within the series.

Use the semicolon for clarity between clauses when there are commas within a clause.

> If you leave early, we will not finish the project; but if you stay, we will complete the assignment.

Use the semicolon for clarity between items in a series that contains a comma.

> On our business trip, we stopped at Miami, Florida; Omaha, Nebraska; and Boston, Massachusetts.

3. Colons

The colon indicates a pause in the sentence. It is used before a list; before a long, formal statement; and before an explanatory statement.

a. Before a List

Use a colon before a list of items, including a list that is introduced by the words *the following* or *as follows.*

> Our trip included all the following cities: London, Paris, Rome, and Florence.

Note: Do not use a colon right after a verb or a preposition.

> You can learn about cities in France by looking in an encyclopedia, in a book about Europe, or on the Internet. (You don't insert a colon after the preposition *by.*)
>
> The distinguishing characteristics of collies are long pointy snouts, distinctive color coats, bushy tails, and affectionate dispositions. (You don't insert a colon after the verb *are.*)

b. Before a Long, Formal Statement

Use a colon to introduce a formal quotation. In this case, begin the quotation with a capital letter.

> President Lincoln began the Gettysburg Address with these words: "Four score and seven years ago our fathers brought forth on this continent, a new nation, conceived in Liberty, and dedicated to the proposition that all men are created equal."

c. Before an Explanatory Statement

Use a colon after a main clause when it is followed by a second clause or phrase that offers an explanation or a restatement of the first clause. In this case, if the statement after the colon is a complete clause and is important, you may begin it with a capital letter. (This is not a hard-and-fast rule. You'll see it both ways: with and without the capital letter. The key is to be consistent.)

> The all-day conference did not live up to our expectations: The presenters were ill informed and the handouts were inadequate. (complete clause after the colon)

> Mr. Alexander was driven by one deep desire: to become partner before he was 35. (phrase after the colon)

4. Dashes

Use the dash to indicate an important or abrupt break in thought or before a summary.

a. Abrupt Break in Thought

The dash gives the information that is set off special emphasis or indicates a sudden change in thought.

> When I left my laptop on the plane, it was lost—or so I thought until the flight attendant came running after me.

> Those rights that Americans hold dear—life, liberty, and the pursuit of happiness—are not universally respected.

b. Before a Summary

Use the dash before a summary. In these cases, the dash and the colon are interchangeable. The dash is used after items in a series to indicate a summarizing statement.

> Late flights, diverted flights, cancelled flights—the many inconveniences of flying are familiar to passengers who rely on the airlines.

5. End Marks

Question marks and exclamation marks are end marks that indicate the writer's intention: to ask a question or to make a strong or startling statement.

a. Question Marks

Use a question mark at the end of an interrogative sentence. An interrogative sentence is one that asks a question.

> Do you have plans for the new advertising campaign?

Do not use a question mark with an indirect question.

> Mr. Ramirez wants to know who came up with this crazy idea.

b. Exclamation Marks

Use an exclamation mark after a startling statement or at the end of an exclamatory sentence.

Wow! I aced the GMAT!

6. Sample Questions

Here are some sample sentence correction questions with punctuation errors:

1. The new president faces serious economic <u>problems, he has to grapple with the meltdown of the stock market, soaring unemployment figures, and failing</u> American car manufacturers.

   A. problems, he has to grapple with the meltdown of the stock market, soaring unemployment figures, and failing
   B. problems: he has to grapple with the meltdown of the stock market, soaring unemployment figures, and failing
   C. problems—he has to grapple with the meltdown of the stock market—soaring unemployment figures, and failing
   D. problems, he has to grapple with the meltdown of the stock market; soaring unemployment figures; and failing
   E. problems; he has to grapple with the meltdown of the stock market; soaring unemployment figures; and failing

The correct answer is **B.** It correctly uses the colon before an explanation. Choice A is a run-on; it contains a comma-splice error. Choice C incorrectly uses the dash because it sets off only one of the phrases in a series. Choice D has a comma-splice error and incorrectly uses the semicolon between phrases. Choice E incorrectly uses the semicolon between phrases.

2. Tensions escalated during the staff <u>meeting, nevertheless everyone</u> attended the farewell party for the plant manager when the meeting was over.

   A. meeting, nevertheless everyone
   B. meeting, nevertheless, everyone
   C. meeting, nevertheless; everyone
   D. meeting; nevertheless: everyone
   E. meeting; nevertheless, everyone

The correct answer is **E.** Only Choice E correctly uses a semicolon before a conjunctive adverb and a comma after it. Choice A uses the comma before the conjunctive adverb and no punctuation after it. Choice B uses only commas. Choice C reverses the placement of the comma and the semicolon. Choice D incorrectly uses a colon after the conjunctive adverb.

3. The personnel director refused to allow the <u>plant closing—so many people</u> would be hurt if the company proceeded with this action.

    A.   plant closing—so many people
    B.   plant closing so many people
    C.   plant closing, so many people
    D.   plant closing, so, many people
    E.   plant closing? So many people

The correct answer is **A.** The sentence correctly uses the dash to indicate a sudden break in thought. Choice B is incorrect because it has no punctuation. Choice C incorrectly uses the comma to join main clauses. Choice D incorrectly uses two commas. Choice E illogically uses the question mark.

B. Grammar

When you're working on grammar for the sentence correction questions on the GMAT, you may find the acronym PRIMPED CATS can help remind you of the errors you'll encounter on the test. Each letter stands for a grammatical error.

    P: Pronoun errors

    R: Redundancy

    I: Idioms

    M: Modification

    P: Parallelism

    E: Errors in adjective/adverb confusion

    D: Diction

    C: Comparisons

    A: Agreement

    T: Tense and voice

    S: Sentence structure

1. Pronoun Errors

a. Pronoun Antecedent Agreement Errors

Pronouns are words that are used to replace nouns. The noun that the pronoun replaces is called the *antecedent.* Usually, but not always, the antecedent comes before the pronoun.

A pronoun must agree with its antecedent in gender and number. If the antecedent of a pronoun is singular, the pronoun must be singular; if the antecedent is plural, the pronoun must be plural. If the antecedent is feminine, the pronoun must be feminine; if the antecedent in masculine, the pronoun must be masculine. For example:

Debbie brought her laptop to the software convention.

Debbie is the feminine singular antecedent for the feminine singular pronoun *her*.

The *project managers* brought *their* laptops to the software convention.

The word *managers* is the plural antecedent for the plural pronoun *their*.

If the antecedent refers to both genders, the phrase *his or her* is acceptable to avoid sexist language. When this phrasing is repeated several times in a sentence or paragraph, it may become awkward, though; you can avoid the problem by changing the sentence to the plural form:

Awkward: Each attendee put his or her laptop on his or her desk.

Better: The attendees put their laptops on their desks.

When indefinite pronouns are antecedents, determine whether they are singular or plural. Here are some singular indefinite pronouns:

- Each
- Either
- Neither
- One
- Everyone
- Everybody
- No one
- Nobody
- Anyone
- Someone
- Somebody
- Anybody

Here are some examples:

Each of the buyers on the trip purchases a different product.

Everyone purchases his or her favorite product.

Exceptions: Sometimes, with *everyone* and *everybody,* the sense of the sentence is compromised when the singular pronoun is used. In these cases, the plural form is acceptable.

Awkward: Everyone in the crowd stood and applauded when he or she saw the PowerPoint presentation.

Better: Everyone in the crowd stood and applauded when they saw the PowerPoint presentation.

Here are some plural indefinite pronouns:

- Several
- Few
- Both
- Many

Here are some indefinite pronouns that are either singular or plural, depending on how they're used:

- Some
- Most
- Any
- All
- None

For example:

> Some of the food has lost *its* taste. (singular in meaning)
> Some of the dealers have lost *their* franchises. (plural in meaning)

Two or more singular antecedents joined by *or* or *nor* take the singular pronoun:

> Either Marlee or Olivia will bring her car to the office.
> Neither Noah nor Alex has taken his GMAT yet.

Every pronoun must clearly refer to a specific antecedent. To avoid vague pronoun reference, be sure you can pinpoint the antecedent of the pronoun.

> *Vague:* Jessica wants to be a doctor because it is so rewarding. (The pronoun *it* has no antecedent.)
> *Better:* Jessica wants to be a doctor because the work is so rewarding.

> *Vague:* Barbara came late to every meeting, which annoyed her supervisor. (The word *which* is a vague pronoun because it has no antecedent.)
> *Better:* Barbara came late to every meeting, a habit that annoyed her supervisor.
> *Best:* Barbara's chronic lateness annoyed her supervisor.

b. Pronoun Case Errors

Pronouns change their form depending on how they're used. The different forms of the pronouns are called *cases.* Pronouns have three cases:

- **Nominative:** The nominative case of pronouns is used when the pronoun is the subject or the predicate nominative.
- **Objective:** The objective case is used when the pronoun is the object of a verb or the object of a preposition.
- **Possessive:** The possessive case is used to indicate possession.

Nominative	Objective	Possessive
I	me	my, mine
we	us	our, ours
you	you	your, yours
he	him	his
she	her	her, hers

Nominative	Objective	Possessive
it	it	its
they	them	their, theirs
who	whom	whose

First, look at the whole sentence and determine what role the pronoun plays in the sentence. If it's the subject, use the nominative case. If it's an object of a verb or the object of a preposition, choose the objective case. If the pronoun is showing ownership, use the possessive case.

Nominative case:

- The pronoun as subject:
  - *He* and *I* want to be assistants to the manager.
  - Mr. Simon and *she* expect promotions very soon.
  - *Who* is going to be president next year?
- The pronoun as *predicate nominative* (a word in the predicate part of the sentence that is linked to the subject):
  - The financial experts must have been *they*.
  - The accountants for the firm are Ms. Stein and *she*.

Objective case:

- The pronoun as *object of a verb* (direct object or indirect object):
  - The company gave *her* the retirement gift. (*Her* is the indirect object of the verb *gave*.)
  - Mr. Holmes invited Jana and *him* to the meeting. (*Jana* and *him* are the direct objects of the verb *invited*.)
- The pronoun as object of a preposition:
  - The head of the committee wanted to share the responsibility with *them*. (*Them* is the object of the preposition *with*.)
  - To *whom* should I address the letter of recommendation? (*Whom* is the object of the preposition *to*.)

Possessive case:

- Use the possessive case to show ownership and before a *gerund* (the -ing form of a verb used as a noun):
  - The director appreciates *your* being prompt for all meetings. (*Your* is the possessive pronoun used before the gerund *being*.)
  - *His* quick thinking saved the day. (*His* is the possessive pronoun used before the gerund *thinking*.)

EXAMPLE:

Mr. Aaron wrote his first series of articles about young entrepreneurs, <u>and in it he described the tensions between my partner and I in graphic detail.</u>

A. and in it he described the tensions between my partner and I in graphic detail.
B. and in them he described the tensions between my partner and me in graphic detail.
C. and in it he described the tensions between my partner and me in graphic detail.
D. and in them he described the tensions between my partner and I in graphic detail.
E. and in that he described the tensions between my partner and me in graphic detail.

This sentence contains two pronoun errors: an error in pronoun-antecedent agreement *(articles . . . it)* and an error in pronoun case *(between my partner and I)*. Choice **B** corrects both errors: The pronoun *them* agrees with the plural antecedent *articles* and the pronoun *me* is the objective pronoun used for the object of the preposition *between*. Choice C doesn't correct the error in pronoun-antecedent agreement. Choice D doesn't correct the error in pronoun case. Choice E incorrectly uses the pronoun *that* to refer to the *articles*.

2. Redundancy and Wordiness

In standard written English, conciseness is a goal. It is best to express your ideas in as few well-chosen words as possible. Always be alert for such repetitive and wordy expressions as

- True fact
- Important essentials
- Two equal halves
- Consensus of opinion
- Unexpected surprise
- Various different
- Extreme in degree
- Large in size
- Round in shape
- Close proximity
- New innovations
- The future to come
- Due to the fact that
- Ten years in age
- Problem that needs a solution

EXAMPLE:

The president proposed an economic bail-out plan for the auto industry <u>for the reason of its being healthy is essential</u> to the economic welfare of this country.

A. for the reason of its being healthy is essential
B. because its health is essential
C. because being healthy is essential
D. on account of its health is essential
E. in which its health is essential

The sentence is wordy and nonidiomatic. Choice **B** corrects the error. All the other choices are awkward, wordy, or non-idiomatic.

3. Idioms

Idioms are expressions or verb phrases that are used in English. The problem arises when the incorrect preposition is used with a verb. Unfortunately, there are no rules—you just need to know what is accepted as correct. Usually, you can trust your ears—go with what sounds right. When a sentence sounds awkward and is not phrased properly, we say it is nonidiomatic.

Here are some common idioms:

- Abide by
- Agree to (something)
- Agree with (someone)
- Apply for
- Approve of
- Argue about (something)
- Argue with (someone)
- Arrived at
- Believe in
- Capable of
- Comment on
- Complain about
- Conform to
- Consists of
- Depend on
- Differ from
- Discriminate against
- Escape from
- In contrast to
- Insensitive to
- Insight into
- Insist upon
- Method of
- Object to
- Opinion of
- Participate in
- Prefer to
- Preoccupied with

- Prohibited from
- Protect from
- Relevant to
- Subscribe to
- Succeeded in

EXAMPLE:

Unfortunately, the union <u>did not approve about the new contract, and the representatives were not capable to change their minds.</u>

A.   did not approve about the new contract, and the representatives were not capable to change
B.   did not approve the new contract, and the representatives were not capable of changing
C.   was not approving about the new contract, and the representatives were not capable to changing
D.   approve with the new contract, and the representatives were not being capable of changing
E.   approve about the new contract, and the representatives were not capable of making a change to

The correct answer is B. Choice B corrects both idiom problems: *approve about* and *capable to.* Choices C, D, and E are all nonidiomatic.

4. Modification

a. Misplaced Modifiers

Modifiers are words, phrases, or clauses that describe, change, or specify other parts of a sentence. Modifiers are often participial phrases. For example:

Riding on the plane, we read the article about the store opening.

Riding on the plane describes *we.*

As I turned the corner, I heard my phone *ringing loudly.*

Ringing loudly describes *phone.*

Sometimes modifiers are infinitive phrases:

To understand English grammar, students must practice writing and speaking correctly.

To understand English grammar modifies *students.*

In English, changes in word order (syntax) lead to changes in meaning. A modifier that is misplaced can cause confusion. For example:

Maria spotted a messenger sitting on a bench eating a sandwich. (In this example, the messenger is sitting and eating, but it sounds like the bench is eating.)

Sitting on a bench eating a sandwich, Maria spotted a messenger. (Here, Maria is sitting and eating, but it sounds like the bench is eating the sandwich.)

To avoid confusion, always place modifying phrases and clauses as close as possible to the words they modify. Here is how you could correct the two sentences above:

Sitting on a bench, Maria spotted a messenger eating a sandwich. (In this sentence there is no modification confusion, because it is clear that Maria is sitting and the messenger is eating.)

b. Dangling Modifiers

Dangling modifiers have no word or phrase to modify. For example, the following sentence is confusing:

Standing on the bridge overlooking the city, the buildings look like children's toys.

Who is standing? The sentence implies that the buildings are standing, so it needs to be revised:

As we stand on the bridge overlooking the city, the buildings look like children's toys.

Now it is clear that *we* are doing the standing.

When you read the GMAT sentence correction questions, check that modifiers are as close as possible to the word they modify and that there is no ambiguity.

EXAMPLE:

By merely visiting a retail Web site, <u>an order can be placed</u> for any conceivable item a business might need.

A. an order can be placed
B. and by placing an order
C. a purchaser can place an order
D. a purchase, placing an order
E. a purchaser's order can be placed

The correct answer is **C**. The sentence has a misplaced modifier: The *order* is not doing the *entering*. Choice C corrects the error by placing the word *purchaser* right after the modifying phrase. Choices B and D are sentence fragments. Choice E has the modifying phrase describing the *order*.

5. Parallelism

Parallel ideas should be in the same grammatical form.

When you join ideas using conjunctions, nouns should be joined with nouns, prepositional phrases joined with prepositional phrases, and clauses joined with clauses.

	Unparallel	Parallel
Nouns	Martin Luther King, Jr., was honored for his courage, faith, and he had a willingness to stick to his beliefs.	Martin Luther King, Jr., was honored for his courage, faith, and perseverance.
Verb phrases	I like to ski, to hike, and swimming.	I like to ski, to hike, and to swim. I like skiing, hiking, and swimming.

	Unparallel	**Parallel**
Prepositional phrases	We left the meeting early because of the inclement weather, and it was late.	We left the meeting because of the inclement weather and the lateness of the hour. We left the meeting because of the inclement weather and because it was late.
Clauses	The investigator found it difficult to believe that the boss had died of natural causes and in the innocence of his aide.	The investigator found it difficult to believe that the boss had died of natural causes and that his aide was innocent.

Correlative conjunctions (such as *both . . . and, either . . . or, neither . . . nor,* and *not only . . . but also*), which always occur in pairs, can be tricky: Be sure what comes after the first conjunction is parallel to what comes after the second conjunction.

Unparallel: The printer *not only* did a great job on my presentation, *but also* on my partner's.

Parallel: The printer did a great job *not only* on my presentation, *but also* on my partner's.

Unparallel: The general had *neither* the support of his troops *nor* did he have the loyalty of his officers.

Parallel: The general had *neither* the support of his troops *nor* the loyalty of his officers.

EXAMPLE:

In their investigation into illegal transfers of funds from the factory workers' pension fund, the auditors found <u>many of the workers were difficult to pin down, taciturn, and they were</u> evasive.

A. many of the workers were difficult to pin down, taciturn, and they were
B. many of the workers to be difficult to pin down, taciturn, and they were
C. that many of the workers were difficult to pin down, taciturn, and
D. many of the workers were difficult to pin down and taciturn, and they were
E. that many of the workers were difficult to pin down, taciturn, and they were

The correct answer is **C**. The sentence is not parallel; items in a series must be in the same grammatical form, in this case, an adjective or adjective phrase. Only Choice C corrects the parallelism error and correctly adds the relative pronoun *that* to introduce the clause. Choices B, D, and E incorrectly use a clause *(they were evasive)* rather than a phrase.

6. Errors with Adjectives and Adverbs

a. Comparisons

Use the comparative form of the adjective to compare *two* nouns or pronouns. The comparative form is formed in two ways:

- **One-syllable adjectives:** Add *-er.* (This ending is also used for some two-syllable adjectives.) For example:
    Of the two locations, the downtown store is larger.
    Wind energy is cheaper than fossil fuels.

- **Most two syllable adjectives:** Put the word *more* in front of the word. For example:

    My computer is more efficient than Herb's.

Use the superlative form of the adjective to compare *three or more* nouns or pronouns. The superlative form is formed in two ways:

- **One-syllable adjectives and some two-syllable adjectives:** Add *-est.* (This ending is also used for some two-syllable adjectives.) For example:

    Yugo was the *cheapest* car on the market.

    The commercial for coffee is the *silliest* I have ever seen.

- **Most two-or-more-syllable adjectives:** Put the word *most* in front of the word. For example:

    The Prius won the award for the *most efficient* vehicle.

Here are some irregular comparison forms:

	Comparative	Superlative
good	better	best
bad	worse	worst
little	less or lesser	least
much	more	most
far	farther or further	farther or furthest

Some adjectives, such as the following, are absolute values and cannot be intensified with *more* or *most:*

- Complete
- Round
- Unique
- Perfect
- Superior
- Correct
- Square
- Supreme
- Totally
- Preferable

b. Adjective/Adverb Confusion

Use an adjective to modify a noun or a pronoun, and use an adverb to modify a verb, an adjective, or another adverb.

Incorrect: The company announced that it will take the new regulations regarding government contracts very serious and implement any necessary changes in financial arrangements. (This sentence uses the adjective *serious* instead of the adverb *seriously.*)

Correct: The company announced that it will take the new regulations regarding government contracts very *seriously* and implement any necessary changes in financial arrangements.

EXAMPLE:

Of the hundreds of challenges facing economic leaders today, <u>the more demanding ones focus on handling each crisis decisively and correct.</u>

A. the more demanding ones focus on handling each crisis decisively and correct.
B. the most demanding ones focus on handling each crisis with decisiveness and correctly.
C. the more demanding ones focus on handling each crisis in a correct manner and decisively.
D. the most demanding ones focus on the handling of each crisis in a way both decisive and correct.
E. the most demanding ones focus on handling each crisis decisively and correctly.

The correct answer is **E.** The sentence contains two adjective/adverb errors: incorrect comparison and adjective/adverb confusion. The word *most* is needed to modify *demanding* because more than two (in this case, hundreds) are being compared. The adverb *correctly* is needed to modify the verb *handled.* Choice B uses the unparallel phrase *with decisiveness and correctly.* Choice C incorrectly uses *more* and uses the unparallel phrase *in a correct manner and decisively.* Choice D uses the wordy phrase *in a way both decisive and correct.*

7. Diction

Diction means word choice. A diction error occurs when a word is used incorrectly or inappropriately.

Diction errors occur most often with words that look alike such as *refer/infer, prospective/perspective, formally/formerly, defensible/defensive,* or *reliable/reliant.* Be alert and careful as you read the sentences.

Here are some commonly misused words:

- *Among/between:* Use *between* for two people or things ("between my brother and me"). Use *among* for three or more ("among all my friends").
- *Fewer/less:* Use *fewer* for anything you can count ("fewer meetings in California"). Use *less* for whole quantities ("less pain").
- *Amount/number:* Use *amount* for whole quantities ("amount of effort"). Use *number* for things you can count ("number of employees").

EXAMPLE:

Because their policies were indistinguishable, <u>there was little choice among the two perspective candidates</u> for mayor.

A. there was little choice among the two perspective candidates
B. there were little choice among the two candidates
C. there was little choice among the two prospective candidates
D. there was little choice between the two perspective candidates
E. there was little choice between the two prospective candidates

The correct answer is **E.** The sentence contains two diction errors: improper use of *among* and the wrong word *perspective.* To compare two people, *between* is the correct preposition. *Prospective* is the right word to use for potential candidates. Only Choice E corrects both idiom errors.

8. Comparisons

a. Illogical Comparisons

Use the word *other* or the word *else* to compare one thing or person to the rest of the group.

> *Illogical comparison:* Our sales team is more successful than any team. (This is illogical because your team *is* a team.)
>
> *Logical comparison:* Our sales team is more successful than any *other* team.

b. Unbalanced Comparisons

Comparisons must be balanced and parallel. Use the words *than* or *as* to balance the sentence.

> *Unbalanced:* The attorney won as many cases if not more than the opposing counsel.
>
> *Balanced:* The attorney won *as* many cases *as,* if not *more than,* the opposing counsel.

c. Faulty Comparisons

You must compare like things—apples to apples, not apples to oranges.

> *Incorrect:* After tasting all the exotic dishes at the convention, I found that I like the foods from India better than China. (In this sentence, you're comparing *foods* to *China.*)
>
> *Correct:* After tasting all the exotic dishes at the convention, I found that I like the foods from India better than the foods from China. (Here you're comparing *foods* to *foods.*)

EXAMPLE:

> In contrast to large advertising firms that purchase huge blocks of television air time, <u>squeezing every dollar out of a small firm's budget requires a skilled leader and creative thinking.</u>
>
> A. squeezing every dollar out of a small firm's budget requires a skilled leader and creative thinking.
> B. squeezing every dollar out of a small firm's budget is done by a skilled leader who uses creative thinking.
> C. those who squeeze every dollar out of a small firm's budget are a skilled leader and creative thinking.
> D. a small firm must use skilled leadership and creative thinking to squeeze every dollar out its budgets.
> E. a small firm squeezes every dollar out of a budget that requires a skilled leader and creative thinking.

The correct answer is **D.** The sentence has an illogical comparison: *large advertising firms* must be compared to *small advertising firms*, not *squeezing.* Choice D is the best answer because it corrects the illogical comparison and compares large firms to small firms. Choice B compares large firms to squeezing. Choice C corrects the illogical comparison, but then uses nonidiomatic phrasing *(those who squeeze every dollar out of a small firm's budget are a skilled leader)*. Choice E corrects the illogical comparison but improperly places an adjective clause *(that requires a skilled leader and creative thinking)* after budget.

9. Agreement

a. Agreement of Subject and Verb

A verb must agree with its subject in number. A singular subject takes the singular form of a verb; a plural subject takes the plural form of the verb.

> *Singular:* My *sales prediction agrees* with yours. (one prediction)
>
> *Plural:* My *sales predictions agree* with yours. (more than one prediction)

Note: Although most nouns form the plural by adding the letter *s,* most verbs in their plural form do not end in the letter *s.*

Phrases may intervene between the subject and the verb. In most cases, ignore the intervening phrase:

> My sales predictions *for the month* agree with yours.

The phrase *for the month* is a prepositional phrase.

Intervening prepositional phrases do not affect agreement of subject and verb, so the best approach is to cross out or bracket intervening phrases. This will avoid confusion.

Note: The subject of a sentence is never part of a prepositional phrase.

> The hotel room with a bathroom and two beds is available.
>
> The hotel *room* [with a bathroom and two beds] *is* available.

Be sure to find the subject and match it with the verb:

> Creating new products to appeal to consumers in specific demographics keeps a company current.

Bracket the intervening phrases:

> *Creating* new products [to appeal to consumers in specific demographics] *keeps* a company current.

Creating is the singular subject; *keeps* is the singular form of the verb.

Intervening parenthetical or explanatory phrases also do not affect agreement of subject and verb, so the best approach is to cross out or bracket intervening phrases. This will avoid confusion.

> My cousin, along with three of her closest friends, trains in a hospital.

Bracket the intervening phrase or phrases and match the subject with the verb:

> My *cousin,* [along with three of her closest friends,] *trains* in a hospital.

b. Agreement Problems with Indefinite Pronouns

Singular indefinite pronouns take the singular form of the verb; plural indefinite pronouns take the plural form of the verb.

> *Each* of the games on the computer *requires* skillful manipulation. (singular)
>
> *Both* of the games on the computer *require* skillful manipulation. (plural)

Singular subjects joined by the correlative conjunctions *either . . . or* and *neither . . . nor* are singular.

> Either Facebook or Twitter *is* an effective new outlet for commercial messages.

Plural subjects joined by these correlative conjunctions are plural.

> Neither the *banks* nor the *trustees were* aware of the fraud.

When one subject is singular and one subject is plural, the verb agrees with the closer subject:

> Neither the *trustees* nor the bank *is* aware of the fraud.
>
> Either the *bank* or the trustees *are* aware of the fraud.

c. Agreement Problems with Inverted Sentences

These sentences will be tricky because you'll encounter the verb before the subject. Again, the key to success is to find the subject, wherever it is in the sentence.

Note: The words *here* and *there* are never subjects.

> Two months before the stock market crash there *were* warning *signs.*

The plural subject *signs* agrees with the plural form of the verb *were.*

> There *are* many *problems* with the economy today.

The plural subject *problems* agrees with the plural form of the verb *are.*

Be sure to read the whole sentence through to find the subject:

> Into the projections for next year *go* the *cost and overhead.*

The plural subject *cost and overhead* agrees with the plural form of the verb *go.*

> Over the skyscrapers *flies* a small *helicopter.*

The singular subject *helicopter* agrees with singular form of the verb *flies.*

d. Noun Agreement

Use a singular noun to refer to a singular noun and a plural noun to refer to a plural noun.

> *Incorrect:* People who want to be a sales executive should apply here.

This sentence is incorrect because the plural noun *people* requires the plural noun *executives* to be logical.

Correct: People who want to be *sales executives* should apply here.

Incorrect: Travelers with a visa must sign in at Passport Control.
Correct: Travelers with *visas* must sign in at Passport Control.

EXAMPLE:

In the French Sculpture Galleries in the city museum, <u>there is two bronzes by Edgar Degas, each of which depicts a young ballet dancer.</u>

- A. there is two bronzes by Edgar Degas, each of which depicts a young ballet dancer.
- B. there are two bronzes by Edgar Degas, each of which depict a young ballet dancer.
- C. there are two bronzes by Edgar Degas, each of which depicts a young ballet dancer.
- D. there are two bronzes by Edgar Degas, each of who depict a young ballet dancer.
- E. two bronzes by Edgar Degas, each of which depict a young ballet dancer.

The correct answer is **C.** The plural subject *bronzes* needs the plural verb *are.* The singular pronoun *each* needs the singular verb *depicts.* Only Choice C has correct agreement.

10. Tense and Voice

a. Tense

Verbs tell the action or state of being in a sentence. They are also the time words, the principal indicators of tense. As you read, be aware of the tense of the sentence and note any inconsistencies.

The six tenses in English are

- **Present:** Action taking place in the present
- **Past:** Action that has already taken place in the past
- **Future:** Action that will take place in the future
- **Present perfect:** Action that began in the past and continues into the present
- **Past perfect:** Action that began in the past and was completed before some other action
- **Future perfect:** Action completed in the future, before some other action in the future

Present Tense		
	Singular	**Plural**
First person	I work.	We work.
Second person	You work.	You work.
Third person	He/she/it works.	They work.

Past Tense

	Singular	Plural
First person	I worked.	We worked.
Second person	You worked.	You worked.
Third person	He/she/it worked.	They worked.

Future Tense

	Singular	Plural
First person	I will work.	We will work.
Second person	You will work.	You will work.
Third person	He/she/it will work.	They will work.

Present Perfect Tense

	Singular	Plural
First person	I have worked.	We have worked.
Second person	You have worked.	You have worked.
Third person	He/she/it has worked.	They have worked.

Past Perfect Tense

	Singular	Plural
First person	I had worked.	We had worked.
Second person	You had worked.	You had worked.
Third person	He/she/it had worked.	They had worked.

Future Perfect Tense

	Singular	Plural
First person	I will have worked.	We will have worked.
Second person	You will have worked.	You will have worked.
Third person	He/she/it will have worked.	They will have worked.

Perfect tenses are always formed by using *have, has,* or *had* plus the past participle form of the verb. You also have the option of using the progressive form *(-ing)* in each tense to show ongoing action:

- Present progressive: I am working.
- Past progressive: I was working.
- Future progressive: I will be working.

- Present perfect progressive: I have been working.
- Past perfect progressive: I had been working.
- Future perfect progressive: I will have been working.

The present participle is the *-ing* form of the verb. In the case of the verb *to work*, it's *working*. (These *-ing* forms cannot be verbs alone; they need a helping verb.)

The past participle is the *-ed, -d, -t, -en,* or *-n* form of the verb. In the case of the verb *to work*, it's *worked*.

Many verbs have irregular forms:

Present	Past	Past Participle
arise	arose	(have) arisen
become	became	(have) become
bring	brought	(have) brought
catch	caught	(have) caught
do	did	(have) done
drink	drank	(have) drunk
drive	drove	(have) driven
eat	ate	(have) eaten
fall	fell	(have) fallen
fly	flew	(have) flown
lend	lent	(have) lent
ring	rang	(have) rung
sing	sang	(have) sung
swim	swam	(have) swum
write	wrote	(have) written

Often verbs occur in verb phrases with a helping verb and a main verb. Some verbs like *do, have,* and *be* can be both main verbs and helping verbs:

Roberto will *do* his project. (main verb)

Roberto and Anna *do need* to practice their presentation. (helping verb)

Watch for sentences that have illogical shifts in tense or use incorrect verb forms.

Illogical shift: Mr. Burns *searched* for signs of emerging markets when he *notices* the trends in India.

Correct: Mr. Burns *is searching* for signs of emerging markets when he *notices* the trends in India. (present tense)

Correct: Mr. Burns *was searching* for signs of emerging markets when he *noticed* the trends in India. (past tense)

Incorrect verb form: We were shocked that he *had drank* all the water in the cooler.

Correct: We were shocked that he *had drunk* all the water in the cooler.

b. Voice

English grammar has two "voices": active and passive.

In active voice, the subject performs the action of the verb:

> Analysts raised their target 13,000 points in light of recent stock market highs.

The subject *(Analysts)* is doing the action of the verb *(raised)*, which is received by the object *(target)*.

In passive voice, the subject receives the action expressed in the verb:

> Targets were raised 13,000 points by analysts in light of recent stock market highs.

The object *(Targets)* becomes the subject and receives the action of the verb *(raised)*. The subject *(Analysts)* becomes the object of the preposition *by.*

Passive-voice sentences are often wordy and awkward. For concise writing, you should use active voice whenever possible. In sentences with two clauses, always maintain consistency of voice. A switch from active to passive creates an unbalanced sentence. Also, overuse of passive voice throughout an essay causes it to seem flat and uninteresting. Try to stick to lively, active verbs.

> *Awkward and wordy:* Because the country is experiencing critical power failures, a sweeping overhaul of their energy policies has been proposed by the leaders of several major corporations.
>
> *Better:* Because the country is experiencing critical power failures, the leaders of several major corporations have proposed a sweeping overhaul of their energy policies.

EXAMPLE:

> While she works as a laboratory technician in Texas, a love for the mechanics of electrophoresis was developed in Susan.
>
> A. While she works as a laboratory technician in Texas, a love for the mechanics of electrophoresis was developed in Susan.
> B. While she worked as a laboratory technician in Texas, a love for the mechanics of electrophoresis was developed in Susan.
> C. While she was working as a laboratory technician in Texas, Susan developed a love for the mechanics of electrophoresis.
> D. While she is working as a laboratory technician in Texas, a love for the mechanics of electrophoresis is being developed in Susan.
> E. While she works as a laboratory technician in Texas, in Susan, a love for the mechanics of electrophoresis was developed.

The correct answer is **C**. The original sentence contains both a tense shift error and a passive voice error. Choice C corrects both errors; the first clause is correctly changed to the past tense, and the second clause is correctly changed from passive voice to active voice. Choice B corrects the tense error, but not the voice error. Choice D has the passive voice error. Choice E has both errors.

11. Sentence Structure

a. Run-On Sentences

Two or more complete thoughts joined in one sentence without proper punctuation constitutes a run-on sentence:

> The lecture was on the life cycle of the frog it seemed to go on for hours.

The run-on can be corrected in several ways:

- **Break up the sentence into separate sentences:** The lecture was on the life cycle of the frog. It seemed to go on for hours.
- **Join the main clauses with semicolons:** The lecture was on the life cycle of the frog; it seemed to go on for hours.
- **Change one or more of the main clauses to subordinate clauses:** Because the lecture was on the life cycle of the frog, it seemed to go on for hours.
- **Use a comma and a conjunction:** The lecture was on the life cycle of the frog, and it seemed to go on for hours.
- **Use the semicolon and a conjunctive adverb:** The lecture was on the life cycle of the frog; consequently, it seemed to go on for hours.

The most common run-on occurs when a comma joins two sentences:

> Nancy really likes her new boss, she thinks he can help her achieve her goals.

Correct the comma splice by any one of the run-on correction methods:

> Nancy really likes her new boss; she thinks he can help her achieve her goals.

b. Sentence Fragments

Most sentence fragments are phrases or subordinate clauses.

> Being interested in setting up a charity promotion. (participial phrase)
> To be interested in setting up a charity promotion. (infinitive phrase)
> Since we are all interested in setting up a charity promotion. (subordinate clause)

To avoid fragments remember:

- A sentence must have subject and a verb and express a complete thought.
- No word ending in -*ing* can stand alone as a verb without a helping verb (except one-syllable verbs like *sing* and *ring*). Be on the alert for the word *being* used alone as a verb rather than as a helping verb or a participle.

IPLE:

<u>Acclaimed cellist Yo-Yo Ma, a brilliant musician who is famed for his virtuoso performances</u> that stimulate the imagination as he seeks to explore music as a means of communication.

A. Acclaimed cellist Yo-Yo Ma, a brilliant musician who is famed for his virtuoso performances
B. Acclaimed cellist Yo-Yo Ma, who is a brilliant musician who is famed for his virtuoso performances
C. Acclaimed cellist Yo-Yo Ma is a brilliant musician famed for his virtuoso performances
D. Acclaimed cellist Yo-Yo Ma, being a brilliant musician who is famed for his virtuoso performances
E. A brilliant musician, Yo-Yo Ma, who is famed for his virtuoso performances

The correct answer is **C**. The original sentence is a sentence fragment; it has no verb for the subject *Yo-Yo Ma*. Choice C corrects the error by inserting the verb *is*. Choices B, D, and E are all sentence fragments.

Practice

Directions (1–6): These questions test your ability to recognize correctness and effectiveness of expression. In each sentence, part of the sentence or the entire sentence is underlined. Underneath each sentence, you'll find five ways of phrasing the underlined material. Choice A is the same as the original sentence in the question; the other four choices are different. If you think the original sentence is correct as written, select Choice A; if not, carefully consider choices B, C, D, and E and select the one you think is the best.

In making your selection, follow the requirements of standard written English. Carefully consider the grammar, *diction* (word choice), sentence construction, and punctuation of each sentence. When you make your choice, select the most effective sentence—the one that is clear and precise, without any awkwardness or ambiguity.

1. Hoping for faster completion of infrastructure projects like highways and airports, <u>the clearances proposed by the legislature have been delayed by disagreements about money.</u>

    A. the clearances proposed by the legislature have been delayed by disagreements about money.
    B. the clearances proposed by the legislature were delayed by disagreements about money.
    C. the legislature proposed clearances that will be delayed by disagreements about money.
    D. the legislature proposed clearances that have been delayed by disagreements about money.
    E. disagreements about money have delayed the clearances proposed by the legislature.

2. The heated rhetoric <u>during the proposed merger—from all sides of the issue—revolved around</u> location of the main office and subsidiary branches.

    A. during the proposed merger—from all sides of the issue—revolved around
    B. during the proposed merger; from all sides of the issue, revolved around
    C. during the proposed merger; from all sides of the issue—revolved around
    D. during the proposed merger being from all sides of the issue, revolved around
    E. during the proposed merger, which was coming from all sides of the issue and revolving around

3. In many cases, scientists studying geological formations of volcanic <u>origin have been surprised when they studied and found that the depth of many volcanoes exceed 1,000 feet.</u>

    A.   origin have been surprised when they studied and found that the depth of many volcanoes exceed 1,000 feet.

    B.   origin have been surprised when they found that the depth of many volcanoes exceed 1,000 feet.

    C.   origin have been surprised when they studied and found that the depth of many volcanoes exceeds 1,000 feet.

    D.   origin has been surprised when they found that the depth of many volcanoes exceeds 1,000 feet.

    E.   origin have been surprised when they found that the depth of many volcanoes exceeds 1,000 feet.

4. The lovely Indian dancer Madhavi Mudgal, a member of a family deeply committed to the classical arts, <u>is the epitome of elegance and grace, her style blends ancient Hindustani traditions with a modern sensibility.</u>

    A.   is the epitome of elegance and grace, her style blends ancient Hindustani traditions with a modern sensibility.

    B.   is the epitome of elegance and grace: Her style blends ancient Hindustani traditions with a modern sensibility.

    C.   the epitome of elegance and grace, her style blends ancient Hindustani traditions with a modern sensibility.

    D.   is the epitome of elegance and grace and her style blends ancient Hindustani traditions with a modern sensibility.

    E.   who is the epitome of elegance and grace, her style blends ancient Hindustani traditions with a modern sensibility.

5. Some governments are often forced to turn to financial experts for help, <u>but officials worry that some advisors who are called in to give advice may overstep its bounds and influence policy.</u>

    A.   but officials worry that some advisors who are called in to give advice may overstep its bounds and influence policy.

    B.   but officials worry that some advisors called in to give advice may overstep their bounds and influence policy.

    C.   but officials worry that some advisors who are called in to give advice may be overstepping its bounds and influencing policy.

    D.   but officials worry that some advisors, called in to give advice, may overstep its bounds and influence policy.

    E.   but officials are worrying that some advisors being called in to give advice may be overstepping their bounds and influencing policy.

6. The new robotic surgical apparatus is valued by surgeons not so much for its speed <u>but because it is more precise</u> in performing delicate procedures.

    A.   but because it is more precise

    B.   but for its increased precision

    C.   but for being more precise

    D.   as for its precision

    E.   as it is because it is more precise

swers

1. **D** The sentence contains a modification error. *Hoping . . . airports* must be followed by the *legislature* because that is what is being modified by *Hoping*. Choice B has the modification error and a tense error *(were delayed)*. Choice C corrects the modification error, but has a tense error *(will be delayed)*. Choice E has a modification error. Only Choice D is correct. *(See Section B.4.)*

2. **A** The sentence has no grammatical errors. The dashes are correctly used to set off an important break in thought. Choices B and C incorrectly use the semicolon. Choice D uses the awkward phrasing *being from all sides of the issue*. Choice E is a sentence fragment. *(See Section A.)*

3. **E** Choice A is incorrect because the sentence is wordy *(studied and found)* and contains a subject-verb error *(depth . . . exceed)*. Choice B corrects the wordiness error, but not the subject-verb agreement error. Choice C corrects the subject-verb agreement error, but not the wordiness error. Choice D corrects both of the original errors, but makes a new subject-verb error *(scientists . . . has)*. *(See Section B.2 and Section B.9.)*

4. **B** Choice B properly uses the colon to introduce an explanation. Choice A is a comma splice error. Choices C and E are awkward and nonidiomatic sentences. Choice D is wordy and incorrectly joins two main clauses without a comma. *(See Section A and Section B.9.)*

5. **B** The sentence contains a pronoun-antecedent agreement error *(advisors . . . it)*. Choices C and D also have this error. Choice E is awkward and nonidiomatic *(worrying that some advisors being called in to give advice may be overstepping)*. *(See Section B.1.)*

6. **D** The sentence contains an unparallel comparison. The comparison *not so much for its* must be followed by *as for its*. Choices B and C incorrectly use *but for*. Choice E is wordy. *(See Section B.8.)*

X. Quantitative Section

In the quantitative section of the GMAT, you're given 37 multiple-choice math questions, which you must answer in 75 minutes. The 37 questions are divided into two different categories: problem solving (see Chapter XI) and data sufficiency (see Chapter XII). These two types of questions are intermingled throughout the quantitative section, with roughly 22 problem-solving questions and 15 data sufficiency questions on the GMAT.

Both types of questions cover basic knowledge of arithmetic, elementary algebra, and geometry. The number of questions for each of these three subjects is roughly

- Arithmetic: 21
- Elementary algebra: 10
- Geometry: 6

When working on the quantitative section of the GMAT, keep in mind the following:

- **It is important to pace yourself.** You have 75 minutes to do 37 questions, which is approximately 2 minutes per question.

- **You may not skip over a question.** The computer will not present the next question until you've answered the current one on the screen.

- **Make an educated guess if you aren't sure about the answer.** There is a penalty for wrong answers, but there is also a penalty for unanswered questions, so if you're struggling with a particular question, you're better off making an educated guess and moving on.

- **Calculators are not allowed.**

A. Reviewing Math Concepts

1. Arithmetic

a. Integers and Real Numbers

As you prepare for the GMAT, you'll find that many questions test your understanding of the properties of real numbers—specifically, the properties of prime numbers, multiplication by 0, and odd and even integers. Here is a summary of some of these properties:

Primes

- A prime number is a positive integer greater than 1, whose only positive factors are itself and 1.
- Prime numbers are 2, 3, 5, 7, 11, 13, . . .
- 1 is not a prime number.
- 2 is the only even prime number.

0 is the only number that is neither positive nor negative.

- 0 is an even number.
- If $ab = 0$, then $a = 0$ or $b = 0$ (or both a and b equal 0).

Even/Odd

- even + even = even and (even)(even) = even
- odd + odd = even and (odd)(odd) = odd
- even + odd = odd and (even)(odd) = even

Use substitution to determine if an algebraic expression is even or odd.

Integers

- Because the set of integers is $\{\ldots, -2, -1, 0, 1, 2, \ldots\}$, if a question asks for integral values only, be sure to eliminate numbers that are not integers such as $\frac{1}{2}$, 2.5, or $\sqrt{7}$.

b. Fractions and Decimals

Fraction and decimal questions are common on the GMAT. Many of these questions require you to identify the correct numerical value of a given point on a number line in either decimal or fraction form. For example:

The approximate numerical values of points A, B, and C, on the number line above are -1.5, -0.5, and 2.5, or $-\frac{3}{2}$, $-\frac{1}{2}$, and $\frac{5}{2}$, respectively.

Some questions may require you to determine a correct inequality involving x, x^2, and x^3 when a numerical value of x is given. For example:

- When $x < -1$, $x^3 < x < x^2$. (For example, if $x = -2$, then $x^2 = 4$ and $x^3 = -8$.)
- When $-1 < x < 0$, $x < x^3 < x^2$. (For example, if $x = -\frac{1}{2}$, then $x^2 = \frac{1}{4}$ and $x^3 = -\frac{1}{8}$.)
- When $0 < x < 1$, $x^3 < x^2 < x$. (For example, if $x = \frac{1}{2}$, then $x^2 = \frac{1}{4}$ and $x^3 = \frac{1}{8}$.)
- When $x > 1$, $x < x^2 < x^3$. (For example, if $x = 2$, then $x^2 = 4$ and $x^3 = 8$.)

For the purpose of comparing x, x^2, and x^3, there are four intervals on a number line from which a number can be selected.

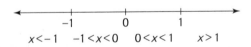

The order of the inequality involving x, x^2, and x^3 depends on from which of the four intervals the value of x is selected. Memorizing the order of the inequality in relation to the intervals on a number line is difficult. Your best bet is to simply substitute a numerical value into x, x^2, and x^3, and compare the results.

c. Percent and Proportions

A *percent* is the ratio of a number to 100. When you have to find the percent of a number, always express the given percent as either an equivalent fraction or a decimal. For example, write 5% as 0.05 or $\frac{5}{100}$, and write $n\%$ as $0.01n$ or $\frac{n}{100}$.

A proportion is an equation that states that two ratios are equal. For example, $\frac{2}{3} = \frac{10}{15}$ or $3 : 6 = 4 : 8$. When setting up a proportion, make sure that you use the same unit of measurement for the corresponding quantities and write the ratios in the same order. For example, given the question "If 5 pens cost 60¢, how much will 2 dozen pens cost at the same rate?", you should express 2 dozen pens as 24 pens and use the proportion $\frac{5}{60} = \frac{24}{x}$, where x represents the cost of 24 pens. Notice that the order of the proportion is $\frac{3 \text{ pens}}{\text{cost of 3 pens}} = \frac{24 \text{ pens}}{\text{cost of 24 pens}}$. You could also use other proportions such as $\frac{3 \text{ pens}}{24 \text{ pens}} = \frac{\text{cost of 3 pens}}{\text{cost of 24 pens}}$.

d. Divisibility and Remainders

A GMAT question on divisibility and remainders may require you to find the remainder when an algebraic expression is divided by a given number. For example, you might be asked the remainder when $2n + 6$ is divided by 3, given that the remainder of n divided by 3 is 1. The strategy here is to substitute a number for n so that when n is divided by 3, the remainder is 1. Notice that there are many numbers that satisfy this requirement (4, 7, 10, and so on). You could select any of these numbers. For example, if you pick 4 for n, then $2n + 6 = 2(4) + 6 = 14$. Therefore, the remainder of 14 divided by 3 is 2. Problem solved. This approach works because remainders repeat in cycles when integers that form an arithmetic sequence are divided by an integer.

e. Patterns and Sequences

Here are two common types of sequences:

- **Arithmetic sequences:** An arithmetic sequence is a sequence whose consecutive terms have a common difference. For example, in the sequence 3, 5, 7, 9, . . . , the common difference is 2.
- **Geometric sequences:** A geometric sequence is a sequence such that the ratios of consecutive terms are the same. For example, in the sequence 2, 6, 18, 54, . . . , the ratio is 3.

Here is a summary of formulas for finding the nth term and the sum of the first n terms for both arithmetic and geometric sequences.

	nth term	**Sum of the first n terms**
Arithmetic sequences	$a_n = a_1 + (n - 1)d$ a_1 = first term d = common difference	$s_n = (a_1 + a_n)\left(\frac{n}{2}\right)$ or $s_n = \left(\frac{n}{2}\right)\left[2a_1 + (n-1)d\right]$
Geometric sequences	$a_n = (a_1)r^{n-1}$ a_1 = first term r = common ratio	$s_n = \frac{a_1 - a_1(r)^n}{1-r}$

For example, given the sequence 2, 5, 8, 11, . . . , note that the first term $a_1 = 2$ and the common difference $d = 3$; therefore, the tenth term $a_{10} = a_1 + (10 - 1)(3) = 29$, and the sum of the first ten terms is $s_{10} = (a_1 + a_{10})\left(\dfrac{10}{2}\right)$ or $s_{10} = (2 + 29)\left(\dfrac{10}{2}\right) = 155$.

f. Sets

Questions involving sets on the GMAT can often be solved using Venn diagrams. A Venn diagram is a diagram using overlapping circles to show relationships among given sets. For example, if A is the set {1, 2, 3, 4, 5} and B is the set {2, 4, 6, 8, 10}, then the relationship between Set A and Set B can be shown using a Venn diagram as illustrated below.

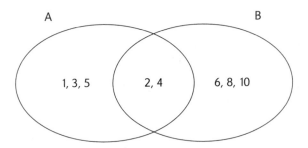

If a Venn diagram has multiple overlapping regions, try outlining the circles in different colors or markings to help you identify the regions.

If you're listing elements in order to identify the elements that two sets have in common, you can save time if you first list the elements that belong to the smaller set and then identify which of those elements are also in the larger set. For example, given that Set A contains all the prime numbers less than 10 and Set B contains all positive even integers less than 100, list all the elements of Set A, {2, 3, 5, 7}, and notice that 2 is an element of both sets.

g. Counting Problems, Combinations, and Permutations

On the GMAT, some questions require you to count the number of ways an event can happen. Here are some of the rules to remember:

- **Fundamental counting principle:** If one activity can occur in m ways, and then following that a second activity can occur in n ways, then the number of ways both activities can occur in that order is mn. For example, if you own three different jackets and four different pairs of slacks, then the number of outfits consisting of one jacket and one pair of slacks is $4 \times 3 = 12$.
- **Combinations:** The number of combinations of n things taken r at a time is $_nC_r = \dfrac{_nP_r}{r!}$, where $n! = n(n-1)(n-2) \ldots 1$. For example, $5! = 5 \cdot 4 \cdot 3 \cdot 2 \cdot 1 = 120$. For example, if there are three players on the school's tennis team, the number of ways of selecting two players to play doubles is $_3C_2 = 3$. Note that the order in which the players are selected does not matter.
- **Permutations:** The number of permutations of n things taken r at a time is $_nP_r = \dfrac{n!}{(n-r)!}$. For example, given the digits 3, 4, and 5, the number of two-digit numbers that we can get by selecting two of the three given digits without repetition is $_3P_2 = 6$. Note that the order in which the digits appear (34 versus 43) does matter.

When you're solving these problems on the GMAT, keep the following tips in mind:

- Use combination if order does *not* matter. Use permutation if order *does* matter.
- $_nP_1 = n$ and $_nP_n = n!$
- $_nC_1 = n$ and $_nC_n = 1$

h. Probability

On the GMAT, you'll be tested on simple probability. Here are some of the rules to keep in mind:

- Probability that an event A will occur is $P(A) = \dfrac{\text{number of ways event } A \text{ can occur}}{\text{total number of possible outcomes}}$.
- Probability that event A will occur is $0 \le P(A) \le 1$.
- Probability that event A will not occur is $P(\text{not } A) = 1 - P(A)$.
- The probability that event A or event B will occur is: $P(A \text{ or } B) = P(A) + P(B) - P(A \text{ and } B)$.

i. Mean, Median, and Mode

On the GMAT, you'll be asked to find the mean, median, and mode of a given set of numbers or algebraic expressions. Here are the key definitions:

- The **mean** of a set of numbers or algebraic expressions is the average of the set. For example:
  - The average of 5, 6, and 10 is $\dfrac{5+6+10}{3} = 7$.
  - The average of $x + 8$ and $5x - 4$ is $\dfrac{x+8+5x-4}{2} = \dfrac{6x+4}{2} = 3x + 2$.
- If you know the average of a set of numbers, then you know the sum. For example: The average of x and y is 10, then the sum of $x + y$ is $2(10) = 20$.
- The **median** of a list of numbers is the middle value, when arranged in numerical order. For example:
  - The median of 2, 6, 10, 11, and 14 is 10.
  - The median of 2, 6, 8, and 20 is $\dfrac{6+8}{2}$ or 7. (When there are an even number of values, you take the average of the two middle numbers.)
- The **mode** of a list of numbers is the number that appears most often. For example:
  - The mode of 2, 3, 5, 5, 5, 6, 6, and 8 is 5.
  - The mode of 2, 3, 6, 6, 8, 8, 12, and 15 is 6 and 8.
- Given a set of data
  - The population variance, v, is the average of the squares of the deviations from the mean, $\bar{x}$:
  $$v = \frac{1}{n}\sum_{i=1}^{n}(x_i - \bar{x})^2$$
  - The population standard deviation, s, is the square root of the variance:
  $$s = \sqrt{v} = \sqrt{\frac{1}{n}\sum_{i=1}^{n}(x_i - \bar{x})^2}$$

2. Algebra

a. Algebraic Expressions

When you're working with algebraic expressions, you need to follow the rules for order of operations. These rules of operation are sometimes referred to as PEMDAS:

- **P:** Parentheses—for example, $3(4 + 6) = 3(10) = 30$.
- **E:** Exponents—for example, $5(3)^2 = 5(9) = 45$.
- **M:** Multiplication—for example, $3 + 2(4) = 3 + 8 = 11$.
- **D:** Division—for example, $40 \div 2 \times 5 = 20 \times 5 = 100$. (***Note:*** Division and multiplication are done from left to right.)
- **A:** Addition—for example, $4 + 6 - 3 = 10 - 3 = 7$.
- **S:** Subtraction—for example, $10 - 2 + 3 = 8 + 3 = 11$. (***Note:*** Addition and subtraction are done from left to right.)

b. Equations

On the GMAT, you'll be tested on solving equations—linear, quadratic, absolute value, and radical equations. Keep in mind the following when you're solving equations:

- **When you're given an equation, the solution to the equation is sometimes not the answer to the question.** For example, if $2x + 4 = 10$, what is the value of $x + 5$? In this case, you must first solve $2x + 4 = 10$ obtain $x = 3$, and then substitute $x = 3$ in the expression $x + 5$, and finally conclude that $x + 5$ is 8.
- **Sometimes, instead of solving the equation for a value, you change the equation to match an expression that can be used to find the answer to the question.** For example, if $3x - y = 8$, what is the value of $6x - 2y$? In this case, multiply both sides of the equation by 2 and you have $6x - 2y$ equal to 16.
- **Quadratic equations on the GMAT usually can be solved by factoring.** However, if a given quadratic equation is not factorable, you could use the quadratic formula: $x = \dfrac{-b \pm \sqrt{b^2 - 4ac}}{2a}$ for $ax^2 + bx + c = 0$.
- **When you have to solve an equation that has the variable under the radical sign, usually you'll have to first isolate the radical on one side of the equation and then raise both sides to a power.** Because this process can create an extraneous answer, be sure to check that the answers satisfy the original equation. For example, the equation $x = \sqrt{x+7} - 1$ could be solved as follows:
  - $x + 1 = \sqrt{x+7}$
  - $(x+1)^2 = \left(\sqrt{x+7}\right)^2$ or $x^2 + 2x + 1 = x + 7$ or $x^2 + x - 6 = 0$
  - $(x + 3)(x - 2) = 0$, which implies $x = -3$ or $x = 2$
  - Note that $x = -3$ is an extraneous root because $-3 \ne \sqrt{-3+7} - 1$. Thus, $x = 2$ is the only solution.

c. Inequalities

Solving inequalities is part of the GMAT. In general, you can solve a simple inequality the same way you would solve an equation, except when multiplying or dividing an inequality by a negative number. If you multiply or divide both sides of an inequality by a negative quantity, the direction of the inequality sign is reversed.

Also, an equality question may involve the order of x, x^2, and x^3, where x is a real number.

The four intervals where the order of x, x^2, and x^3 changes are when:

- **x is less than –1:** In this case, $x^3 < x < x^2$.
- **x is between –1 and 0:** In this case, $x < x^3 < x^2$.
- **x is between 0 and 1:** In this case, $x^3 < x^2 < x$.
- **$x > 1$:** In this case, $x < x^2 < x^3$.

d. Absolute Values

When solving problems involving absolute values on the GMAT, it helps to remember the following:

- The absolute value of a number is never negative. It's either positive or 0. For example, $|-3| = 3$, $|3| = 3$, and $|0| = 0$.
- The definition of the absolute value of a number is: $|x| = \begin{cases} x, \text{if } x \geq 0 \\ -x, \text{if } x < 0 \end{cases}$.
- There are three common types of questions involving absolute value:
  - If $|x| = a$, $a > 0$, then solve the two equations $x = a$ and $x = -a$.
  - If $|x| > a$, $a > 0$, then solve the two inequalities $x < -a$ or $x > a$.
  - If $|x| < a$, $a > 0$, then solve the two inequalities $x > -a$ and $x < a$ or solve $-a < x < a$.

e. Systems of Equations

On the GMAT, you may be asked to solve a system of two or more equations. If so, keep in mind the following:

- Read the question carefully. When you solve a system of equations, the solution may not be the answer to the question. You may have to substitute the value of a variable in another expression to find the answer to the question. For example, if $x + y = 6$ and $x - y = 4$, what is the value of $2x + 3y$? In this case, first solve the simultaneous equations $x + y = 6$ and $x - y = 4$ by addition, and obtain $x = 5$ and $y = 1$. Then $2x + 3y$ becomes $2(5) + 3(1)$ or 13.
- Applying the multiplication property of 0, if $xyz = 0$ and $xy \neq 0$, then you have $z = 0$.
- When you're solving a system of equations, if one equation has variables x and y and another has x^2 and y^2, substituting (usually the preferred method for solving) can lead to very complicated equations. Instead of using substitution, begin by factoring the equations. Often, this produces an expression with x and y that match part of the other equation and can make the problem easier to solve. For example, if $a + b = 4$ and $a^2 - b^2 = 12$, what is the value of $a - b$? In this case, $a^2 - b^2 = 12$ is equivalent to $(a + b)(a - b) = 12$ or $4(a - b) = 12$ or $a - b = 3$.

f. Exponents

If a and b are integers

- $(x^a)(x^b) = x^{a+b}$. For example, $(x^3)(x^4) = x^7$.
- $\dfrac{x^a}{x^b} = x^{a-b}$. For example, $\dfrac{x^{10}}{x^4} = x^6$.

- $(ax^b)^n = a^n(x^{bn})$. For example, $(2x^5)^3 = (2)^3(x^5)^3 = 8x^{15}$.
- $x^0 = 1$, $x \neq 0$. For example, $(-4)^0 = 1$ but $-4^0 = -1$ because $-4^0 = -(4^0) = -1$.
- $x^{-n} = \dfrac{1}{x^n}$, $x \neq 0$. For example, $3^{-2} = \dfrac{1}{3^2}$.
- $x^{\frac{a}{b}} = \left(\sqrt[b]{x}\right)^a$ or $\sqrt[b]{x^a}$, if $\sqrt[b]{x}$ exists. For example, $8^{\frac{2}{3}} = \left(\sqrt[3]{8}\right)^2$ or $\sqrt[3]{8^2} = 4$.

When you're solving questions involving exponents, keep these tips in mind:

- Remember that the base does not change when you're multiplying powers of the same base or raising a power to a power—for example, $(7^3)(7^2) = (7)^5$ and $(7^3)^2 = 7^6$.
- When you're trying to find the value of an exponent in an equation, one way to solve the problem is to try to express each side of the equation as a single power. If the base of the power is the same on both sides of the equation, set the exponents equal to each other. For example, if $2^3 + 2^3 = 4^x$, what is the value of x? Rewrite $2^3 + 2^3 = 4^x$ as $2(2^3) = 4^x$, which is equivalent to $2^4 = 4^x$. Express 4^x as $(2^2)^x$, which becomes 2^{2x}. Thus, $2^4 = 2^{2x}$. Now set $2x = 4$ or $x = 2$.

g. Direct and Inverse Variation

On the GMAT, you'll be tested on direct and inverse variation. Here are the key rules to remember:

- When two quantities x and y are directly proportional, then
  - $y = kx$ or $\dfrac{y}{x} = k$, $x \neq 0$ for some constant k, with $k \neq 0$.
  - As x increases, y increases, for $k > 0$.
  - The graph is a line whose slope is k and the y-intercept is 0.
  - If (x_1, y_1) and (x_2, y_2) are points on the graph, then $\dfrac{x_1}{y_1} = \dfrac{x_2}{y_2}$.
- When two quantities, x and y, are inversely proportional, then
  - $y = \dfrac{k}{x}$, $x \neq 0$, or $xy = k$ for some constant k, with $k \neq 0$.
  - As x increases, y decreases, for $k > 0$.
  - The graph is a hyperbola.
  - If (x_1, y_1) and (x_2, y_2) are points on the graph, then $(x_1)(y_1) = (x_2)(y_2)$.

h. Functions

On the GMAT, you're expected to answer questions involving functions and their graphs. Here are some important rules to keep in mind:

- If $y = f[g(x)]$, then y is a composition of f and g. Evaluating $y = f[g(x)]$ for a given value of x requires first substituting x in $g(x)$ and then substituting the answer for $g(x)$ in f. The order of substitution may not be reversed, because composition may not be commutative.
- Because the graph of a function is a picture of the ordered pairs that satisfy the equation, you can find values of the function by reading the graph. The accompanying figure is a typical graph that you may encounter.

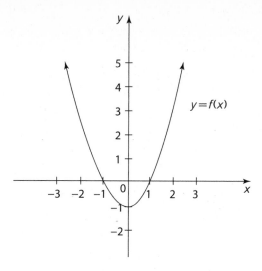

- If you need to find a function value, such as $f(2)$, from the graph, find the y-coordinate of the point on the graph where $x = 2$. In the accompanying figure, this is the point $(2,3)$. Because $y = 3$ when $x = 2$, using function notation, you would say $f(2) = 3$.
- If you need to use the graph to find b when $f(b) = 3$ find the point(s) with y-coordinate 3. Remember that b is the x-coordinate when the y-coordinate is 3. Because there are two points, $(2,3)$ and $(-2,3)$, $b = \pm2$.

3. Geometry

a. Measurement of Angles and Line Segments

On the GMAT, you'll be tested on angles and line segments. Here are the key rules to keep in mind:

- The sum of the measures of the three interior angles of a triangle is $180°$.
- The measure of an exterior angle of a triangle is equal to the sum of the measures of the two nonadjacent interior angles.

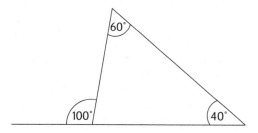

- The measure of an exterior angle of a regular polygon with n sides is $\frac{360}{n}$.

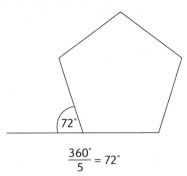

$$\frac{360°}{5} = 72°$$

- If two parallel lines are cut by a transversal, then the alternate interior angles are congruent.

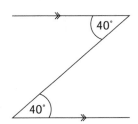

- If two parallel lines are cut by a transversal, then the corresponding angles are congruent.

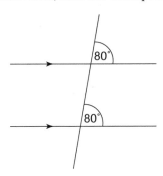

- If two lines intersect, then the vertical angles are congruent.

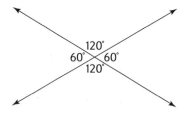

- The midpoint of a line segment divides the line segment into two congruent line segments.

b. Properties of Triangles

Some of the questions on the GMAT require you to apply the properties of triangles. Here are some of the important properties to remember:

- The triangle inequality: $a + b > c$

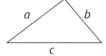

- The sum of the lengths of any two sides of a triangle is always greater than the length of the third side.
- If the lengths of two sides of a triangle are unequal, the measures of the angles opposite these sides are unequal and the greater angle lies opposite the greater side. Example: $\overline{BC} > \overline{BA}$ $m\angle A > m\angle C$.

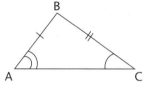

- The shortest distance from a vertex of a triangle to the opposite side is the length of the altitude from the same vertex to the opposite side.

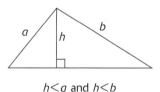

$h < a$ and $h < b$

- The Pythagorean theorem: $a^2 + b^2 = c^2$

- Special right triangle: 30°-60° right triangle.

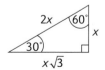

- Special right triangle: 45°-45° right triangle.

c. Similarity

If two triangles are similar, then

- Corresponding angles have the same measure.
- The lengths of any two corresponding line segments (including sides, altitudes, medians, and angle bisectors) have the same ratio.
- The ratio of the *perimeters* is equal to the ratio of the lengths of any pair of corresponding line segments.
- The ratio of the *areas* is equal to the square of the ratio of the lengths of any pair of corresponding line segments.

d. Areas and Perimeters

On the GMAT, perimeter and area problems are common questions. Here are the important formulas to keep in mind:

		Perimeter	Area
Triangle		$a + b + c$	$\frac{1}{2}bh$
Equilateral triangle		$3s$	$\frac{s^2\sqrt{3}}{4}$
Rectangle		$2(l + w)$	lw
Square		$4s$	s^2 or $\dfrac{d^2}{2}$

		Perimeter	Area
Parallelogram		$2(a + b)$	bh
Trapezoid		$a + b + c + d$	$\frac{1}{2}h(a+b)$

e. Solids, Volumes, and Surface Areas

On the GMAT, some questions require you to find the volume and surface areas of solids. Here are the important formulas to keep in mind:

		Volume	Surface Area
Cube		s^3	$6s^2$
Rectangular box		lwh	$2(lh + hw + lw)$
Right Circular Cylinder		$\pi r^2 h$	Total surface area: $2\pi r^2 + 2\pi rh$ Lateral surface area: $2\pi rh$
Sphere		$\frac{4}{3}\pi r^3$	$4\pi r^2$

		Volume	Surface Area
Pyramids		$\frac{1}{3}$(base area)(height)	Base area + lateral surface areas
Right Circular Cone		$\frac{1}{3}\pi r^2 h$	Lateral: $\pi r\sqrt{r^2+h^2}$ Total: $\pi r\sqrt{r^2+h^2}+\pi r^2$

f. Properties of Circles

Given a circle O with radius r and diameter d:

- Circumference: $C = 2\pi r$ or $C = \pi d$
- Area: $A = \pi r^2$
- The length of an arc: $\dfrac{m\,\overset{\frown}{AB}}{2\pi r} = \dfrac{m\angle AOB}{360}$

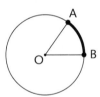

- The area of a sector: $\dfrac{\text{area of sector } AOB}{\pi r^2} = \dfrac{m\angle AOB}{360}$

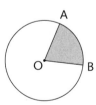

g. Coordinate Geometry

Given $A\,(x_1,y_1)$ and $B\,(x_2,y_2)$:

- The midpoint of $\overline{AB}$: $\left(\dfrac{x_1+x_2}{2}, \dfrac{y_1+y_2}{2}\right)$. Think of a midpoint as the "average."
- The distance between A and B (the length of $\overline{AB}$): $d_{\overline{AB}} = \sqrt{(x_2-x_1)^2+(y_2-y_1)^2}$.
- The slope of $\overline{AB}$: $m_{\overline{AB}} = \dfrac{y_2-y_1}{x_2-x_1}$. (Practice problems for slope are given in the next section.)

h. Slopes and Lines

On the GMAT, you'll be asked to find the slope of a line. Here are some important facts you should know:

- The slope of the line through the points (x_1,y_1) and (x_2,y_2) is $\frac{y_2 - y_1}{x_2 - x_1}$.
- The graph of $y = mx + b$ is a straight line with slope m and y-intercept b.
- If two lines are parallel, their slopes are equal.
- If two lines are perpendicular, their slopes are negative reciprocals and the product of their slopes is -1.

B. Solving Word Problems

The key to solving word problems is to read the problem closely. Start by identifying what you need to find. Then find it by setting up and solving an equation or by guessing and checking.

Be sure to answer the question that is asked. The solution to your equation may not be the final answer to the question. For example: If the sum of two consecutive integers is 15, then $x + (x + 1) = 15$ and $x = 7$. However, if the question asks for the value of the larger integer, the larger integer is 8.

Beware that sometimes a question may contain information not relevant to the solution.

Below are examples of some common word problems:

1. Percent

EXAMPLE:

The graph below shows how John's salary was determined in 2008. If John earned a total of $18,000 in overtime pay in 2008, how much did he receive as bonuses?

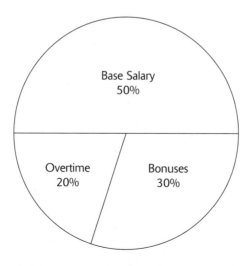

A. $6,000
B. $9,000
C. $27,000
D. $54,000
E. $90,000

The correct answer is **C**. Let x be John's annual salary. Because the overtime pay was 20% of John's salary, $0.2x = 18,000$ and $x = 90,000$. The bonuses were 30% of John's salary, so $0.3x = 0.3(90,000) = 27,000$. Thus, John's bonuses for 2008 were $27,000.

You can also do this problem by setting up a proportion to find the bonuses. Let y be the bonuses. Then $\frac{0.2}{18000} = \frac{0.3}{y}$, $0.2y = (0.3)(18,000)$, and $y = 27,000$.

2. Numbers

EXAMPLE:

The cube root of a positive number is the same as the number divided by four. What is the number?

A. –8
B. 0
C. 2
D. 4
E. 8

The correct answer is **E**. Let x be the number. Then $\sqrt[3]{x} = \frac{x}{4}$ or $x^{\frac{1}{3}} = \frac{x}{4}$. Raising both sides to the third power, you have $\left(x^{\frac{1}{3}}\right)^3 = \left(\frac{x}{4}\right)^3$, which is equivalent to $x = \frac{x^3}{64}$. Multiplying both sides by 64, you have $64x = x^3$ or $0 = x^3 - 64x$. Factor $x^3 - 64x$ and you have $0 = x(x^2 - 64)$ or $0 = x(x - 8)(x + 8)$. Thus, $x = -8, 0,$ or 8. Because x is a positive number, you know that $x = 8$.

3. Distance

EXAMPLE:

If Marissa drove for h hours at an average rate of m miles per hour and then she drove for k hours at an average rate of n miles per hour, what is the total distance, in miles, that she had driven?

A. $m + n$

B. $\frac{m+n}{h+k}$

C. $\frac{m}{h} + \frac{n}{k}$

D. $(h + k)(m + n)$

E. $mh + nk$

The correct answer is **E.** Because distance = rate × time, when Marissa drove for h hours at an average of m miles per hour, the distance was mh miles. Similarly, when she drove for k hours at an average rate of n miles per hour, the distance was nk miles. The total distance, in miles, is $mh + nk$.

EXAMPLE:

Erica used a car service that charges $5 per mile plus an additional initial fee of $20. If the total cost for the car service was $110, what was the distance traveled, in miles?

A. 16
B. 18
C. 20
D. 22
E. 26

The correct answer is **B.** Let x be the number of miles of Erica's trip. Then $5x + 20 = 110$, which is equivalent to $5x = 90$ or $x = 18$. Thus, the distance of Erica's trip is 18 miles.

4. Proportion

EXAMPLE:

Kaela is 5 feet 6 inches tall and casts a shadow that is 11 feet long. If Dan is standing behind Kaela and he is 6 feet tall, how long is his shadow?

A. 10 feet
B. 11 feet
C. 11 feet 6 inches
D. 12 feet
E. 12 feet 6 inches

The correct answer is **D.**

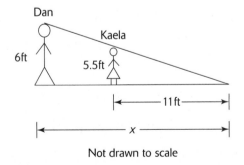

Not drawn to scale

Because each triangle has a right angle and the triangles share an angle, they are similar. As long as all numbers are expressed in the same units with Kaela's height 5.5 feet instead of 5 feet 6 inches, Dan's height can be found using the following equation:

$$\frac{\text{Kaela's height}}{\text{length of Kaela's shadow}} = \frac{\text{Dan's height}}{\text{length of Dan's shadow}} \text{ or } \frac{5.5}{11} = \frac{6}{x} \text{ or } 5.5x = 66 \text{ or } x = 12.$$ Dan's shadow is 12 feet long.

5. Work

EXAMPLE:

If Bill can mow the lawn in 60 minutes and Mary can mow the same lawn in 30 minutes, how long would it take the two of them working together to complete the job?

A. 15 minutes
B. 20 minutes
C. 24 minutes
D. 30 minutes
E. 45 minutes

The correct answer is **B.** Let n be the number of minutes required for Bill and Mary working together to complete the job.

	Time Needed to Complete the Job, If Working Alone	Part of the Job Completed per Minute	Time Needed to Complete the Job, If Working Together	Part of the Job Completed in n Minutes
Bill	60 minutes	$\frac{1}{60}$	n minutes	$\frac{n}{60}$
Mary	30 minutes	$\frac{1}{30}$	n minutes	$\frac{n}{30}$

Because it takes n minutes for Bill and Mary working together to complete the job, and in n minutes Bill can mow $\frac{n}{60}$ of the lawn and Mary can mow $\frac{n}{30}$ of the lawn, you have $\frac{n}{60} + \frac{n}{30} = 1$. Multiplying both sides of the equation by 60, you have $n + 2n = 60$, or $n = 20$. It would take Bill and Mary 20 minutes working together to mow the lawn.

EXAMPLE:

If three painters working together can paint a house in two hours, how long will it take for nine painters working together at the same rate to paint the same house?

A. 8 hours
B. 6 hours
C. 3 hours
D. 48 minutes
E. 40 minutes

The correct answer is **E**. Because there are more painters painting the house, it should take less time than two hours. Thus, you can eliminate choices A, B, and C. This is an inverse proportion because the more painters you have, the less time it will take. The formula for an inverse proportion is $(x_1)(y_1) = (x_2)(y_2)$, and in this case, $(3)(2) = (9)(y)$ or $y = \frac{2}{3}$ hour, which is 40 minutes.

You could also solve the problem by approaching it the following way: Because it takes three painters two hours to paint the house, the job requires a total of $3 \times 2 = 6$ people hours to complete. Let y be the number of hours needed for nine painters working together to complete the job. Then $9y = 6$ or $y = \frac{2}{3}$ hour, which is 40 minutes.

6. Probability

EXAMPLE:

In Janet's classroom, she labeled all her books as either fiction or nonfiction. She has 30 nonfiction books. If a book is picked at random, the probability that it is fiction is $\frac{3}{5}$. What is the total number of books in her classroom?

A.   50
B.   60
C.   75
D.   90
E.   150

The correct answer is **C**. Because $P(\text{nonfiction}) = 1 - \frac{3}{5} = \frac{2}{5}$, use x to represent the total number of books. There are 30 nonfiction books. Therefore, $\dfrac{\text{the number of nonfiction books}}{\text{total number of books}} = \frac{2}{5}$, which is equivalent to $\dfrac{30}{x} = \frac{2}{5}$ or $2x = 30(5)$ or $x = 75$. There are 75 books in total in Janet's classroom.

7. Counting

EXAMPLE:

At a restaurant, the menu consists of two varieties of salad, five different entrees, and three desserts, of which one is apple pie. If the Tuesday night dinner special consists of one salad, one entree, and apple pie for dessert, how many different Tuesday night dinner specials are there?

A.   5
B.   7
C.   10
D.   15
E.   30

The correct answer is **C**. Use the fundamental counting principle to determine the number of different dinner specials. Because there are two choices for salad, five choices for the entree, and one choice for dessert (because dessert must be apple pie), there are $(5)(2)(1) = 10$ different dinner specials.

EXAMPLE:

Four table-tennis players—Bill, Mary, Janet, and Karen—put their paddles on a table during a break. After the break, Bill picked up his own paddle. However, Mary, Janet, and Karen picked up each other's paddles but not their own. In how many ways can this happen?

A. 2
B. 4
C. 6
D. 8
E. 16

The correct answer is **A.**

Janet	Karen	Mary
K	M	J
M	J	K

There are three decisions to investigate:

- Which paddle did Janet pick up?
- Which paddle did Mary pick up?
- Which paddle did Karen pick up?

Janet picked up either Mary's paddle or Karen's paddle. If Janet picked up Mary's paddle, then Mary had Karen's paddle, and Karen had Janet's paddle. This is one possible outcome. If Janet picked up Karen's paddle then Mary had Janet's paddle and Karen had Mary's paddle. This is the only other possible outcome. Thus, there are two possible ways that Janet, Karen, and Mary could have picked up the wrong paddles.

8. Geometry

EXAMPLE:

If the area of a rectangle is 32 and the length and width of the rectangle are integers, what is the smallest possible perimeter of the rectangle?

A. 12
B. 24
C. 36
D. 64
E. 66

The correct answer is **B.** To find the smallest perimeter, find the possible values for the length and width and calculate the perimeter. The possibilities are listed in the following table:

Area	Length	Width	Perimeter
32	1	32	66
32	2	16	36
32	4	8	24
32	8	4	24
32	16	2	36
32	32	1	66

Thus, the smallest possible perimeter of the rectangle is 24.

EXAMPLE:

A container in the shape of a cube is completely filled with water. An edge of the cube measures 12 cm. A second container is in the shape of a rectangular box with length 8 cm, width 12 cm, and height 20 cm. If all the water from the cubic container is emptied into the rectangular container, what is the height, in cm, of the water level in the rectangular container?

A.   3
B.   9
C.   12
D.   16
E.   18

The correct answer is **E.**

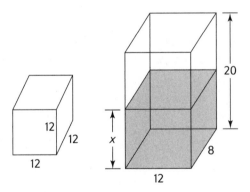

Not drawn to scale

Because the original container is completely filled, the volume of the water is $V = (12)^3$ cm^3 = 1,728 cm^3. When the water is poured into the second container, the volume of the water is unchanged. Let x be the height of the water level in the rectangular box. Then $(8)(12)(x) = 1,728$ or $96x = 1,728$ or $x = 18$. The height of the water level is 18 cm.

183

9. Data Interpretation

EXAMPLE:

In the accompanying diagram, the line graph shows the number of books sold by Whitman Bookstore in each month from January through May. What percent of the number of books sold in February is equal to the number of books sold in May?

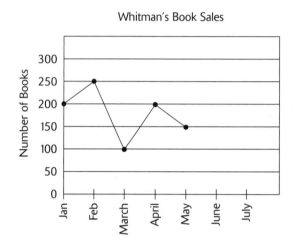

Whitman's Book Sales

A. 25
B. 40
C. 60
D. 75
E. 80

Solution: C. According to the graph, you know that the number of books sold in February is 250 and the number of books sold in May is 150. Use the proportion $\frac{150}{250} = \frac{x}{100\%}$, which is equivalent to $x = \frac{100(150)}{250}\% = 60\%$.

EXAMPLE:

In 2008, students who attended Washington High School and Adams High School were allowed to participate in only one sport for the year: tennis, soccer, swimming, or basketball. Based on the information provided in the accompanying bar graph, how many more students at Washington High School than Adams High School participated in a sport in 2008?

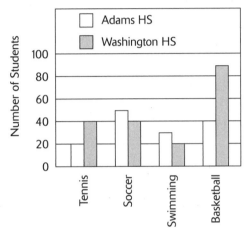

Number of Students in Four Sports
at Washington HS and Adams HS

A. 40
B. 50
C. 70
D. 140
E. 190

The correct answer is **B.** At Washington High School, 40 students played tennis, 40 played soccer, 20 were swimmers, and 90 played basketball; that means 40 + 40 + 20 + 90 = 190 students participated in a sport. At Adams High School, 20 students played tennis, 50 played soccer, 30 were swimmers, and 40 played basketball; that means 20 + 50 + 30 + 40 = 140 students participated in a sport. The number of additional students who participated in sports at Washington High School than at Adams High School is 190 – 140 = 50.

10. Set

EXAMPLE:

In a music class with 20 students, each student plays only the violin, plays only the cello, or plays both. If four students play both the violin and the cello and, of all the students in the class, twice as many play the violin as play the cello, how many students play only the cello?

A.   4
B.   6
C.   8
D.   12
E.   1

The correct answer is **A.**

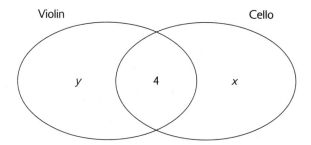

Set up a Venn diagram with x representing the number of students who only play the cello and y representing the number of students who only play the violin. Because there are 20 students in the class, $x + y + 4 = 20$ or $x + y = 16$. Because twice as many students who play the violin as play the cello, $y + 4 = 2(x + 4)$ or $y = 2x + 4$. Substitute $2x + 4$ for y in the equation $x + y = 16$ and solve to find that $x = 4$ and $y = 12$. The number of students who only play the cello is 4.

XI. Problem Solving

In the quantitative section of the GMAT, roughly 22 of the 37 multiple-choice questions are problem-solving questions, and the remaining 15 are data-sufficiency questions (see Chapter XII). These two types of questions are intermingled throughout the quantitative section.

Problem-solving questions are standard multiple-choice questions with five answer choices: A, B, C, D, and E. These problems test your basic math skills, your ability to apply elementary math concepts, and your ability to reason quantitatively. Problem-solving questions cover three subject areas: arithmetic, elementary algebra, and geometry. The number of questions for each of these three subjects is roughly

- Arithmetic: 13
- Elementary algebra: 6
- Geometry: 3

When working on a problem-solving question, make sure that you read the question carefully, know exactly what you have to find, solve the problem, and select the best of the answer choices given.

Remember: All numbers in the quantitative section are real numbers, and all figures shown are drawn as accurately as possible, unless stated otherwise. Straight lines may sometimes appear jagged on the computer screen.

When working on the quantitative section of the GMAT, keep in mind the following:

- **It is important to pace yourself.** You have 75 minutes to do 37 questions, which is approximately 2 minutes per question.
- **You may not skip over a question.** The computer will not present the next question until you've answered the current one on the screen.
- **Make an educated guess if you aren't sure about the answer.** There is a penalty for wrong answers, but there is also a penalty for unanswered questions, so if you're struggling with a particular question, you're better off making an educated guess and moving on.
- **Calculators are not allowed.**

A. Arithmetic

1. In a math class, there are 12 girls. If 25% of the students in the class are boys, what is the total number of students in the class?

    A. 15
    B. 16
    C. 24
    D. 36
    E. 48

The correct answer is **B.** If 25% of the students are boys, then 75% are girls. Set up a proportion with s being the number of students in the class. You have $\frac{12}{75\%} = \frac{s}{100\%}$ or $\frac{12}{0.75} = \frac{s}{1}$, which is equivalent to $\frac{12}{\frac{3}{4}} = \frac{s}{1}$ or $s = 12\left(\frac{4}{3}\right) = 16$. *(See Chapter X, Section A.1.c.)*

2. If x and y are integers, which of the following must be an odd integer?

   A. $x + y$
   B. $2x + y$
   C. $x + 2y$
   D. $3(x + y)$
   E. $2(x + y) + 1$

The correct answer is **E.** Note that the sum $(x + y)$ can be either even or odd. However, $2(x + y)$ must be even. Thus, $2(x + y) + 1$ is odd. *(See Chapter X, Section A.1.a.)*

3. In the accompanying diagram, five points, A, B, C, D, and E, are on a number line in the positions indicated. Which point has m as its coordinate if $m < m^3 < m^2$?

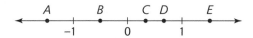

   A. A
   B. B
   C. C
   D. D
   E. E

The correct answer is **B.** To find the correct answer, assign approximate numerical values for A, B, C, D, and E in the indicated intervals and see which one produces a true statement when substituted in $m < m^3 < m^2$. If $A = -10$, then $m < m^3 < m^2$ becomes $-10 < -1,000 < 100$; this isn't true, so m is not the coordinate of A. If $B = -0.5$, then $m < m^3 < m^2$ becomes $-0.5 < -0.125 < 0.25$; this is true, so m could be the coordinate of B. If $C = 0.5$, then $m < m^3 < m^2$ becomes $0.5 < 0.125 < 0.25$; this isn't true, so m is not the coordinate of C. Because C and D are in the same interval (they're both greater than 0 and less than 1), the relationships are the same and m could not be the coordinate of D. If $E = 3$, then $m < m^3 < m^2$ becomes $3 < 27 < 9$; this isn't true, so m is not the coordinate of E. The only point that could have m as its coordinate is B. *(See Chapter X, Section A.1.a.)*

4. If $b < -1 < a < 0$, which of the following has the smallest value?

   A. $-b^3$
   B. $-b$
   C. ab
   D. $-a^2$
   E. a^3

The correct answer is **D.** You can either consider each choice or select a variety of values and substitute. If you consider each choice, here's what you find:

- Choice A: Because b is less than -1, b^3 is also less than -1 and $-b^3$ is greater than 1.
- Choice B: Because b is less than -1, $-b$ is greater than 1.
- Choice C: Because a and b are both negative, their product is positive and ab is positive.
- Choice D: Because a^2 is always positive, $-a^2$ is negative.
- Choice E: Because a is negative, a^3 is negative.

Negative numbers are smaller than positive numbers, so you can eliminate choices A, B, and C. To compare a^3 with $-a^2$, you need to substitute a number for a to see which is smaller. For example, if $a = -0.5$, then $a^3 = -0.125$ and $-a^2 = -0.25$. So, $-a^2 < a^3$. The smallest value is $-a^2$.

If you substitute values, you might let $b = -10$ and $a = -0.5$. Then $-b^3 = 1{,}000$, $-b = 10$, $ab = 5$, $-a^2 = -0.25$, and $a^3 = -0.125$. The smallest value is -0.25 which is $-a^2$. *(See Chapter X, Section A.1.a.)*

5. What is the numerical value of $\dfrac{1}{2+\dfrac{1}{1+\dfrac{1}{2}}}$?

    A. $\dfrac{2}{7}$

    B. $\dfrac{3}{8}$

    C. $\dfrac{1}{2}$

    D. $\dfrac{8}{3}$

    E. $\dfrac{7}{2}$

The correct answer is **B.** Begin by simplifying the fraction $\dfrac{1}{1+\dfrac{1}{2}}$, which is equivalent to $\dfrac{1}{\dfrac{2}{2}+\dfrac{1}{2}}=\dfrac{1}{\dfrac{3}{2}}=\dfrac{2}{3}$.

Therefore, $\dfrac{1}{2+\dfrac{1}{1+\dfrac{1}{2}}}=\dfrac{1}{2+\dfrac{2}{3}}=\dfrac{1}{\dfrac{6}{3}+\dfrac{2}{3}}=\dfrac{1}{\dfrac{8}{3}}=\dfrac{3}{8}$. *(See Chapter X, Section A.1.b.)*

6. Given a number such that $\dfrac{2}{5}$ of the number is 30, what is $\dfrac{1}{3}$ of the number?

    A.   4
    B.   10
    C.   12
    D.   25
    E.   75

The correct answer is **D.** Let x be the number. Because $\dfrac{2}{5}$ of the number is 30, you have $\dfrac{2}{5}x = 30$ or $x = 75$. Thus, $\dfrac{1}{3}$ of the number is $\dfrac{1}{3}(75) = 25$.

You can also do this problem by using a proportion: $\dfrac{\frac{2}{5}}{30} = \dfrac{\frac{1}{3}}{x}$. Thus, $\frac{2}{5}x = \frac{1}{3}(30)$, or $x = 25$. *(See Chapter X, Section A.1.c.)*

7. On a blueprint for an office building, 6 inches represents 45 feet. Using this scale, how many inches on the blueprint will represent 30 feet?

   A.   1.5
   B.   2
   C.   2.5
   D.   3
   E.   4

The correct answer is **E**. To find the number of inches on the blueprint, x, use the proportion $\dfrac{6}{45} = \dfrac{x}{30}$. Then $45x = 6(30)$ and $x = 4$. Notice that you don't have to convert inches to feet. When you set up a proportion, corresponding quantities must have the same unit of measurement. In this problem, you're comparing inches on the blueprint to height measured in feet. Both blueprint numbers are in the same units (inches), and both heights are in the same units (feet), so the proportion may be set up without converting. If the height of one building were given in feet and the height of the other building were given in inches, you would have to convert both to feet or both to inches before setting up the proportion. *(See Chapter X, Sections A.1.c and B.4.)*

8. If $x^2y = 16$ and $xyz = 0$, which of the following must be true?

   A. $x > 0$
   B. $y < 0$
   C. $y = 0$
   D. $z < 0$
   E. $z = 0$

The correct answer is **E**. Because $xyz = 0$, at least one of the variables x, y, or z must be 0. If either $x = 0$ or $y = 0$, the product x^2y would have to equal 0. Because $x^2y = 16$, which implies that neither x nor y are equal to 0, the factor that equals 0 must be z. *(See Chapter X, Section A.1.a.)*

9. If a positive integer, n, is divisible by 2, 5, and 6, which of the following must also be divisible by 2, 5, and 6?

   A. $n + 10$
   B. $n + 12$
   C. $n + 13$
   D. $n^2 - 13$
   E. $2n + 30$

The correct answer is **E**. A possible value for n is 30, because the remainder is 0 when 30 is divided by 2, by 5, and by 6. When you evaluate the choices, substitute 30 for n, and you have $n + 10 = 40$, $n + 12 = 42$, $n + 13 = 43$, $n^2 - 13 = 887$, and $2n + 30 = 90$. Only Choice E produces an answer that is divisible by 2, 5, and 6. Thus, $2n + 30$ is divisible by 2, 5, and 6.

You could also use a different approach based on the fact that if n is divisible by 2, 5, and 6, then n is a multiple of 2, 5, and 6, and if two numbers are divisible by 2, 5, and 6, then their sum is also divisible by 2, 5, and 6. Because 10, 12, and 13 are not divisible by 2, 5, and 6, choices A, B, C, and D are eliminated. For Choice E, you know that 30 is a multiple of 2, 5, and 6 and that $2n$ is a multiple of 2, 5, and 6 because n is a multiple of 2, 5, and 6. So the sum $2n + 30$ is a multiple of 2, 5, and 6. The expression that is divisible by 2, 5, and 6 is $2n + 30$. *(See Chapter X, Section A.1.d.)*

10. If k is an integer and 3 is the remainder when k is divided by 5, how many values for k are possible when $0 < k < 100$?

   A. 10
   B. 19
   C. 20
   D. 23
   E. 40

The correct answer is **C**. To solve this problem, list the possible integers for k and look for a pattern. The smallest value for k is 3; some of the other values are 8, 13, 18, 23, 28, 33, and 38. The remainder will be 3 when the units digit is 3 or 8. Between 0 and 100, there are ten integers with 3 as the units digit and ten integers with 8 as the units digit. The number of possible values for k is $10 + 10 = 20$. *(See Chapter X, Section A.1.d.)*

11. If the first term of a sequence is 2 and each successive term is found by multiplying the preceding term by -3, what is the sum of the fourth and fifth terms?

   A. −216
   B. −108
   C. 108
   D. 162
   E. 216

The correct answer is **C**. This is a geometric sequence, so using the formula $a_n = a_1(r^{n-1})$, you have the fourth term $a_4 = (2)(-3)^{(4-1)} = 2(-3)^3 = -54$ and the fifth term $a_5 = 2(-3)^{(5-1)} = 162$. The sum of the fourth and fifth terms is $162 + (-54) = 108$. You could also approach this problem by listing the first five terms: 2, −6, 18, −54, and 162. Thus, $-54 + 162 = 108$. *(See Chapter X, Section A.1.e.)*

12. $1^2, 2^2, 3^2, 4^2, \ldots$

   The first four terms of a sequence are shown above. If the sum of the first n terms is greater than 100, what is the smallest value of n?

   A. 6
   B. 7
   C. 8
   D. 10
   E. 20

The correct answer is **B**. To find when the sum will be greater than 100, start adding the terms: $1^2 + 2^2 = 5$, $1^2 + 2^2 + 3^2 = 14$, and so on. When you reach $1^2 + 2^2 + 3^2 + 4^2 + 5^2 + 6^2 = 91$, and $1^2 + 2^2 + 3^2 + 4^2 + 5^2 + 6^2 + 7^2 = 140$, you know that the first time the sum is greater than 100 occurs when $n = 7$. The smallest value of n is 7. *(See Chapter X, Section A.1.e.)*

13. If A is the set of odd integers less than 24 and B is the set of prime numbers less than 20, how many numbers are common to both sets?

    A. 7
    B. 8
    C. 9
    D. 10
    E. 12

The correct answer is **A**. Because Set B has fewer elements than Set A, list the elements in Set B and see how many elements in Set B are odd integers. The elements in Set B are {2, 3, 5, 7, 11, 13, 17, 19}. The elements in Set A that are odd integers less than 24 are {3, 5, 7, 11, 13, 15, 17, 19, 23}. The number of common elements is 7. *(See Chapter X, Sections A.1.f and B.10.)*

14. The distribution of the elements in sets A, B, and C is shown in the accompanying Venn diagram. The numbers and variables in the regions are the numbers of elements in those regions. If there are exactly ten elements that are in both Set B and Set C, what is the value of x?

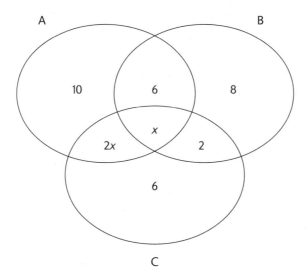

    A. 2
    B. 4
    C. 6
    D. 8
    E. 10

The correct answer is **D**. Because the Venn diagram shows that $x + 2$ elements are in both Set B and Set C, $x + 2 = 10$ or $x = 8$. *(See Chapter X, Sections A.1.f and B.10.)*

15. When x is a member of Set A, the value of $\sqrt{x^2} + x$ is also a member of Set A. Which of the following could be Set A?

    A.   {–2, 1}
    B.   {–1, 0}
    C.   {–1, 0, 1}
    D.   {0, 1}
    E.   {0, 1, 2}

The correct answer is **B**. Substituting gives the results listed in the following table:

x	–2	–1	0	1	2
$\sqrt{x^2} + x$	0	0	0	2	4

Of the choices, the only set that satisfies the condition is {–1, 0}. *(See Chapter X, Sections A.1.f and B.10.)*

16. The junior class is holding an election for president, vice president, and secretary, and six students are candidates. If any of the candidates could be elected president, vice president, or secretary but no one can hold more than one position, how many different outcomes are possible?

    A.   6
    B.   20
    C.   36
    D.   72
    E.   120

The correct answer is **E**. This is a permutation problem because order matters. You could have the same three students elected to different positions. Thus, the number of different outcomes is $_6P_3$, which is $6 \times 5 \times 4 = 120$. *(See Chapter X, Section A.1.g.)*

17. If the local post office only has three denominations of stamps available—1¢ stamps, 10¢ stamps, and 20¢ stamps—how many different sets of stamps can be used to form 41¢?

    A.   4
    B.   5
    C.   8
    D.   9
    E.   10

The correct answer is **D**. This problem involves not only selecting from three subgroups of stamps, but also factoring in the values of these stamps. This is not a permutation or combination problem. One way to do this problem is to list all the possible outcomes. Summarizing the outcomes, you have the following table:

1¢	10¢	20¢
1	0	2
1	2	1
11	1	1
21	0	1
1	4	0
11	3	0
21	2	0
31	1	0
41	0	0

Notice that it is easier to start by taking the largest denomination first, and then working out the others. In this case, start with 20¢ stamps, then 10¢ stamps, and lastly 1¢ stamps. The table shows that there are nine possible sets of stamps to make 41¢. *(See Chapter X, Sections A.1.g and B.7.)*

18. What is the total number of distinct diagonals that can be drawn in an octagon? (An octagon has eight sides.)

   A. 7
   B. 20
   C. 28
   D. 40
   E. 56

The correct answer is **B.** There are eight vertices in an octagon. From each vertex, five diagonals can be drawn. So, you have $8 \times 5 = 40$ diagonals. However, each diagonal was counted twice. For example, a diagonal drawn from vertex A to vertex C is the same as the diagonal drawn from vertex C to vertex A. Therefore, the total number of distinct diagonals in an octagon is $\frac{40}{2} = 20$. *(See Chapter X, Sections A.1.g and B.7.)*

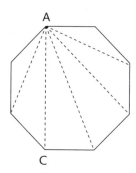

19. If a number is randomly selected from the set {1, 2, 3, 4, 5, 6, 7, 8, 9}, what is the probability that it will be a prime number?

   A. $\dfrac{2}{9}$

   B. $\dfrac{3}{9}$

   C. $\dfrac{4}{9}$

   D. $\dfrac{5}{9}$

   E. 3

The correct answer is **C.** $P(\text{a prime number}) = \dfrac{\text{number of prime numbers in the set}}{\text{total number of elements in the set}}$. There are four prime numbers in the set: 2, 3, 5, and 7. There are nine numbers in total. Therefore the probability of getting a prime number is $\dfrac{4}{9}$. *(See Chapter X, Sections A.1.h and B.6.)*

20. Victoria has 3 quarters and 2 dimes in her piggybank. If 2 coins are taken out of the piggybank at random, what is the probability that both coins are dimes?

   A. $\dfrac{1}{20}$

   B. $\dfrac{1}{10}$

   C. $\dfrac{2}{5}$

   D. $\dfrac{2}{3}$

   E. $\dfrac{4}{5}$

The correct answer is **B.** $P(2 \text{ dimes}) = \dfrac{\text{number of ways of picking 2 dimes}}{\text{total number of ways of picking 2 coins from 5 coins}}$. The number of ways of picking 2 dimes is $_2C_2 = 1$. The number of ways of picking 2 coins from 5 coins is $_5C_2 = 10$. Therefore, $P(2 \text{ dimes}) = \dfrac{1}{10}$.

Another approach is as follows: $P(2 \text{ dimes}) = P(\text{first coin is a dime}) \times P(\text{second coin is a dime}) = \dfrac{2}{5}\left(\dfrac{1}{4}\right) = \dfrac{1}{10}$. *(See Chapter X, Sections A.1.h and B.6.)*

21. In the accompanying diagram, O is the center of both circles with $OB = 6$ and $AB = 2$. If a point is picked at random from the larger circle, what is the probability of getting a point that lies in the shaded region?

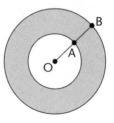

Not drawn to scale

A. $\dfrac{1}{4}$

B. $\dfrac{1}{3}$

C. $\dfrac{1}{2}$

D. $\dfrac{4}{9}$

E. $\dfrac{5}{9}$

The correct answer is **E.** Note that P (getting a point in the shaded region) $= \dfrac{\text{the area of the shaded region}}{\text{the area of the larger circle}}$.

The area of the shaded region = (area of the larger circle) – (area of the smaller circle). The length of the radius of the larger circle is 6. The area of the larger circle is $\pi(6)^2 = 36\pi$. The radius of the smaller circle is $6 - 2 = 4$. The area of the smaller circle is $\pi(4)^2 = 16\pi$. Thus, the area of the shaded region is $36\pi - 16\pi = 20\pi$. The probability of getting a point from the shaded region is $\dfrac{20\pi}{36\pi}$ or $\dfrac{5}{9}$. *(See Chapter X, Sections A.1.h and B.6.)*

22. There are 24 students in Mr. Faseoli's music class, each of whom is a member of either the orchestra or the band or both. If 16 of these students are in the orchestra and 14 are in the band, and if a student is randomly chosen, what is the probability that the student picked is in both the orchestra and the band?

A. $\dfrac{1}{5}$

B. $\dfrac{1}{4}$

C. $\dfrac{1}{3}$

D. $\dfrac{4}{5}$

E. 1

The correct answer is **B.**

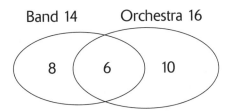

Band 14   Orchestra 16

8   6   10

$P(\text{picking a student in both orchestra and band}) = \dfrac{\text{the number of students in both orchestra and band}}{\text{total number of students in class}}$. The number of students in either orchestra or band is $16 + 14 = 30$. Because there are only 24 students in the class, there must be $30 - 24 = 6$ students in both orchestra and band. Thus, $P(\text{picking a student in both orchestra and band}) = \dfrac{6}{24}$ or $\dfrac{1}{4}$. *(See Chapter X, Sections A.1.h and B.6.)*

23. If the average (arithmetic mean) of x and $3x - 4$ is p and the average of $6 - 2x$ and $14 - 2x$ is q, what is the average of p and q?

A. 4
B. 16
C. $4 - 2x$
D. $2x + 4$
E. $8x + 16$

The correct answer is **A.** Because the average of x and $3x - 4$ is p, you have $p = \dfrac{(x) + (3x - 4)}{2} = \dfrac{4x - 4}{2} = 2x - 2$. Similarly, $q = \dfrac{(6 - 2x) + (14 - 2x)}{2} = \dfrac{20 - 4x}{2} = 10 - 2x$. The average of p and q can be obtained by $\dfrac{(2x - 2) + (10 - 2x)}{2} = \dfrac{8}{2} = 4$. *(See Chapter X, Section A.1.i.)*

24. Rebecca's test grades in her math class for the first quarter are 90, 84, 80, 92, 84, and 98. Of the 6 grades in the first quarter, if p is the mean, q is the median, and r is the mode, which of the following inequalities is true?

   A. $r < q < p$
   B. $r < p < q$
   C. $p < r < q$
   D. $q < p < r$
   E. $p < q < r$

The correct answer is **A**. The mean is the average; $p = \dfrac{90 + 84 + 80 + 92 + 84 + 98}{6} = 88$. The median is q, which is the middle value of 80, 84, 84, 90, 92, and 98 or $\dfrac{84 + 90}{2} = 87$. The mode is r, which is the value that appears the most often: 84. Thus, $r < q < p$. *(See Chapter X, Section A.1.i.)*

25. Given $3x - 2$, $-\dfrac{1}{x}$, and x^2, if x^2 is the median, which of the following could be the value of x?

   A. -3
   B. -2
   C. $-\dfrac{1}{2}$
   D. $\dfrac{1}{2}$
   E. 3

The correct answer is **C**. Substitute the given numbers into the three expressions:

x	$3x - 2$	x^2	$\dfrac{1}{x}$
-3	-11	9	$\dfrac{1}{3}$
-2	-8	4	$\dfrac{1}{2}$
$-\dfrac{1}{2}$	$-3\dfrac{1}{2}$	$\dfrac{1}{4}$	2
$\dfrac{1}{2}$	$-\dfrac{1}{2}$	$\dfrac{1}{4}$	-2
3	7	9	$-\dfrac{1}{3}$

Notice that when $x = -\dfrac{1}{2}$, you have $-3\dfrac{1}{2}$, $\dfrac{1}{4}$, and 2, making x^2 the median. *(See Chapter X, Section A.1.i.)*

26. Janet was saving a part of her salary every month so she could buy a house. In four months, she saved a total of $2,000. If the accompanying table shows the total amount of money that Janet had saved by the end of each month, how much did she save in March?

Janet's Savings

Month	Total Amount in Dollars
January	500
February	800
March	1,400
April	2,000

A. $600
B. $800
C. $1,300
D. $1,400
E. $2,200

The correct answer is **A.** The amount shown in the savings account is cumulative. In other words, the amount shown in March reflects what was saved in January, February, and March. Because Janet saved a total of $800 for January and February and a total of $1,400 for January, February, and March, she must have saved $1,400 – $800 = $600 for the month of March. *(See Chapter X, Section B.9.)*

27. Karen gets a fixed allowance for lunch and entertainment every week. The accompanying bar graph shows the amount that she spent on lunch for the past five weeks. If she spent 60% of her allowance on lunch during the second week, what percent of her allowance did she spend on her lunch during the fourth week?

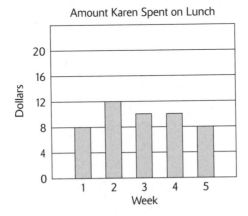

Amount Karen Spent on Lunch

A. 40
B. 50
C. 60
D. 80
E. 100

The correct answer is **B**. According to the bar graph, Karen spent $12 out of her allowance for lunch. Because $12 is 60% of her allowance, use the proportion $\frac{12}{\text{allowance}} = \frac{60}{100}$, which is equivalent to $\frac{100(12)}{60} = 20$. In the fourth week, Karen spent $10 on lunch. Therefore, $\frac{\$10}{\$20}$, which is $\frac{1}{2}$ or 50%. You could also solve this problem by using the proportion $\frac{\$12}{60\% \text{ of allowance}} = \frac{\$10}{x\% \text{ of allowance}}$, giving $x = 50\%$. *(See Chapter X, Section B.9.)*

28. Let $n*$ be defined as $n^2 - 3n$ for all integers n. What is the value of $n*$ if $n = -4$?

    A. -28
    B. -4
    C.   4
    D.   16
    E.   28

The correct answer is **E**. Use -4 for n and do the arithmetic: $(-4)^2 - 3(-4) = 16 + 12 = 28$. *(See Chapter X, Section A.2.a.)*

29. For all real numbers m and n, if $m\nabla n$ is defined as $m\nabla n = m^2 - 2n$, what is the value of $4\nabla(3\nabla2)$?

    A.   5
    B.   6
    C.   21
    D.   23
    E.   123

The correct answer is **B**. Because the symbol ∇ is used twice in the equation, you have to substitute and follow the pattern twice. First, work inside the parenthesis: Use 3 for m, 2 for n, and $m\nabla n = m^2 - 2n$ to find that $3\nabla2 = (3)^2 - 2(2) = 5$. Next, use 5 in place of $(3\nabla2)$ in the original problem. Then $4\nabla(3\nabla2) = 4\nabla5$. Use 4 for m, 5 for n, and $m\nabla n = m^2 - 2n$ to find that $4\nabla5 = (4)^2 - 2(5) = 6$. *(See Chapter X, Section A.2.a.)*

30. There are 200 marbles in a box. All the marbles are either red or blue. If there are 40 more red marbles than blue, how many red marbles are there in the box?

    A.   40
    B.   80
    C.   120
    D.   160
    E.   180

The correct answer is **C**. Let x be the number of blue marbles, and $x + 40$ be the number of red marbles. There are 200 marbles in the box, so you have $x + x + 40 = 200$, which is equivalent to $2x + 40 = 200$, or $x = 80$. Thus, the number of red marbles is $x + 40 = 120$. *(See Chapter X, Section A.2.b.)*

B. Algebra

1. If m and n are nonzero integers and $m = -n$, what is the value of $m^2 - n^2$?

   A. -2
   B. -1
   C. 0
   D. 1
   E. 2

The correct answer is **C.** If $m = -n$, then $m^2 - n^2 = (-n)^2 - n^2 = n^2 - n^2 = 0$. *(See Chapter X, Section A.2.a.)*

2. If x and y are positive integers, $x > y$ and $x + y = 7$, which of the following could be a value of $x^2 - y^2$?

   A. 14
   B. 35
   C. 45
   D. 48
   E. 49

The correct answer is **B.** Because x and y are positive integers and $x + y = 7$, the possible values of x and y are:

x	1	2	3	4	5	6
y	6	5	4	3	2	1

Because $x > y$, you have (4, 3), (5, 2), and (6, 1). Substituting these x and y values in $x^2 - y^2$, you have $x^2 - y^2 = 7$, 21, or 35. Of the given choices, the one that is a possible value of $x^2 - y^2$ is 35. *(See Chapter X, Section A.2.a.)*

3. Points A, B, C, and D lie on the same line. If B is the midpoint of $\overline{AC}$, C is the midpoint of $\overline{BD}$ and $AD = 12k$, what is the length of $\overline{BD}$ in terms of k?

   A. 4k
   B. 8k
   C. 10k
   D. 14k
   E. 16k

The correct answer is **B.**

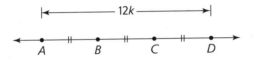

B is the midpoint of $\overline{AC}$, so $AB = BC$. C is the midpoint of $\overline{BD}$, so $BC = CD$. Because $AB = BC$ and $BC = CD$, you know that $AB = BC = CD$. Because $AB + BC + CD = AD$ and $AD = 12k$, each segment is $4k$ in length and $BC + CD = 4k + 4k = 8k$ and $BD = 8k$. *(See Chapter X, Section A.2.a.)*

4. If $a > b$ and $ay - by = 4$, what is the value of y when $(a - b)^2 = 4$?

   A. 0
   B. 1
   C. 2
   D. 4
   E. 8

The correct answer is **C**. Because $(a - b)^2 = 4$, you know that $(a - b) = \pm 2$. Because $a > b$, you know $a - b > 0$ and $a - b = 2$. To find y when $a - b = 2$, express $ay - by = 4$ in the factored form $y(a - b) = 4$ and substitute 2 for $(a - b)$. Then $(y)(2) = 4$ and $y = 2$. *(See Chapter X, Section A.2.b.)*

5. Three times a number is the same as the number added to 60. What is the number?

   A. 15
   B. 20
   C. 30
   D. 45
   E. 180

The correct answer is **C**. Let x be the number. Then, you have $3x = 60 + x$, which is equivalent to $2x = 60$, or $x = 30$. The number is 30. *(See Chapter X, Sections A.2.b and B.2.)*

6. If x is a real number, how many values of x satisfy the equation $(x + 10)^2 = 25$?

   A. 0
   B. 1
   C. 2
   D. 3
   E. 4

The correct answer is **C**. Instead of multiplying $(x + 10)(x + 10)$ and then factoring to solve the quadratic equation $x^2 + 20x + 100 = 0$, keep the equation in its original form and find the square root of both sides. Thus, $(x + 10) = \pm 5$. Solving the equations $x + 10 = 5$ and $x + 10 = -5$, you have $x = -5$ or $x = -15$. Therefore, there are two values of x satisfying the given equation. *(See Chapter X, Section A.2.b.)*

7. If $2x + 3y = 10$, what is the value of $4x + 6y$?

   A. 15
   B. 20
   C. 30
   D. 40
   E. 60

The correct answer is **B**. The question did not ask for the individual values of x and y, but instead the value of $4x + 6y$. Notice that $4x + 6y = 2(2x + 3y)$. Multiply both sides of the equation $2x + 3y = 10$ by 2 and you have $2(2x + 3y) = 20$. Thus, $4x + 6y = 20$. *(See Chapter X, Section A.2.b.)*

8. For which positive number is 16 times the cube root of the number the same as the number?

    A.   8
    B.   16
    C.   27
    D.   64
    E.   128

The correct answer is **D.** If x is the number then $16\left(\sqrt[3]{x}\right)=x$. Cubing both sides, you have $4{,}096x = x^3$ or $x^3 - 4{,}096x = 0$. Factoring the equation $x^3 - 4{,}096x = 0$, you have $x(x^2 - 4{,}096) = 0$. Thus, $x = 0$ or $x = \pm\sqrt{4{,}096} = \pm 64$. Because x is a positive number, $x = 64$. *(See Chapter X, Sections A.2.b and B.2.)*

9. If $\frac{1}{6} < \frac{3}{n} < \frac{1}{4}$, how many integral values of n are possible?

    A.   1
    B.   3
    C.   5
    D.   6
    E.   7

The correct answer is **C.** The inequalities $\frac{1}{6} < \frac{3}{n} < \frac{1}{4}$ is equivalent to $\frac{1}{6} < \frac{3}{n}$ and $\frac{3}{n} < \frac{1}{4}$. Solving $\frac{1}{6} < \frac{3}{n}$, you have $n < 18$. Similarly, solving $\frac{3}{n} < \frac{1}{4}$, we have $12 < n$ or $n > 12$. Because $n > 12$ and $n < 18$, n must be 13, 14, 15, 16, or 17. There are five integral values for n. *(See Chapter X, Section A.2.c.)*

10. Five years ago, Mary was at least three more than twice Karen's age. If k represents Karen's age now and m represents Mary's age now, which of the following describes the relationship of their ages five years ago?

    A. $m > 2k + 3$
    B. $m > 2k - 3$
    C. $m + 5 > 2(k + 5) - 3$
    D. $m - 5 \le 2(k + 5) + 3$
    E. $m - 5 \ge 2(k - 5) + 3$

The correct answer is **E.** Five years ago, Mary's age was $m - 5$ and Karen's age was $k - 5$. If five years ago Mary had been three years more than twice Karen's age, the relationship of their ages would have been described as $m - 5 = 2(k - 5) + 3$. Because five years ago, Mary was at least three years more than twice Karen's age, the equation becomes an inequality instead: $m - 5 \ge 2(k - 5) + 3$.

	Current Age	Age 5 Years Ago
Mary	m	$m - 5$
Karen	k	$k - 5$

(See Chapter X, Section A.2.c.)

11. Given that $x^2 - y^2 < 12$ and $x + y > 10$, if x and y are positive integers and $x > y$, what is the value of y?

 A. 3
 B. 4
 C. 5
 D. 6
 E. 8

The correct answer is **C**. Factor $x^2 - y^2$ as $(x + y)(x - y)$ and rewrite $x^2 - y^2 < 12$ as $(x + y)(x - y) < 12$. Because $x + y > 10$, let $x + y = 11$. Note that if you let $x + y = 12$ or 13 or more, the inequality $(x + y)(x - y) < 12$ will not work. Now $(x + y)(x - y) < 12$ becomes $(11)(x - y) < 12$. The only possible integer value for $x - y$ is 1. Solve the simultaneous equations $x + y = 11$ and $x - y = 1$ by adding the 2 equations. You have $2x = 12$ or $x = 6$. Thus, $y = 5$. *(See Chapter X, Section A.2.c.)*

12. $10 - |n + 2| = 4$

 If n is a negative number, what is the value of n?

 A. –2
 B. –6
 C. –8
 D. –10
 E. –16

The correct answer is **C**. The inequality is equivalent to $6 = |n + 2|$. Then $n + 2 = 6$ or $n + 2 = -6$ and you have $n = 4$ or $n = -8$. Because n is a negative number, $n = -8$. *(See Chapter X, Section A.2.d.)*

13. In the xy-plane, which of the following points lies on the graph of the equation $-2|x| + y = 2$?

 A. $(-3, 8)$
 B. $(-1, 0)$
 C. $(0, -2)$
 D. $(4, -1)$
 E. $(6, -2)$

The correct answer is **A**. If a point lies on the graph of an equation, then the coordinates of the point satisfy the equation. Substitute the coordinates of each point in the five choices, into the equation and check. In Choice A, using $x = -3$ and $y = 8$, you have $-2|-3| + 8 = 2$ or $-6 + 8 = 2$ or $2 = 2$. Thus, the coordinates satisfy the equation. The point that is on the graph is $(-3, 8)$. *(See Chapter X, Section A.2.d.)*

14. If n satisfies both of the equations below, what is the value of n?

$$|2n - 4| = 10$$

$$|3 - 2n| = 11$$

    A.   −7
    B.   −4
    C.   −3
    D.   4
    E.   7

The correct answer is **E**. Solve $|2n - 4| = 10$, and you have $2n - 4 = 10$ or $2n - 4 = -10$, which gives you $n = 7$ or $n = -3$. Solve $|3 - 2n| = 11$, and you have $3 - 2n = 11$ or $3 - 2n = -11$, which gives you $n = -4$ or $n = 7$. Therefore, the value of n that satisfies both equations is 7. *(See Chapter X, Section A.2.d.)*

15. If $4a - 5b = 20$ and $b = 4$, what is the value of $2b + 5a$?

    A.   −42
    B.   0
    C.   8
    D.   30
    E.   58

The correct answer is **E**. Because $b = 4$ and $4a - 5b = 20$, you know that $4a - 5(4) = 20$ or $4a = 40$ or $a = 10$. Because $a = 10$ and $b = 4$, $2b + 5a = 2(4) + 5(10)$ or 58. *(See Chapter X, Section A.2.e.)*

16. If a, b, c, and d are positive integers and $a = 2b$, $b = 3c$, and $2a = cd$, what is the value of d?

    A.   1
    B.   3
    C.   6
    D.   12
    E.   Cannot be determined

The correct answer is **D**. Because you have to find the value of d, begin by working with the equation that has d as a variable, $2a = cd$. Solve $2a = cd$ for d, you have $d = \frac{2a}{c}$. If you knew the values of a and c, you could find the value of d. Because $b = 3c$, solving for c, you have $c = \frac{b}{3}$. Substituting $a = 2b$ and $c = \frac{b}{3}$ in $d = \frac{2(2b)}{\left(\frac{b}{3}\right)} = (4b)\left(\frac{3}{b}\right) = 12$.

Another approach is to begin with $a = 2b$ and substitute $3c$ for b and obtain $a = 6c$. Then the equation $2a = cd$ becomes $2(6c) = cd$, which gives $12c = cd$ and then you get $d = 12$. *(See Chapter X, Section A.2.e.)*

17. If $a > 0$, $c > 0$, and $a^2b = 9$ and $bc^2 = 25$, what is the value of abc?

    A.   15
    B.   25
    C.   45
    D.   75
    E.   225

The correct answer is **A**. When you multiply the equations $a^2b = 9$ and $bc^2 = 25$, you have $(a^2b)(bc^2) = (9)(25)$ or $a^2b^2c^2 = 225$ and $abc = \pm15$. Because $a > 0$ and $c > 0$ and $a^2b > 0$, you know that $b > 0$. Thus, $abc = 15$. *(See Chapter X, Section A.2.e.)*

18. If $(2x^2)^3 = 8x^n$ for all values of x, what is the value of n?

    A.   3
    B.   4
    C.   5
    D.   6
    E.   7

The correct answer is **D**. Because you're trying to find an exponent, express each side as a power with the same base and set the exponents equal. Because $(2x^2)^3 = 2^3(x^2)^3 = 8x^{2 \times 3} = 8x^6$ and $(2x^2)^3 = 8x^n$, you know that $8x^6 = 8x^n$ or $n = 6$. *(See Chapter X, Section A.2.f.)*

19. If $5^4(5^a) = 5^{20}$, what is the value of a?

    A.   5
    B.   6
    C.   10
    D.   16
    E.   80

The correct answer is **D**. You're trying to find an exponent, so express each side as a power with the same base and set the exponents equal. Because $5^4(5^a) = 5^{4+a}$ and $5^4(5^a) = 5^{20}$, you know that $5^{4+a} = 5^{20}$ and $4 + a = 20$ or $a = 16$. *(See Chapter X, Section A.2.f.)*

20. If m and n are inversely proportional and $n = 6$ when $m = 4$, what is the value of m when $n = 12$?

    A.   −2
    B.   2
    C.   8
    D.   14
    E.   18

The correct answer is **B**. Because *inversely proportional* means that the product is always the same, solve $(12)(m) = (4)(6)$ to find that $24 = 12m$ and $m = 2$. *(See Chapter X, Section A.2.g.)*

21. Some of the values of p and q are shown in the accompanying table. If p is directly proportional to q, what is the value of k?

p	4	6	10
q	6	k	15

   A. 6
   B. 8
   C. 9
   D. 10
   E. 12

The correct answer is **C**. Because p is directly proportional to q, the ratio of p to q is a constant. You have $\frac{4}{6} = \frac{6}{k}$ or $\frac{6}{k} = \frac{10}{15}$. In either case, solve for k and you have $k = 9$. *(See Chapter X, Section A.2.g.)*

22. Given a function $y = f(x)$ such that y is inversely proportional to x, which of the following could be $f(x)$?

   A.

x	y
2	4
3	6
4	8

   B.

x	y
3	5
5	7
7	9

   C.

x	y
−1	2
1	2
3	2

   D.

x	y
5	0
5	2
5	4

   E.

x	y
1	16
2	8
4	4

The correct answer is **E.** Because y is inversely proportional to x, $xy =$ constant. Of the given choices, the only table of values where the product of x and y is a constant is Choice E. Note that $(1)(16) = (2)(8) = (4)(4) = 16$. Therefore, of the given choices, Choice E is the only possible table of values for $f(x)$. *(See Chapter X, Section A.2.g.)*

23. If the function f is defined by $f(x) = 2x - 6$, which of the following is equivalent to $5f(x) + 10$?

    A. $10x - 40$
    B. $10x - 20$
    C. $10x + 4$
    D. $10x + 20$
    E. $7x + 4$

The correct answer is **B.** Because $f(x) = 2x - 6$, you have $5f(x) + 10 = 5(2x - 6) + 10$, which is equivalent to $10x - 20$. *(See Chapter X, Section A.2.h.)*

24. Some of the values of the function f are shown in the accompanying table. If a function h is defined by $h(x) = 2f(x - 1)$, what is the value of $h(2)$?

x	$f(x)$
−3	−1
−2	0
−1	4
0	2
1	−3
2	4
3	5

    A. −6
    B. −3
    C. 4
    D. 5
    E. 7

The correct answer is **A.** Because $h(x) = 2f(x - 1)$, $h(2) = 2f(2 - 1)$ or $h(2) = 2f(1)$. The table shows that $f(1) = -3$. Thus, $2f(1) = 2(-3)$ or -6. *(See Chapter X, Section A.2.h.)*

25. The graph of $y = f(x)$ for $-2 \le x \le 5$ is shown in the accompanying diagram. If $k < 0$ and $f(k) = 0$, what is the value of k?

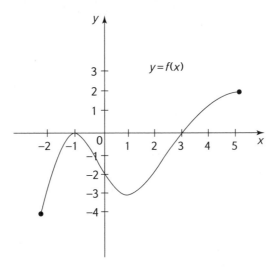

A.   –4
B.   –2
C.   –1
D.   0
E.   3

The correct answer is **C.** Because $f(k) = 0$ implies that k is a root of $f(x)$. The roots of $f(x)$ are the x-intercepts of the graph of $f(x)$. In this case, the x-intercepts are –1 and 3. Because $k < 0$, $k = -1$. *(See Chapter X, Section A.2.h.)*

C. Geometry

1. Points A, B, C, and D lie on a line in that order. If C is the midpoint of $\overline{BD}$, $CD = 2AB$ and $AD = 60$, what is the length of $\overline{AC}$?

A.   12
B.   24
C.   36
D.   40
E.   48

The correct answer is **C.** Let $AB = x$. Because $CD = 2AB$, you have $CD = 2x$. Also, C is the midpoint of $\overline{BD}$; therefore, $BC = CD = 2x$. Because $AD = 60$, you have $x + 2x + 2x = 60$ or $5x = 60$, which leads to $x = 12$. The length of $\overline{AC}$ is $3x$ or $3(12) = 36$. *(See Chapter X, Section A.3.a.)*

2. In △*DEF*, *DE* = 6 and *DF* = 10. What is the smallest possible integer length of side $\overline{EF}$?

   A. 4
   B. 5
   C. 6
   D. 15
   E. 16

The correct answer is **B.**

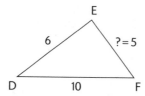

Because you're looking for the smallest possible length of $\overline{EF}$, assume that $\overline{EF}$ is not the longest side of △*DEF*. Applying the triangle inequality, you have *DE* + *EF* > *DF* or 6 + *EF* > 10, which is equivalent to *EF* > 4. Because *EF* is an integer, the smallest possible value for *EF* is 5. *(See Chapter X, Section A.3.b.)*

3. In the accompanying diagram, *a*, *b*, and *c* are the lengths of the three sides of the triangle. Which of the following must be true?

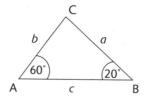

Not drawn to scale

   A. $a > b > c$
   B. $b > a > c$
   C. $c > b > a$
   D. $a > c > b$
   E. $c > a > b$

The correct answer is **E.** Because the sum of the measures of the three angles of a triangle is 180, $m\angle c =$ 180 – 60 – 20 = 100. In a triangle, the longest side is always opposite the biggest angle. Thus, $c > a > b$. *(See Chapter X, Section A.3.b.)*

4. In the accompanying diagram, $\overline{DE}\|\overline{BC}$. If $AE = 2$, $EC = 4$, and $BC = 12$, find the length of DE.

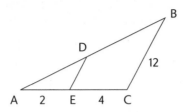

Not drawn to scale

A. 2
B. 4
C. 6
D. 8
E. 9

The correct answer is **B**. Because $\overline{DE}\|\overline{BC}$, congruent corresponding angles are formed with $\angle DEA \cong \angle BCA$ and $\triangle ADE \sim \triangle ABC$. Because the triangles are similar, their corresponding sides are in proportion and $\frac{DE}{BC} = \frac{AE}{AC}$. Notice that $EC = 4$ may not be used in this proportion because EC is not a side of either triangle. To find DE, solve $\frac{DE}{BC} = \frac{AE}{AC}$ or $\frac{DE}{12} = \frac{2}{2+4}$ or $(DE)(2 + 4) = (2)(12)$ or $DE = \frac{24}{6}$ or $DE = 4$. *(See Chapter X, Section A.3.c.)*

5. In the accompanying diagram, $AB\|CD$ and $\overline{AD}$ intersects $\overline{BC}$ at E. If $AB = 6$, $CD = 9$, and $BC = 30$, what is the length of $\overline{BE}$?

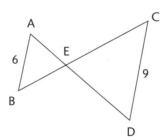

A. 6
B. 9
C. 12
D. 15
E. 18

The correct answer is **C**. Because $AB\|CD$, pairs of congruent alternate interior angles are formed, $\angle B \cong \angle C$ and $\angle A \cong \angle D$, so $\triangle ABE \sim \triangle DCE$. Because the triangles are similar, corresponding sides in proportion and $\frac{BE}{AB} = \frac{EC}{DC}$. To find BE, use x as the length $\overline{BE}$ and $(30 - x)$ as the length of $\overline{CE}$ and $\frac{x}{6} = \frac{30-x}{9}$ or $9x = 6(30 - x)$ or $9x = 180 - 6x$ or $x = 12$. *(See Chapter X, Section A.3.c.)*

6. $\triangle LMN$ is similar to $\triangle PQT$. The area of $\triangle LMN$ is 16, and the length of its shortest side is 2. If the area of $\triangle PQT$ is 36, what is the length of its shortest side?

    A.   3
    B.   4.5
    C.   6
    D.   9
    E.   22

The correct answer is **A**. Because $\triangle LMN \sim \triangle PQT$, the ratio of the areas is equal to the square of the ratio of any corresponding sides. Because the two shortest sides are a pair of corresponding sides, $\frac{16}{36} = \left(\frac{2}{x}\right)^2$ or $\frac{4}{9} = \frac{4}{x^2}$ or $4x^2 = 36$ or $x = \pm 3$. Because x must be positive, $x = 3$. The length of the shortest side of $\triangle PQT$ is 3. *(See Chapter X, Section A.3.c.)*

7. The area of an equilateral triangle is $9\sqrt{3}$. What is its perimeter?

    A.   6
    B.   12
    C.   18
    D.   24
    E.   36

Solution: C. The area of the equilateral triangle is $9\sqrt{3}$ and $A = \frac{s^2\sqrt{3}}{4}$, so $9\sqrt{3} = \frac{s^2\sqrt{3}}{4}$ or $s^2 = (4)(9)$ or $s = \pm 6$. Because s is the length of a side, $s = 6$, and the perimeter is $3(6) = 18$. *(See Chapter X, Sections A.3.d and B.8.)*

8. If two sides of a triangle measure 6 and 8, what is the largest possible area for the triangle?

    A.   7
    B.   24
    C.   32
    D.   48
    E.   64

The correct answer is **B**.

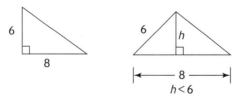

The largest possible area for a triangle with two sides measuring 6 and 8 is the area of a right triangle. In this case, the area is $\frac{1}{2}(6)(8) = 24$. Notice that if the two sides, 6 and 8, were not perpendicular, the altitude would be less than 6. Therefore, the area of the triangle would be less than 24. *(See Chapter X, Section A.3.d.)*

9. In the accompanying diagram, *ABCD* is a rectangle with side *AB* containing points *E* and *F* and *AE* = *EF* = *FB*. If the area of △*ADF* is 12, what is the area of quadrilateral *FBCD*?

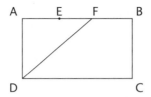

- **A.** 12
- **B.** 18
- **C.** 24
- **D.** 36
- **E.** 48

The correct answer is **C.**

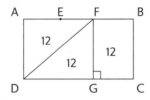

Draw a perpendicular line from *F* to $\overline{DC}$ at point *G*. Note that the area of △*AFD* equals the area of △*FDG* = 12. Because *AE* = *EF* = *FB*, we have $FB = \frac{1}{2} AF$. The area of rectangle $FBCG = \frac{1}{2}$ (area of rectangle *AFGD*), and the area of rectangle *AFGD* is 12 + 12 = 24. Therefore, the area of quadrilateral *FBCD* is $12 + \frac{1}{2}(24) = 24$. *(See Chapter X, Section A.3.d.)*

10. If the length, width, and height of a rectangular box measure 1, 3, and 8, respectively, what is the total surface area of the box?

- **A.** 24
- **B.** 35
- **C.** 70
- **D.** 72
- **E.** 144

The correct answer is **C.**

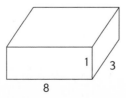

Not drawn to scale

A rectangular box has six faces. The top and bottom faces both have surface areas (8)(3) = 24 for a total of 2(24) = 48. The front and back faces both have surface area (8)(1) = 8, for a total of (2)(8) = 16. The left and right faces both have surface area (3)(1) = 3 for a total of (2)(3) = 6. The surface area of the box is 48 + 16 + 6 = 70. *(See Chapter X, Section A.3.e.)*

11. A sphere with a diameter measuring 3 cm is inscribed in a cube. What is the length of a diagonal, in cm, of the cube?

   A. 3
   B. $3\sqrt{2}$
   C. $3\sqrt{3}$
   D. 6
   E. 27

The correct answer is **C**.

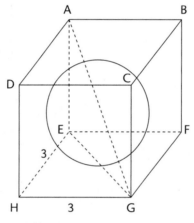

Not drawn to scale

Because the diameter of the sphere is 3 cm, the length of each edge of the cube—including edges $\overline{AE}$, $\overline{EH}$, and $\overline{HG}$—is 3 cm. To find a diagonal of the cube, you must use the Pythagorean theorem twice—first to find EG and then to find AG. Because $\overline{EG}$ is a side in right triangle EHG, $(EG)^2 = 3^2 + 3^2 = \sqrt{18}$. Because $\overline{AG}$ is a side in right triangle AEG, $(AG)^2 = 3^2 + (\sqrt{18})^2 = 9 + 18 = 27$ and $AG = \pm\sqrt{27} = \pm3\sqrt{3}$. The length of a diagonal is $3\sqrt{3}$ cm. *(See Chapter X, Section A.3.e.)*

12. If the total surface area of a cube is 96, what is its volume?

   A. 64
   B. 125
   C. 128
   D. 216
   E. 512

The correct answer is **A.** To find the volume of the cube, you need to know the length of an edge. Because an edge of the cube is also a side, s, of the face of the cube and because the surface area is 96, s can be found using $6s^2 = 96$, $s^2 = 16$, and $s = \pm 4$. Because s is an edge, $s = 4$, the volume, $V = s^3 = 4^3 = 64$. *(See Chapter X, Sections A.3.e and B.8.)*

13. In the accompanying diagram , O is the center of the circle. If the area of the shaded region, sector AOB, is 25π, what is the length of $\overset{\frown}{AB}$?

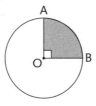

   A.   5

   B.   10

   C. $\dfrac{5\pi}{2}$

   D. 5π

   E. 10π

The correct answer is **D.** First, find the radius of the circle. Use the proportion, $\dfrac{\text{area of sector } AOB}{\text{area of a circle}} = \dfrac{90}{360}$, which is equivalent to $\dfrac{25\pi}{\pi r^2} = \dfrac{1}{4}$ or $r^2 = 4(25)$. Thus, $r = 10$. Now use another proportion to find the length of $\overset{\frown}{AB}$, $\dfrac{\text{length of } \overset{\frown}{AB}}{\text{circumference of a circle}} = \dfrac{90}{360}$ or $\dfrac{\text{length of } \overset{\frown}{AB}}{2\pi(10)} = \dfrac{1}{4}$. Thus, the length of $\overset{\frown}{AB} = 5\pi$. *(See Chapter X, Section A.3.f.)*

14. In the accompanying diagram, a regular hexagon is inscribed in a circle. If $AB = 6$, what is the length of $\overset{\frown}{AB}$?

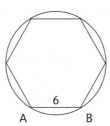

   A.   2

   B. π

   C. 2π

   D. 4π

   E. 6π

The correct answer is **C.**

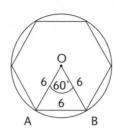

A regular hexagon is both equilateral and equiangular. Therefore, $m\angle AOB = 60$. Also, $\overline{AO}$ and $\overline{BO}$ are radii and, thus, $m\angle OAB = m\angle OBA = 60$, and $\triangle AOB$ is an equilateral triangle. To find the length of $\overset{\frown}{AB}$, we use the proportion $\dfrac{\text{length of } \overset{\frown}{AB}}{\text{circumference of circle}} = \dfrac{60}{360}$, which is equivalent to $\dfrac{\text{length of } \overset{\frown}{AB}}{2\pi 6} = \dfrac{1}{6}$ or length of $\overset{\frown}{AB} = 2\pi$. *(See Chapter X, Section A.3.f.)*

15. In the accompanying diagram, O is the center of the larger circle and $\overline{OA}$ and $\overline{OB}$ are diameters of the smaller circles. If the length of $\overline{AOB}$ is 12. What is the total area of the shaded regions?

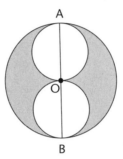

   A. 9π
   B. 18π
   C. 24π
   D. 27π
   E. 36π

The correct answer is **B**. Because $\overline{OA}$ and $\overline{OB}$ are radii of the larger circle and $\overline{AOB}$ is 12, we have $OA = OB = 6$. The area of the larger circle is $\pi(6)^2 = 36\pi$. The two smaller circles are congruent and the length of the radius, for both small circles is 3. The area of each small circle is $\pi(3)^2 = 9\pi$, and the total area of both small circles is 18π. Therefore, the area of the shaded regions is $36\pi - 18\pi = 18\pi$. *(See Chapter X, Section A.3.f.)*

16. In the coordinate plane, if $M(2, -1)$ is the midpoint of the line segment joining points $A(4, a)$ and $B(0, b)$, what is the value of $a + b$?

   A. -2
   B. -1
   C. 0
   D. 3
   E. 6

The correct answer is **A**. Applying the midpoint formula, you have the coordinates of $\left(\frac{4+0}{2}, \frac{a+b}{2}\right)$. Because the coordinates of M are given as (2, –1), you have $\frac{a+b}{2} = -1$ or $a + b = -2$. Notice that you do not need to find the individual values of a and b. They are not relevant to the question. *(See Chapter X, Section A.3.g.)*

17. In an xy-coordinate plane, point C with coordinates (2, 1) is the center of a circle and point A with coordinates (7, 1) is on the circle, which of the following could be the coordinates of point B, if B is also a point on the circle?

    A. (–7, 1)
    B. (1, 7)
    C. (4, 6)
    D. (6, 4)
    E. (7, 6)

The correct answer is **D**.

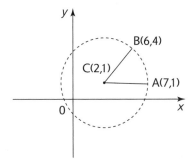

Because $\overline{CA}$ is a radius of the circle, the length of the radius of the circle is $\sqrt{(7-2)^2 + (1-1)^2} = 5$. Because B is a point on the circle, $\overline{CB}$ must also be a radius with length 5. Using the distance formula with each choice, only when the coordinates of B are (6, 4) does the length equal to $\sqrt{(6-2)^2 + (4-1)^2} = 5$.

Another approach is to note that the equation of the circle is $(x-2)^2 + (y-1)^2 = 5^2$ because the center is (2, 1) and the length of the radius is 5. Substitute the coordinates of the point in each choice in the equation and see if the equation is true.

Note: You can save time if you graph the points. Because $\overline{CA}$ is horizontal, you can find the length of the radius using $7 - 2 = 5$, and you can see that choices A, B, and E appear to be too far from C to be on the circle. Now only two points require checking with the distance formula. *(See Chapter X, Section A.3.g.)*

18. Which of the following points on the accompanying graph has coordinates that satisfy the equation, $-|3x|+|y|=2$?

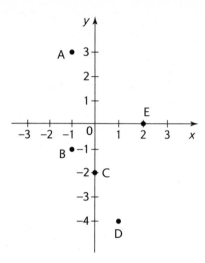

- **A.** *A*
- **B.** *B*
- **C.** *C*
- **D.** *D*
- **E.** *E*

The correct answer is **C.** A point satisfies an equation if substituting produces an equation that is true. Substitute the coordinates of each point into the equation $-|3x|+|y|=2$. Only when the coordinates of $C(0, -2)$ are substituted is the resulting equation true: $-|3(0)|+|2|=0+2=2$. *(See Chapter X, Section A.3.g.)*

19. In the xy-plane, $y = 4x + 1$ and $cx + 2y = d$ are parallel lines. What is the value of c?

- **A.** -8
- **B.** -4
- **C.** $-\dfrac{1}{4}$
- **D.** 4
- **E.** 8

The correct answer is **A.** If two lines are parallel, their slopes are equal. The line $y = 4x + 1$ is written in slope-intercept form $y = mx + b$. The slope of this line is $m = 4$. To find the slope of $cx + 2y = d$, rewrite the equation in $y = mx + b$ form. Subtract cx from both sides of the equation, and you have $2y = -cx + d$ and dividing both sides by 2, you have $y = \frac{-cx}{2} + \frac{d}{2}$. Therefore, the slope of this line is $m = -\frac{c}{2}$. Because the two lines are parallel, the slopes are equal. Set $-\frac{c}{2} = 4$ and you have $c = -8$. *(See Chapter X, Section A.3.h.)*

20. In the xy-plane, the coordinates of three given points are $A(2, 4)$, $B(1, 1)$, and $C(4, 2)$. If line l is drawn passing through point A and perpendicular to $\overline{BC}$, what is the slope of line l?

   A. -3
   B. -1
   C. $-\dfrac{1}{3}$
   D. $\dfrac{1}{3}$
   E. 3

The correct answer is **A.**

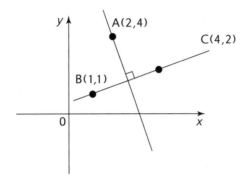

Draw a sketch of the xy-plane including the points A, B, and C. If two lines are perpendicular, their slopes are negative reciprocals. The slope of $\overline{BC}$ is $m_{\overline{BC}} = \dfrac{2-1}{4-1} = \dfrac{1}{3}$. Therefore, the slope of a line perpendicular to $\overline{BC}$ is -3.

Note: The fact that the line passes through point A is not relevant. There are infinitely many lines perpendicular to $\overline{BC}$, and the slope of all of these lines is -3.

XII. Data Sufficiency Questions

In the quantitative section of the GMAT, roughly 15 of the 37 multiple-choice questions are data-sufficiency questions, and the remaining 22 are problem-solving questions (see Chapter XI). These two types of questions are intermingled throughout the quantitative section.

Data-sufficiency questions test your knowledge of three subject areas: arithmetic, elementary algebra, and geometry. The number of questions for each of these three subjects is roughly

- Arithmetic: 8
- Elementary algebra: 4
- Geometry: 3

Data-sufficiency questions are multiple-choice questions with five answer choices. These questions, however, do not require you to find a solution to the problem. Instead, you need to examine the given data and determine which of the given data provides sufficient information to solve the problem. The format of data-sufficiency questions is as follows:

You are given a problem accompanied by two statements labeled (1) and (2). Based on the information, you must select one of the following choices:

A. Statement (1) *alone* is sufficient, but statement (2) alone is not sufficient.
B. Statement (2) *alone* is sufficient, but statement (1) alone is not sufficient.
C. *Both* statements *together* are sufficient, but *neither* statement *alone* is sufficient.
D. *Each* statement *alone* is sufficient.
E. Statements (1) and (2) *together* are *not* sufficient.

When solving data-sufficiency questions, remember the following:

- You don't have to solve the problem. You only need to determine whether the given information is sufficient to solve the problem according to the answer choices.
- When a question asks for the value of a quantity, it is considered sufficient only if you can determine exactly one value for the quantity.
- As with the rest of the quantitative section, all figures are drawn as accurately as possible to match the information in the problem, unless indicated otherwise. However, in data-sufficiency questions, the figure may *not* match the information given in statements (1) and/or (2).
- Straight lines may appear jagged on the computer screen.
- All numbers used are real numbers.

When working on the quantitative section of the GMAT, keep in mind the following:

- **It is important to pace yourself.** You have 75 minutes to do 37 questions, which is approximately 2 minutes per question.
- **You may not skip over a question.** The computer will not present the next question until you've answered the current one on the screen.

- **Make an educated guess if you aren't sure about the answer.** There is a penalty for wrong answers, but there is also a penalty for unanswered questions, so if you're struggling with a particular question, you're better off making an educated guess and moving on.
- **Calculators are not allowed.**

A. Arithmetic

1. Is n smaller than -4.5?

   (1) $n > -5.2$

   (2) $n < -4.8$

  A. Statement (1) *alone* is sufficient, but statement (2) alone is not sufficient.

  B. Statement (2) *alone* is sufficient, but statement (1) alone is not sufficient.

  C. *Both* statements *together* are sufficient, but *neither* statement *alone* is sufficient.

  D. *Each* statement *alone* is sufficient.

  E. Statements (1) and (2) *together* are *not* sufficient.

The correct answer is **B.**

(1) The set of real numbers n such that $n > -5.2$ include numbers smaller than -4.5, such as -5.0 and numbers greater than -4.5, such as -3.0. Not enough information is given to determine whether $n < -4.5$. Not sufficient.

(2) Because $n < -4.8$ and $-4.8 < -4.5$, n must be smaller than -4.5. Sufficient.

Statement (2) alone is sufficient. *(See Chapter X, Section A.1.b.)*

2. If n is an integer, is $n + 5$ odd?

   (1) $2n - 3$ is odd

   (2) $3n + 1$ is even

  A. Statement (1) *alone* is sufficient, but statement (2) alone is not sufficient.

  B. Statement (2) *alone* is sufficient, but statement (1) alone is not sufficient.

  C. *Both* statements *together* are sufficient, but *neither* statement *alone* is sufficient.

  D. *Each* statement *alone* is sufficient.

  E. Statements (1) and (2) *together* are *not* sufficient.

The correct answer is **B.**

(1) For all integer values of n, even or odd, $2n - 3$ is odd. For example, if $n = 4$, $2n - 3 = 2(4) - 3 = 5$ and if $n = 5$, $2n - 3 = 2(5) - 3 = 7$. Not sufficient.

(2) Because $3n + 1$ is even, $3n$ is odd and, therefore, n is odd. Therefore $n + 5$ is even. Sufficient.

Statement (2) alone is sufficient. *(See Chapter X, Section A.1.a.)*

3. Given that $a > 0$ and $b > 0$, is $\frac{a}{b} > 1$?

   (1) $a - b = 3$

   (2) $2a = 3b$

   A. Statement (1) *alone* is sufficient, but statement (2) alone is not sufficient.

   B. Statement (2) *alone* is sufficient, but statement (1) alone is not sufficient.

   C. *Both* statements *together* are sufficient, but *neither* statement *alone* is sufficient.

   D. *Each* statement *alone* is sufficient.

   E. Statements (1) and (2) *together* are *not* sufficient.

The correct answer is **D.**

(1) Because $a - b = 3$, you have $a = b + 3$. Therefore, $\frac{a}{b} = \frac{b+3}{b} = 1 + \frac{3}{b}$, which is greater than 1. Sufficient.

(2) Because $2a = 3b$, you have $\frac{a}{b} = \frac{3}{2} > 1$. Sufficient.

Each statement alone is sufficient. *(See Chapter X, Section A.1.c.)*

4. If the average of Janet's four math tests is 80, did she receive a 90 or more on at least one of her tests?

   (1) One of her test scores is 60.

   (2) One of her test scores is 80.

   A. Statement (1) *alone* is sufficient, but statement (2) alone is not sufficient.

   B. Statement (2) *alone* is sufficient, but statement (1) alone is not sufficient.

   C. *Both* statements *together* are sufficient, but *neither* statement *alone* is sufficient.

   D. *Each* statement *alone* is sufficient.

   E. Statements (1) and (2) *together* are *not* sufficient.

The correct answer is **C.**

(1) The fact that the average of Janet's four tests is 80 implies that the sum of the four tests is 4(80) or 320. Because one of the test scores is 60, the sum of the other three tests is 320 – 60 or 260. Therefore the three test scores could be 86, 86, and 88 or 84, 84 and 92. Insufficient.

(2) Because one of Janet's test scores is 80 and the sum of the four tests is 320, the sum of the other three scores is 320 – 80 or 240. Therefore, the other three test scores could be 80, 80, and 80 or 70, 80, and 90. Insufficient.

Using statements (1) and (2) together, you know that two of Janet's tests are 60 and 80, and that the sum of the remaining two tests is 320 – (80 + 60) or 180. Therefore, the remaining two tests could be 90 and 90 or, if one test score is below 90, the other test score must be greater than 90. Both statements together are sufficient. *(See Chapter X, Section A.1.i.)*

5. If n is a real number, is $n > 1$?

(1) $n^2 - 4 > 0$

(2) $n^3 + 8 < 0$

A.   Statement (1) *alone* is sufficient, but statement (2) alone is not sufficient.

B.   Statement (2) *alone* is sufficient, but statement (1) alone is not sufficient.

C.   *Both* statements *together* are sufficient, but *neither* statement *alone* is sufficient.

D.   *Each* statement *alone* is sufficient.

E.   Statements (1) and (2) *together* are *not* sufficient.

The correct answer is **B.**

(1)   Because $n^2 - 4 > 0$, you have $n^2 > 4$ and, therefore, $n > 2$ or $n < -2$. Insufficient.

(2)   Because $n^3 + 8 < 0$, you have $n^3 < -8$ or $n < -2$. Sufficient.

Statement (2) alone is sufficient. *(See Chapter X, Sections A.1.a and B.2.)*

6. If 20% of n is k, what is the value of k?

(1)   60% of n is 120.

(2) $\frac{2}{5}$ of n is 80.

A.   Statement (1) *alone* is sufficient, but statement (2) alone is not sufficient.

B.   Statement (2) *alone* is sufficient, but statement (1) alone is not sufficient.

C.   *Both* statements *together* are sufficient, but *neither* statement *alone* is sufficient.

D.   *Each* statement *alone* is sufficient.

E.   Statements (1) and (2) *together* are *not* sufficient.

The correct answer is **D.**

(1)   Because 60% of n is 120, you have $0.6n = 120$ or $n = 200$. Therefore, $0.2(200) = k$. Sufficient.

(2)   Because $\frac{2}{5}$ of n is 80, you have $n = 200$. Therefore, $0.2(200) = 6$. Sufficient.

Each statement alone is sufficient. *(See Chapter X, Sections A.1.c and B.1)*

7. Karen took a ride with Speedy Car Services that charges x dollars per mile and an additional surcharge of y dollars per ride. What is the value of y?

(1)   Karen's ride was 12 miles.

(2)   Karen paid $70 for her ride.

A.   Statement (1) *alone* is sufficient, but statement (2) alone is not sufficient.

B.   Statement (2) *alone* is sufficient, but statement (1) alone is not sufficient.

C.   *Both* statements *together* are sufficient, but *neither* statement *alone* is sufficient.

D.   *Each* statement *alone* is sufficient.

E.   Statements (1) and (2) *together* are *not* sufficient.

The correct answer is **E.**

(1) Karen's ride was 12 miles, and the total cost of the ride was $12x + y$. Not enough information to determine the value of y. Insufficient.

(2) Because Karen paid $70 for her ride, you have (x)(number of miles) $+ y = 70$. Not enough information to determine the value of y. Insufficient.

Using statements (1) and (2) together, you have $12x + y = 70$, which has infinitely many solutions (x, y), including $(5, 10)$ and $(4, 22)$. Not sufficient. Both statement (1) and (2) together are not sufficient. *(See Chapter X, Sections A.2.b and B.3)*

8. During a special promotion week, a store charges no tax and offers a 50% discount off the original price on a jacket. Mary, being an employee of the store, gets another 10% off the discounted sale price. If Mary paid n for the jacket, what is the value of n?

    (1)   10% of the discounted price is $8.

    (2)   Mary saved $88 on the jacket.

    A.   Statement (1) *alone* is sufficient, but statement (2) alone is not sufficient.
    B.   Statement (2) *alone* is sufficient, but statement (1) alone is not sufficient.
    C.   *Both* statements *together* are sufficient, but *neither* statement *alone* is sufficient.
    D.   *Each* statement *alone* is sufficient.
    E.   Statements (1) and (2) *together* are *not* sufficient.

The correct answer is **D.**

Let x be the original price of the jacket.

(1) The discounted price is $(x)(0.5)$, and 10% of the discounted price is $(x)(0.5)(0.1)$. Thus, $(x)(0.5)(0.1) = 8$ or $0.05x = 8$ or $x = 160$. The original price is $160. Mary received 10% off the discounted price, which means that Mary paid 90% of the discounted price. Thus, $n = (160)(0.5)(0.9)$. Sufficient.

(2) From the 50% discount, Mary saved $(x)(0.5)$ dollars, and from the additional 10% employee discount, Mary saved $(x)(0.5)(0.1)$ dollars. Therefore, $0.5x + 0.05x = 88$ or $0.55x = 88$ or $x = 160$. Mary paid $(160)(0.5)(0.9)$ dollars. Sufficient.

Each statement alone is sufficient. *(See Chapter X, Sections A.1.c and B.1.)*

9. What is the value of the two-digit integer n?

    (1)   The difference of the two digits is 6.

    (2) n is a prime number.

    A.   Statement (1) *alone* is sufficient, but statement (2) alone is not sufficient.
    B.   Statement (2) *alone* is sufficient, but statement (1) alone is not sufficient.
    C.   *Both* statements *together* are sufficient, but *neither* statement *alone* is sufficient.
    D.   *Each* statement *alone* is sufficient.
    E.   Statements (1) and (2) *together* are *not* sufficient.

The correct answer is **E.**

Let a be the units digit and b be the tens digit.

(1) The difference of a and b is 6. Therefore, the values of a and b are:

a	0	1	2	3	7	8	9
b	6	7	8	9	1	2	3

Therefore n could be 60, 71, 82, 93, 17, 28, and 27. Not sufficient.

(2) Because n is a two-digit prime number, n could be one of many numbers, including 11, 13, 17, 19, 23, and so on. Not sufficient.

Using statements (1) and (2) together, you have 71 and 17 that are prime and that the difference of their digits is 6. Not enough information to determine the exact value of n. Not sufficient. Both statements together are not sufficient. *(See Chapter X, Section A.1.a.)*

10. An urn contains 2 white balls, 4 black balls, and n red balls. What is the value of n?

(1) The probability of randomly picking a ball and the ball being white is $\frac{1}{6}$.

(2) The probability of randomly picking a ball and the ball being red is $\frac{1}{2}$.

A. Statement (1) *alone* is sufficient, but statement (2) alone is not sufficient.
B. Statement (2) *alone* is sufficient, but statement (1) alone is not sufficient.
C. *Both* statements *together* are sufficient, but *neither* statement *alone* is sufficient.
D. *Each* statement *alone* is sufficient.
E. Statements (1) and (2) *together* are *not* sufficient.

The correct answer is **D**.

(1) Because the total number of balls in the urn is $2 + 4 + n$, the probability of picking a white ball is $\frac{2}{2+4+n} = \frac{1}{6}$ or $\frac{2}{6+n} = \frac{1}{6}$. Cross-multiply and you have $6 + n = 12$ or $n = 6$. Sufficient.

(2) The probability of picking a red ball is $\frac{n}{2+4+n} = \frac{1}{2}$ or $\frac{n}{6+n} = \frac{1}{2}$. Cross-multiply and you have $2n = 6 + n$ or $n = 6$. Sufficient.

Each statement alone is sufficient. *(See Chapter X, Sections A.1.h and B.6.)*

B. Algebra

1. If n is an integer, is $4n < |n|$?

(1) $2n < 0$

(2) $n = -8$

A. Statement (1) *alone* is sufficient, but statement (2) alone is not sufficient.
B. Statement (2) *alone* is sufficient, but statement (1) alone is not sufficient.
C. *Both* statements *together* are sufficient, but *neither* statement *alone* is sufficient.
D. *Each* statement *alone* is sufficient.
E. Statements (1) and (2) *together* are *not* sufficient.

The correct answer is **D**.

(1) Because $2n < 0$, you know $n < 0$ which is to say n is negative. Therefore $4n$ is also negative, and $4n$ is less than $|n|$ which is either zero or positive. Sufficient.

(2) Because $n = -8$, you have $4n = -32$. $|-8| = 8$, and $4n < |-8|$. Sufficient.

Each statement alone is sufficient. *(See Chapter X, Section A.2.d.)*

2. If x and y are integers, and $x^y = 16$, what is the value of x?

(1) $x > 0$

(2) $x < y$

A. Statement (1) *alone* is sufficient, but statement (2) alone is not sufficient.
B. Statement (2) *alone* is sufficient, but statement (1) alone is not sufficient.
C. *Both* statements *together* are sufficient, but *neither* statement *alone* is sufficient.
D. *Each* statement *alone* is sufficient.
E. Statements (1) and (2) *together* are *not* sufficient.

The correct answer is **C**.

(1) Given that x and y are integers, and $x^y = 16$, the expression x^y could be written as $(-4)^2$, $(-2)^4$, $(2)^4$, $(4)^2$, and $(16)^1$. Because $x > 0$, x could be 2, 4, or 16. Not sufficient.

(2) Because $x < y$, x could be -4, -2, or 2. Not sufficient.

Using statements (1) and (2) together, you have $x > 0$ and $x < y$, which imply that x has to be 2, 4, or 16 and x has to be -4, -2, or 2. Thus, x is 2. Sufficient. Both statements together are sufficient. *(See Chapter X, Sections A.2.f and B.2.)*

3. What is the value of $2a + 3$?

(1) $2a^2 - 18 = 0$

(2) $3 - a > 0$

A. Statement (1) *alone* is sufficient, but statement (2) alone is not sufficient.
B. Statement (2) *alone* is sufficient, but statement (1) alone is not sufficient.
C. *Both* statements *together* are sufficient, but *neither* statement *alone* is sufficient.
D. *Each* statement *alone* is sufficient.
E. Statements (1) and (2) *together* are *not* sufficient.

The correct answer is **C**.

(1) Solve $2a^2 - 18 = 0$, and you have $2a^2 - 18$ or $a = \pm 3$. Not sufficient.

(2) Since $3 - a > 0$, you have $3 > a$, which is equivalent to $a < 3$. Not sufficient.

Using statements (1) and (2) together, you have $a = \pm 3$ and $a < 3$, and therefore $a = -3$. Thus, you can evaluate $2a + 3$. Both statements together are sufficient. *(See Chapter X, Sections A.2.a and A.2.b.)*

4. Given that x and y are real numbers, what is the value of $4xy$?

(1) $x^2 + y^2 = 100$
(2) $(x + y)^2 = 196$

A.   Statement (1) *alone* is sufficient, but statement (2) alone is not sufficient.
B.   Statement (2) *alone* is sufficient, but statement (1) alone is not sufficient.
C.   *Both* statements *together* are sufficient, but *neither* statement *alone* is sufficient.
D.   *Each* statement *alone* is sufficient.
E.   Statements (1) and (2) *together* are *not* sufficient.

The correct answer is **C.**

(1) The graph of $x^2 + y^2 = 100$ is a circle. There are infinitely many solutions (x, y) satisfying the equation, including (0, 10) and (6, 8). Not enough information to determine the value of $4xy$. Not sufficient.

(2) There are infinitely many solutions (x, y) satisfying the equation $(x + y)^2 = 196$, including (0, 14) and (6, 8). Not sufficient.

Using statements (1) and (2) together, you have $(x + y)^2 = x^2 + 2xy + y^2$; hence,

$$\left(x^2 + 2xy + y^2\right) - \left(x^2 + y^2\right) = 196 - 100$$
$$2xy = 96$$
$$4xy = 192$$

Both statements together are sufficient. *(See Chapter X, Sections A.2.a and A.2.b.)*

5. During no-tax week, Mary bought n identical blouses, each the same price, for \$180. What was the price of each blouse?

(1)   Had Mary bought twice as many blouses, it would've cost her \$360.
(2)   Had Mary bought two fewer blouses, it would've cost her \$120.

A.   Statement (1) *alone* is sufficient, but statement (2) alone is not sufficient.
B.   Statement (2) *alone* is sufficient, but statement (1) alone is not sufficient.
C.   *Both* statements *together* are sufficient, but *neither* statement *alone* is sufficient.
D.   *Each* statement *alone* is sufficient.
E.   Statements (1) and (2) *together* are *not* sufficient.

The correct answer is **B.** Let x be the price of each blouse.

(1) The equations $nx = 180$ and $2nx = 360$ are equivalent. Not enough information to determine the value of x. Not sufficient.

(2) Solve the equation $(n - 2)x = 120$ and $nx = 180$ together. Rewrite $(n - 2)x = 120$ as $nx - 2x = 120$ and substituting $nx = 180$, you have $180 - 2x = 120$ or $x = 30$. Sufficient.

Statement (2) alone is sufficient. *(See Chapter X, Sections A.2.b.)*

6. Bill is ten years older than Mary. What is Mary's age?

(1)   Mary's age is $\frac{3}{4}$ Bill's age.

(2)   Ten years ago, Bill's age was one and a half times Mary's age.

A.   Statement (1) *alone* is sufficient, but statement (2) alone is not sufficient.
B.   Statement (2) *alone* is sufficient, but statement (1) alone is not sufficient.
C.   *Both* statements *together* are sufficient, but *neither* statement *alone* is sufficient.
D.   *Each* statement *alone* is sufficient.
E.   Statements (1) and (2) *together* are *not* sufficient.

The correct answer is **D.**

(1)   Because $b = m + 10$ and $m = \frac{3}{4}b$, solving simultaneously, you have $b = 40$. Therefore, $m = 30$. Sufficient.

(2)   Ten years ago, Bill's age was $b - 10$ and Mary's age was $m - 10$. Therefore, $b - 10 = \frac{3}{2}(m - 10)$ or $2b - 20 = 3m - 30$, or $2b = 3m - 10$. Solve the simultaneous equations $2b = 3m - 10$ and $b = m + 10$, and you have $2(m + 10) = 3m - 10$ or $m = 30$. Sufficient.

Each statement alone is sufficient. *(See Chapter X, Sections A.2.e.)*

7. What is the value of y?

(1) $x + y = 2$

(2) $y = x^2$

A.   Statement (1) *alone* is sufficient, but statement (2) alone is not sufficient.
B.   Statement (2) *alone* is sufficient, but statement (1) alone is not sufficient.
C.   *Both* statements *together* are sufficient, but *neither* statement *alone* is sufficient.
D.   *Each* statement *alone* is sufficient.
E.   Statements (1) and (2) *together* are *not* sufficient.

The correct answer is **E.**

(1)   The equation $x + y = 2$ has infinitely many solutions (x, y), including $(-2, 4)$, $(0, 2)$, $(1, 1)$, and $(2, 0)$. Not sufficient.

(2)   The equation $y = x^2$ has infinitely many solutions (x, y), including $(-2, 4)$, $(0, 0)$, $(1, 1)$. Not sufficient.

Using statements (1) and (2), solve the equations $x + y = 2$ and $y = x^2$ simultaneously, and you have $x + x^2 = 2$ or $x^2 + x - 2 = 0$, which is equivalent to $(x + 2)(x - 1) = 0$. Thus, $x = -2$ or 1 and $y = 4$ or 1. Not sufficient. information to determine the value of y. Both statements together are not sufficient. *(See Chapter X, Sections A.2.e.)*

8. In Ms. Chen's physical education class, every student plays either soccer or table tennis or both. If 30 students play soccer and 20 students play table tennis, how many students are there in Ms. Chen's class?

   (1) There are ten students who play both soccer and table tennis.
   (2) There are twice as many students who play only soccer as there are students who play only table tennis.

   A. Statement (1) *alone* is sufficient, but statement (2) alone is not sufficient.
   B. Statement (2) *alone* is sufficient, but statement (1) alone is not sufficient.
   C. *Both* statements *together* are sufficient, but *neither* statement *alone* is sufficient.
   D. *Each* statement *alone* is sufficient.
   E. Statements (1) and (2) *together* are *not* sufficient.

The correct answer is **D.**

(1) Because there are ten students who play both soccer and table tennis, you have

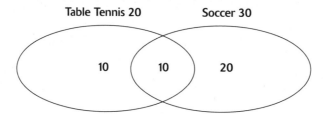

Therefore the total number of students in Ms. Chen's class is 10 + 10 + 20 or 40. Sufficient.

(2) Let x be the number of students who play both soccer and table tennis. You have

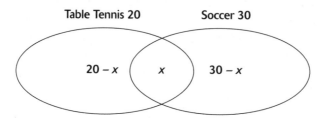

$30 - x = 2(20 - x)$ or $30 - x = 40 - 2x$ or $x = 10$. Therefore, there are 40 students in Ms Chen's class. Sufficient.

Each statement alone is sufficient. *(See Chapter X, Sections A.2.e and B.10.)*

9. What is the value of $\frac{a}{b} - \frac{b}{a}$?

   (1) $(a - b)(a + b) = 12$

   (2) $ab = 8$

   A.   Statement (1) *alone* is sufficient, but statement (2) alone is not sufficient.
   B.   Statement (2) *alone* is sufficient, but statement (1) alone is not sufficient.
   C.   *Both* statements *together* are sufficient, but *neither* statement *alone* is sufficient.
   D.   *Each* statement *alone* is sufficient.
   E.   Statements (1) and (2) *together* are *not* sufficient.

The correct answer is **C**.

The expression $\frac{a}{b} - \frac{b}{a} = \frac{a^2}{ab} - \frac{b^2}{ab} = \frac{a^2 - b^2}{ab}$.

   (1) The equation $(a - b)(a + b) = 12$ is equivalent to $a^2 - b^2 = 12$. Therefore, the value of $\frac{a^2 - b^2}{ab} = \frac{12}{ab}$ cannot be determined unless you know the value of ab. Not sufficient.

   (2) Because $ab = 8$, the value of $\frac{a^2 - b^2}{ab} = \frac{a^2 - b^2}{8}$ cannot be determined unless you know the value of $a^2 - b^2$. Not sufficient.

Using statements (1) and (2) together, you have $a^2 - b^2 = 12$ and $ab = 8$, and, thus, $\frac{a^2 - b^2}{ab} = \frac{12}{8} = \frac{3}{2}$.

Sufficient. Both statements (1) and (2) together are sufficient. *(See Chapter X, Sections A.2.a and A.2.e.)*

10. If a certain long-distance telephone call cost \$7, how long was the call?

   (1)   The first minute cost \$$x$ and each additional minute cost \$$y$.

   (2)   The first minute cost \$2.

   A.   Statement (1) *alone* is sufficient, but statement (2) alone is not sufficient.
   B.   Statement (2) *alone* is sufficient, but statement (1) alone is not sufficient.
   C.   *Both* statements *together* are sufficient, but *neither* statement *alone* is sufficient.
   D.   *Each* statement *alone* is sufficient.
   E.   Statements (1) and (2) *together* are *not* sufficient.

The correct answer is **E**. Let n be the total number of minutes from the phone call.

   (1) You have $(1)x + (n - 1)y = 7$, and this equation has infinitely many solutions (x, y), including $(1, 6)$ for $n = 2$, and $(3, 2)$ for $n = 3$. Not enough information to determine the value of n. Insufficient.

   (2) Because the cost for the first minute was \$2, and the total cost was \$7, the cost for all the additional minutes after the first minute was \$5. However, you don't know the cost for each additional minute and, therefore, can't determine the length of the phone call. For example, it could have been ten minutes at 50 cents per minute or 5 minutes at \$1 per minute. Not sufficient.

Using statements (1) and (2) together, you have $(1)(2) + (n - 1)y = 7$. This equation has infinitely many solutions for n and y, including $n = 3$, $y = 2.5$ and $n = 11$, $y = 0.5$. Not sufficient information to determine the value of n. Both statements together are not sufficient. *(See Chapter X, Sections B.3 and B.5.)*

C. Geometry

1. In the accompanying figure, $AD = 36$. What is BC?

    A   B   C   D

(1) B is the midpoint of $\overline{AC}$.

(2) C is the midpoint of $\overline{BD}$.

    A.   Statement (1) *alone* is sufficient, but statement (2) alone is not sufficient.

    B.   Statement (2) *alone* is sufficient, but statement (1) alone is not sufficient.

    C.   *Both* statements *together* are sufficient, but *neither* statement *alone* is sufficient.

    D.   *Each* statement *alone* is sufficient.

    E.   Statements (1) and (2) *together* are *not* sufficient.

The correct answer is **C.**

(1) Because B is the midpoint of $\overline{AC}$, you have $AB = BC$. The equation $AB + BC + CD = 36$ is equivalent to $2BC + CD = 36$. However, you don't know the length of $\overline{CD}$. Therefore, there is not enough information to determine BC. Not sufficient.

(2) Because C is the midpoint of $\overline{BD}$, you have $BC = CD$. The equation $AB + BC + CD = 36$ is equivalent to $AB + 2BC = 36$. However, because you don't know the length of AB, there is not sufficient information to determine BC. Not sufficient.

Using statements (1) and (2) together, you have $AB = BC$ and $BC = CD$. Therefore, $AB = BC = CD$. The equation $AB + BC + CD = 36$ is equivalent to $3BC = 36$ or $BC = 12$. Both statements together are sufficient. *(See Chapter X, Section A.3.a.)*

2. Given that $\triangle ABC$ is isosceles, what is the $m\angle A$?

(1) $m\angle B = 45°$.

(2)   The measure of the vertex angle is twice the measure of one of the base angles.

    A.   Statement (1) *alone* is sufficient, but statement (2) alone is not sufficient.

    B.   Statement (2) *alone* is sufficient, but statement (1) alone is not sufficient.

    C.   *Both* statements *together* are sufficient, but *neither* statement *alone* is sufficient.

    D.   *Each* statement *alone* is sufficient.

    E.   Statements (1) and (2) *together* are *not* sufficient.

The correct answer is **E.** Note that the measures of the base angles of an isosceles triangle are equal.

(1) In order to find $m\angle A$, you need to know if $\angle A$ is the vertex angle or one of the base angles. If $\angle A$ is the vertex angle, then $\angle B$ and $\angle C$ are base angles, and $m\angle A = 45 + 45 = 90$ or $m\angle A = 90$. If $\angle A$ is a base angle, then either $\angle B$ is the vertex angle or $\angle C$ is the vertex angle. If $\angle B$ is the vertex angle, then $45 + m\angle A + m\angle C = 180$, which is equivalent to $45 + 2m\angle A = 180$ or $m\angle A = 67.5$. If $\angle C$ is the vertex angle, then $m\angle A = m\angle B = 45$. Because you don't know whether $\angle A$ is the vertex angle, there isn't enough information to determine $m\angle A$. Not sufficient.

(2) Let x be the measure of one of the base angles, and $2x$ be the measure of the vertex angle. Therefore, $2x + x + x = 180$ or $x = 45$. However, because you don't know whether $\angle A$ is the vertex angle or one of the base angles, there isn't enough information to determine $m\angle A$. Not sufficient.

Using statements (1) and (2) together, you know that the measures of the three angles are 45, 45, and 90, and that $m\angle B = 45$. However, $m\angle A$ could be 45 or 90. There is not enough information to determine $m\angle A$. Both statements together are still not sufficient. *(See Chapter X, Section A.3.a.)*

3. In the xy-plane, is the point $(-2, 4)$ on line l?

    (1)   Line l passes through the origin.

    (2)   The slope of line l is -1.

    A.   Statement (1) *alone* is sufficient, but statement (2) alone is not sufficient.
    B.   Statement (2) *alone* is sufficient, but statement (1) alone is not sufficient.
    C.   *Both* statements *together* are sufficient, but *neither* statement *alone* is sufficient.
    D.   *Each* statement *alone* is sufficient.
    E.   Statements (1) and (2) *together* are *not* sufficient.

The correct answer is **C**.

(1) There are infinitely many lines passing through the origin, including $y = x$, $y = -x$, and $y = 2x$. There is not enough information to determine whether point $(-2, 4)$ lies on line l. Not sufficient.

(2) There are infinitely many lines with their slopes equal to -1, including $y = -x$, $y = -x + 1$, and $y = -x - 1$. Not sufficient.

Using statements (1) and (2) together, you have the slope of line $l = -1$ and line l passing through the origin. The point slope form of a line is $y - y_1 = m(x - x_1)$. Therefore, the equation of line l is $y - 0 = -1(x - 0)$ or $y = -x$. Substitute the point $(-2, 4)$ into the equation $y = -x$, you have $4 \neq -(-2)$. Thus, the point $(-2, 4)$ does not lie on line l. Both statements together are sufficient. *(See Chapter X, Section A.3.g.)*

4. In the accompanying figure, what is the perimeter of square *ABCD*?

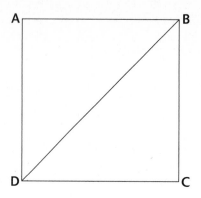

(1) $BD = 10\sqrt{2}$.

(2) The area of $\triangle BDC = 50$.

A. Statement (1) *alone* is sufficient, but statement (2) alone is not sufficient.

B. Statement (2) *alone* is sufficient, but statement (1) alone is not sufficient.

C. *Both* statements *together* are sufficient, but *neither* statement *alone* is sufficient.

D. *Each* statement *alone* is sufficient.

E. Statements (1) and (2) *together* are *not* sufficient.

The correct answer is **D.** Let *x* = *BC*. Because *ABCD* is a square, *AB* = *BC* = *CD* = *AD* = *x*.

(1) Since $BD = 10\sqrt{2}$ and $\triangle BDC$ is an isosceles right triangle with *BC* = *CD*, you have $x^2 + x^2 = \left(10\sqrt{2}\right)^2$ or $2x^2 = 200$ or *x* = 10. Therefore, the perimeter of *ABCD* = 4(10) or 40. Sufficient.

(2) The area of $\triangle BDC = \frac{1}{2}(BC)(DC)$ or $50 = \frac{1}{2}(x)(x)$ or *x* = 10. Therefore the perimeter of *ABCD* = 4(10) or 40. Sufficient.

Each statement alone is sufficient. *(See Chapter X, Sections A.3.d and B.8.)*

5. In the accompanying figure, points A and B are on circle O. What is the area of $\triangle AOB$?

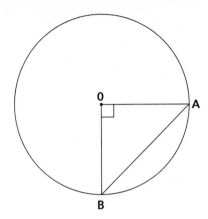

(1)   The measure of minor arc AB is 3π.

(2)   The area of sector AOB is 9π.

A.   Statement (1) *alone* is sufficient, but statement (2) alone is not sufficient.

B.   Statement (2) *alone* is sufficient, but statement (1) alone is not sufficient.

C.   *Both* statements *together* are sufficient, but *neither* statement *alone* is sufficient.

D.   *Each* statement *alone* is sufficient.

E.   Statements (1) and (2) *together* are *not* sufficient.

The correct answer is **D.**

(1) Because $\overline{AO} \perp \overline{BO}$, the measure of minor arc AB is $\frac{1}{4}$ the circumference of circle O. Therefore, the circumference of circle O is $4(3\pi)$ or 12π. The circumference of a circle is $2\pi r$ and, thus, $2\pi r = 12\pi$ or $r = 6$. Now you have $AO = 6$ and $BO = 6$. The area of $\triangle AOB = \frac{1}{2}(AO)(BO) = \frac{1}{2}(6)(6) = 18$. Sufficient.

(2) Because $\overline{AO} \perp \overline{BO}$, the area of sector AOB is $\frac{1}{4}$ of the area of circle O. Therefore, the area of circle O is $4(9\pi)$ or 36π. The area of $\triangle AOB = \frac{1}{2}(6)(6)$ or 18. Sufficient.

Each statement alone is sufficient. *(See Chapter X, Section A.3.f.)*

6. In the accompanying figure, $\overline{BCD}$, $\overline{ABE}$, and $x = 100$. What is the value of y?

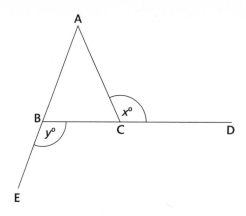

Not drawn to scale

(1) $m\angle A = 20°$

(2) $\overline{AB} \cong \overline{AC}$

A. Statement (1) *alone* is sufficient, but statement (2) alone is not sufficient.

B. Statement (2) *alone* is sufficient, but statement (1) alone is not sufficient.

C. *Both* statements *together* are sufficient, but *neither* statement *alone* is sufficient.

D. *Each* statement *alone* is sufficient.

E. Statements (1) and (2) *together* are *not* sufficient.

The correct answer is **D**.

(1) The measure of an exterior angle of a triangle is equal to the sum of the measure of the two non-adjacent angles of the triangle. Therefore, $m\angle ACD = m\angle A + m\angle ABC$ or $100 = 20 + m\angle ABC$, and $m\angle ABC = 80$. Also, $m\angle ABC + m\angle CBE = 180$, which is equivalent to $80 + y = 180$ or $y = 100$. Sufficient.

(2) Because $\overline{AB} \cong \overline{AC}$, $m\angle ABC = m\angle ACB$. Also, $m\angle ACD + m\angle ACB = 180$, which is equivalent to $100 + m\angle ACB = 180$ and $m\angle ACB = 80$. Therefore, $m\angle ABC = 80$ and $y = 100$. Sufficient.

Each statement alone is sufficient. *(See Chapter X, Section A.3.b.)*

7. In the accompanying figure of $\triangle ABC$, $AB = 5$. Is $\triangle ABC$ a right triangle?

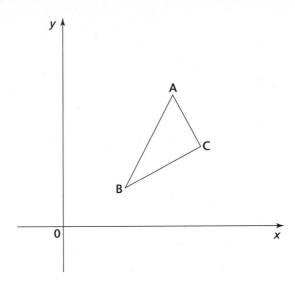

(1) $AC = 3$.

(2) slope of $\overline{AC} = -2$ and slope of $\overline{BC} = \frac{1}{2}$.

A. Statement (1) *alone* is sufficient, but statement (2) alone is not sufficient.

B. Statement (2) *alone* is sufficient, but statement (1) alone is not sufficient.

C. *Both* statements *together* are sufficient, but *neither* statement *alone* is sufficient.

D. *Each* statement *alone* is sufficient.

E. Statements (1) and (2) *together* are *not* sufficient.

The correct answer is **B.**

(1) A triangle is a right triangle if the lengths of its three sides satisfy the Pythagorean theorem. In this case, $AB = 5$ and $AC = 3$, but you do not know the value of BC. Therefore, there is not enough information to determine whether $\triangle ABC$ is a right triangle. Not sufficient.

(2) A triangle is a right triangle if two of its sides are perpendicular to each other. Because the slope of $\overline{AC} = -2$ and the slope of $\overline{BC} = \frac{1}{2}$, the slope of $\overline{AC} \times$ the slope of $\overline{BC} = (-2)\left(\frac{1}{2}\right) = -1$, which implies that their slopes are negative reciprocals. Therefore, $\overline{AC} \perp \overline{BC}$ and $\triangle ABC$ is a right triangle. Sufficient.

Statement (2) alone is sufficient. *(See Chapter X, Sections A.3.b and A.3.h.)*

8. Given a point (h, k) on the xy-plane, if $(h)(k) \neq 0$, in what quadrant does the point (h, k) lie?

(1) $(h^2, -k^2)$ lies in quadrant IV.

(2) $(h, -k)$ lies in quadrant III.

A. Statement (1) *alone* is sufficient, but statement (2) alone is not sufficient.

B. Statement (2) *alone* is sufficient, but statement (1) alone is not sufficient.

C. *Both* statements *together* are sufficient, but *neither* statement *alone* is sufficient.

D. *Each* statement *alone* is sufficient.

E. Statements (1) and (2) *together* are *not* sufficient.

The correct answer is **B**.

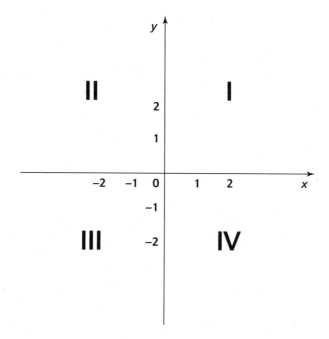

(1) The fact that the point $(h^2, -k^2)$ lies in quadrant IV implies that $h^2 > 0$ and $-k^2 < 0$. However, $h^2 > 0$ for both positive and negative values of h. For example, if (h, k) is $(-4, 3)$ or if (h, k) is $(4, 3)$, in both cases, the point $(h^2, -k^2)$ lies in quadrant IV. Therefore, there is not enough information to determine the quadrant for the point (h, k). Not sufficient.

(2) Because $(h, -k)$ lies in quadrant III, $h < 0$ and $-k < 0$, from $-k < 0$, you know that $k > 0$, so the point (h, k) lies in quadrant II. Sufficient.

Statement (2) alone is sufficient. *(See Chapter X, Section A.3.g.)*

9. In the accompanying figure of $\triangle ABC$ with $m\angle A = 60°$, which of the three sides of $\triangle ABC$ is the longest side?

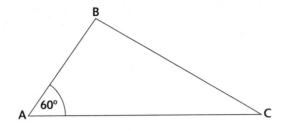

Not drawn to scale

(1) $AB < BC$

(2) $m\angle B = 2m\angle C$

A.   Statement (1) *alone* is sufficient, but statement (2) alone is not sufficient.

B.   Statement (2) *alone* is sufficient, but statement (1) alone is not sufficient.

C.   *Both* statements *together* are sufficient, but *neither* statement *alone* is sufficient.

D.   *Each* statement *alone* is sufficient.

E.   Statements (1) and (2) *together* are *not* sufficient.

The correct answer is **D.** In a triangle, the longest side is always opposite the largest angle.

(1) In $\triangle ABC$, $\overline{BC}$ is opposite $\angle A$ and $\overline{AB}$ is opposite $\angle C$. Because $AB < BC$ and $m\angle A = 60$, $m\angle C$ must be less than 60. Also, $m\angle A + m\angle B + m\angle C = 180$, which is equivalent to $60 + m\angle B + m\angle C = 180$ or $m\angle B + m\angle C = 120$. Because $m\angle C < 60$, $m\angle B > 60$. Therefore, $\angle B$ is the largest angle in $\triangle ABC$, and $\overline{AC}$ is the longest side. Sufficient.

(2) Because $m\angle A + m\angle B + m\angle C = 180$ and $m\angle B = 2m\angle C$, you have $60 + 2m\angle C + m\angle C = 180$ or $m\angle C = 40$. Therefore, $m\angle B = 80$ and $\angle B$ is the largest angle of $\triangle ABC$. Therefore, $\overline{AC}$ is the longest side. Sufficient.

Each statement alone is sufficient. *(See Chapter X, Section A.3.b.)*

10. In the accompanying figure of a cube, what is its volume?

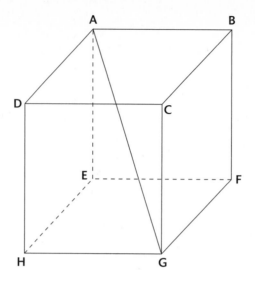

Not drawn to scale

   (1)   The total surface area of the cube is 600.

   (2) $AG = 10\sqrt{3}$.

   A.   Statement (1) *alone* is sufficient, but statement (2) alone is not sufficient.
   B.   Statement (2) *alone* is sufficient, but statement (1) alone is not sufficient.
   C.   *Both* statements *together* are sufficient, but *neither* statement *alone* is sufficient.
   D.   *Each* statement *alone* is sufficient.
   E.   Statements (1) and (2) *together* are *not* sufficient.

The correct answer is **D.** Let x be the length of an edge of the cube.

  (1) A cube has six congruent faces. In this case, the area of each face is x^2, and the total surface area is $6x^2$. Set $6x^2 = 600$ and you get $x = 10$. The volume of the cube is x^3. Therefore, the volume = 10^3. Sufficient.

  (2) Draw $\overline{EG}$.

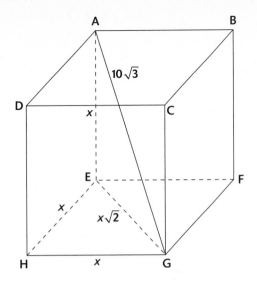

Not drawn to scale

Note that $\triangle EHG$ is a right triangle with $(EH)^2 + (HG)^2 = (EG)^2$ or $x^2 + x^2 = (EG)^2$. Solve the equation and you have $EG = x\sqrt{2}$. Also note that $\triangle AEG$ is a right triangle with $(AE)^2 + (EG)^2 = (AG)^2$ or $x^2 + \left(x\sqrt{2}\right)^2 = \left(10\sqrt{3}\right)^2$. Solving this equation, you have $x^2 + 2x^2 = 300$, which is equivalent to $3x^2 = 300$, and $x = 10$. Thus, the volume of the cube is 10^3. Sufficient.

Each statement alone is sufficient. *(See Chapter X, Section A.3.e.)*

XIII. Full-Length Practice Test with Answer Explanations

This full-length practice test has four sections, which are identical to the four sections on the GMAT:

Number	Section	Number of Questions	Time
1	Analytical Writing: Analysis of an Argument	1 question	30 minutes
2	Integrated Reasoning	10 questions	30 minutes
3	Quantitative	37 questions	75 minutes
4	Verbal	41 questions	75 minutes

When you take this exam, try to simulate the test conditions by following the time allotments carefully. Use word-processing software (such as Microsoft Word) to write the analytical essay. Do not use the spell-check and grammar-check functions of your software. If you don't have access to a computer, use the answer sheets provided. For section 2, mark your answers in the spaces provided. You may use a simple calculator. For sections 3 and 4, use the answer sheets provided and fill in the corresponding circles. (On the actual CAT GMAT, you will select your answer on the computer and then click Confirm.)

Remember: On the actual CAT GMAT, the questions in sections 3 and 4 will begin at a fairly easy level and then become gradually more difficult as you answer questions correctly. If you answer a question incorrectly, your next question will be an easier one. On this full-length practice test, the questions vary in difficulty level.

Answer Sheet

Section 1

CUT HERE

Section 2

Fill in answers with questions.

Section 3

1 Ⓐ Ⓑ Ⓒ Ⓓ Ⓔ	21 Ⓐ Ⓑ Ⓒ Ⓓ Ⓔ	
2 Ⓐ Ⓑ Ⓒ Ⓓ Ⓔ	22 Ⓐ Ⓑ Ⓒ Ⓓ Ⓔ	
3 Ⓐ Ⓑ Ⓒ Ⓓ Ⓔ	23 Ⓐ Ⓑ Ⓒ Ⓓ Ⓔ	
4 Ⓐ Ⓑ Ⓒ Ⓓ Ⓔ	24 Ⓐ Ⓑ Ⓒ Ⓓ Ⓔ	
5 Ⓐ Ⓑ Ⓒ Ⓓ Ⓔ	25 Ⓐ Ⓑ Ⓒ Ⓓ Ⓔ	
6 Ⓐ Ⓑ Ⓒ Ⓓ Ⓔ	26 Ⓐ Ⓑ Ⓒ Ⓓ Ⓔ	
7 Ⓐ Ⓑ Ⓒ Ⓓ Ⓔ	27 Ⓐ Ⓑ Ⓒ Ⓓ Ⓔ	
8 Ⓐ Ⓑ Ⓒ Ⓓ Ⓔ	28 Ⓐ Ⓑ Ⓒ Ⓓ Ⓔ	
9 Ⓐ Ⓑ Ⓒ Ⓓ Ⓔ	29 Ⓐ Ⓑ Ⓒ Ⓓ Ⓔ	
10 Ⓐ Ⓑ Ⓒ Ⓓ Ⓔ	30 Ⓐ Ⓑ Ⓒ Ⓓ Ⓔ	
11 Ⓐ Ⓑ Ⓒ Ⓓ Ⓔ	31 Ⓐ Ⓑ Ⓒ Ⓓ Ⓔ	
12 Ⓐ Ⓑ Ⓒ Ⓓ Ⓔ	32 Ⓐ Ⓑ Ⓒ Ⓓ Ⓔ	
13 Ⓐ Ⓑ Ⓒ Ⓓ Ⓔ	33 Ⓐ Ⓑ Ⓒ Ⓓ Ⓔ	
14 Ⓐ Ⓑ Ⓒ Ⓓ Ⓔ	34 Ⓐ Ⓑ Ⓒ Ⓓ Ⓔ	
15 Ⓐ Ⓑ Ⓒ Ⓓ Ⓔ	35 Ⓐ Ⓑ Ⓒ Ⓓ Ⓔ	
16 Ⓐ Ⓑ Ⓒ Ⓓ Ⓔ	36 Ⓐ Ⓑ Ⓒ Ⓓ Ⓔ	
17 Ⓐ Ⓑ Ⓒ Ⓓ Ⓔ	37 Ⓐ Ⓑ Ⓒ Ⓓ Ⓔ	
18 Ⓐ Ⓑ Ⓒ Ⓓ Ⓔ		
19 Ⓐ Ⓑ Ⓒ Ⓓ Ⓔ		
20 Ⓐ Ⓑ Ⓒ Ⓓ Ⓔ		

Section 4

1 Ⓐ Ⓑ Ⓒ Ⓓ Ⓔ	21 Ⓐ Ⓑ Ⓒ Ⓓ Ⓔ	41 Ⓐ Ⓑ Ⓒ Ⓓ Ⓔ
2 Ⓐ Ⓑ Ⓒ Ⓓ Ⓔ	22 Ⓐ Ⓑ Ⓒ Ⓓ Ⓔ	
3 Ⓐ Ⓑ Ⓒ Ⓓ Ⓔ	23 Ⓐ Ⓑ Ⓒ Ⓓ Ⓔ	
4 Ⓐ Ⓑ Ⓒ Ⓓ Ⓔ	24 Ⓐ Ⓑ Ⓒ Ⓓ Ⓔ	
5 Ⓐ Ⓑ Ⓒ Ⓓ Ⓔ	25 Ⓐ Ⓑ Ⓒ Ⓓ Ⓔ	
6 Ⓐ Ⓑ Ⓒ Ⓓ Ⓔ	26 Ⓐ Ⓑ Ⓒ Ⓓ Ⓔ	
7 Ⓐ Ⓑ Ⓒ Ⓓ Ⓔ	27 Ⓐ Ⓑ Ⓒ Ⓓ Ⓔ	
8 Ⓐ Ⓑ Ⓒ Ⓓ Ⓔ	28 Ⓐ Ⓑ Ⓒ Ⓓ Ⓔ	
9 Ⓐ Ⓑ Ⓒ Ⓓ Ⓔ	29 Ⓐ Ⓑ Ⓒ Ⓓ Ⓔ	
10 Ⓐ Ⓑ Ⓒ Ⓓ Ⓔ	30 Ⓐ Ⓑ Ⓒ Ⓓ Ⓔ	
11 Ⓐ Ⓑ Ⓒ Ⓓ Ⓔ	31 Ⓐ Ⓑ Ⓒ Ⓓ Ⓔ	
12 Ⓐ Ⓑ Ⓒ Ⓓ Ⓔ	32 Ⓐ Ⓑ Ⓒ Ⓓ Ⓔ	
13 Ⓐ Ⓑ Ⓒ Ⓓ Ⓔ	33 Ⓐ Ⓑ Ⓒ Ⓓ Ⓔ	
14 Ⓐ Ⓑ Ⓒ Ⓓ Ⓔ	34 Ⓐ Ⓑ Ⓒ Ⓓ Ⓔ	
15 Ⓐ Ⓑ Ⓒ Ⓓ Ⓔ	35 Ⓐ Ⓑ Ⓒ Ⓓ Ⓔ	
16 Ⓐ Ⓑ Ⓒ Ⓓ Ⓔ	36 Ⓐ Ⓑ Ⓒ Ⓓ Ⓔ	
17 Ⓐ Ⓑ Ⓒ Ⓓ Ⓔ	37 Ⓐ Ⓑ Ⓒ Ⓓ Ⓔ	
18 Ⓐ Ⓑ Ⓒ Ⓓ Ⓔ	38 Ⓐ Ⓑ Ⓒ Ⓓ Ⓔ	
19 Ⓐ Ⓑ Ⓒ Ⓓ Ⓔ	39 Ⓐ Ⓑ Ⓒ Ⓓ Ⓔ	
20 Ⓐ Ⓑ Ⓒ Ⓓ Ⓔ	40 Ⓐ Ⓑ Ⓒ Ⓓ Ⓔ	

CUT HERE

Section 1: Analysis of an Argument

Time: 30 minutes

Directions: Write an essay in response to the prompt:

The following appeared in a memorandum from the CEO of Dynamic Kitchen Appliance Manufacturing Company to the department heads of the company:

"To save money, I am directing the CFO of Dynamic Kitchen Appliance Manufacturing to sign up with Linksup Company, a network marketing company that claims it can reduce networking costs by 37 percent. When Speedco Company, a manufacturer of bathroom parts, signed up with a networking company, it showed a 24 percent increase in profits."

Discuss the logic of this argument. In your discussion, be sure to analyze how well reasoned you think it is and evaluate the use of evidence in the argument. For example, you may need to consider what faulty or questionable assumptions underlie the thinking and what alternative explanations or counterexamples might weaken the conclusion. In your response, you may want to discuss what sort of evidence would strengthen or refute the argument, what changes in the argument would make it more logically sound, and what information would help you more accurately evaluate its conclusion.

IF YOU FINISH BEFORE TIME IS CALLED, CHECK YOUR WORK ON THIS SECTION ONLY. DO NOT WORK ON ANY OTHER SECTION IN THE TEST.

STOP

Section 2: Integrated Reasoning

Time: 30 minutes

Directions: This section contains four types of questions. Answer each question in the space provided. You may use a calculator.

The table below shows the populations of 25 states, according to the US Census in 1980, 1990, 2000, and 2010, as well as the percent change in the population from the previous census. These 25 states were the most populous states in the 2010 Census.

	1980		1990		2000		2010	
STATE	**Population**	**Percent Change**	**Population**	**Percent Change**	**Population**	**Percent Change**	**Population**	**Percent Change**
Alabama	3,893,888	13%	4,040,587	4%	4,447,100	10%	4,779,736	8%
Arizona	2,718,215	54%	3,665,228	35%	5,130,632	40%	6,392,017	25%
California	23,667,902	19%	29,760,021	26%	33,871,648	14%	37,253,956	10%
Colorado	2,889,964	31%	3,294,394	14%	4,301,261	31%	5,029,196	17%
Florida	9,746,324	44%	12,937,926	33%	15,982,378	24%	18,801,310	18%
Georgia	5,463,105	19%	6,478,216	19%	8,186,453	26%	9,687,653	18%
Illinois	11,426,518	3%	11,430,602	0%	12,419,293	9%	12,830,632	3%
Indiana	5,490,224	6%	5,544,159	1%	6,080,485	10%	6,483,802	7%
Louisiana	4,205,900	16%	4,219,973	0%	4,468,976	6%	4,533,372	1%
Maryland	4,216,975	8%	4,781,468	13%	5,296,486	11%	5,773,552	9%
Massachusetts	5,737,037	1%	6,016,425	5%	6,349,097	6%	6,547,629	3%
Michigan	9,262,078	4%	9,295,297	0%	9,938,444	7%	9,883,640	−1%
Minnesota	4,075,970	7%	4,375,099	7%	4,919,479	12%	5,303,925	8%
Missouri	4,916,686	5%	5,117,073	4%	5,595,211	9%	5,988,927	7%
New Jersey	7,364,823	3%	7,730,188	5%	8,414,350	9%	8,791,894	5%
New York	17,558,072	−4%	17,990,455	3%	18,976,457	6%	19,378,102	2%
North Carolina	5,881,766	16%	6,628,637	13%	8,049,313	21%	9,535,483	19%
Ohio	10,797,630	1%	10,847,115	1%	11,353,140	5%	11,536,504	2%
Pennsylvania	11,863,895	1%	11,881,643	0%	12,281,054	3%	12,702,379	3%
South Carolina	3,121,820	21%	3,486,703	12%	4,012,012	15%	4,625,364	15%
Tennessee	4,591,120	17%	4,877,185	6%	5,689,283	17%	6,346,105	12%
Texas	14,229,191	27%	16,986,510	19%	20,851,820	23%	25,145,561	21%
Virginia	5,346,818	15%	6,187,358	16%	7,078,515	14%	8,001,024	13%
Washington	4,132,156	21%	4,866,692	18%	5,894,121	21%	6,724,540	14%
Wisconsin	4,705,767	7%	4,891,769	4%	5,363,675	10%	5,686,986	6%

Consider each of the following statements about the state populations. For each statement, indicate whether the statement is true or false, based on the information provided in the table.

True	False	
		1. Over these four census results, Arizona was consistently the fastest growing state represented in the table.
		2. Of the 10 most populous states in 2010, half showed a population change of less than 5 percent from the previous census.
		3. The state with the lowest population in this group in 2000 also had the lowest population in the group in 2010.

The following graph tracks the Consumer Price Index from 1916 to 2000. The solid line is the regression line for the data. The dotted line connects the value for 1916 to the value for 2000.

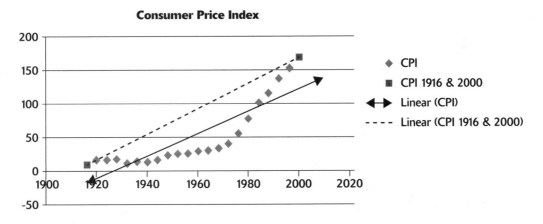

Consumer Price Index

Use the choices provided to fill in the blanks in each of the following statements based on the information given by the graph.

4. The Consumer Price Index (CPI) increased most sharply in the period from _____ (1920 to 1940, 1940 to 1960, 1960 to 1980, 1980 to 2000).

5. If the line connecting the values for 1916 and 2000 were used to estimate the CPI for 1990, that estimate would be _____ (*higher than, lower than, equal to*) the actual value.

Three sources of information are provided below. Examine each entry, and use the information in the sources to judge the validity of the statements that follow.

The following is an excerpt from an internal memo from a consultant.

Does unemployment cause poverty or does poverty cause unemployment? Obviously, the lack of a steady income can cause a person or a family to fall into poverty, but poverty is a persistent state for a portion of the population, limiting the educational opportunities and narrowing the range of jobs available. While it's not surprising that a large proportion of the unemployed fall below the poverty level, not all of the poor are unemployed, nor are all the unemployed poor.

There are a great many reasons why people report that they're not working. Sometimes it's because they can't find work, but other times it's because they choose to leave a job. The current economy is sluggish and isn't creating as many jobs as people want, but our society also encourages people to return to school, or to take family leave. Increased life expectancy means a larger senior population, some of whom opt for retirement while others want or need to keep working. At the same time, the more affluent can opt for early retirement. People are more mobile, changing jobs frequently, and less fit, leading to more injury and illness. A large number of workers, especially older workers, are classified as disabled.

One thing we do know is that the longer a person is unemployed, the harder it is for them to find a new job, both because prospective employers are skeptical of gaps in the work history and because skills atrophy. By the end of 2010, more than 30 percent of the people looking for work had been unemployed for at least a year, (up from about 23 percent a year earlier) and for older workers, that rate was even higher.

The following graph organizes the adult population by age group and employment level and shows the percentage of each group below the poverty level.

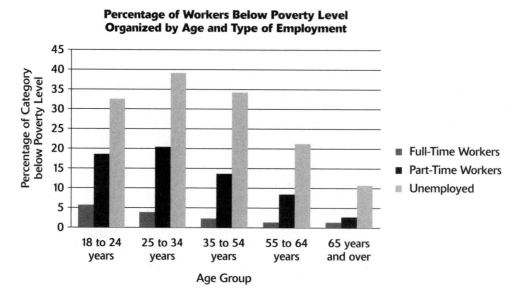

The following graph shows the percentage of each age group reporting various reasons for unemployment.

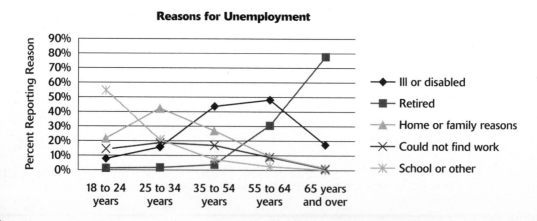

Consider each of the following statements. Does the information in the three sources support the inference as stated?

Yes	No	
		6. The number reporting retirement as their reason for unemployment grows roughly exponentially with age, but the percent of unemployed below the poverty level decreases with age.
		7. Family reasons as a cause of unemployment peaks for the 25–34 age group because those people were quitting their jobs to raise families.
		8. Unemployment due to illness or disability is significant only among workers over 65.

9. The reason that the percentage of unemployed people who fall below poverty level is highest for those under 55

   A.   is because they did not have adequate education to find jobs with adequate salaries.
   B.   is because they decided to retire early and could not live on Social Security.
   C.   is because they had physical disabilities that prevented them from working.
   D.   is because the large mortgages on their homes overbalanced their income.
   E.   cannot be determined from the information given.

10. The price of Roadrunner Racers stock is increasing a constant rate of $5 per month and the price of Coyote Cars is decreasing at a constant rate of $3 per month. Currently, the ratio of the per-share prices is 1:5, but in 6 months, the per-share prices will be identical. Find the current per-share price of each stock.

Roadrunner Racers	Coyote Cars	
		$3
		$5
		$12
		$15
		$25
		$60

IF YOU FINISH BEFORE TIME IS CALLED, CHECK YOUR WORK ON THIS SECTION ONLY. DO NOT WORK ON ANY OTHER SECTION IN THE TEST.

STOP

Section 3: Quantitative

Time: 75 minutes

37 questions

Directions (1–22): Solve the problems and indicate the best answers. All given figures lie in a plane and are drawn accurately unless otherwise indicated. All numbers used are real.

1. On the number line below, a, b, c, d, and e are equally spaced between –2 and 1. Which of the following fractions has the greatest value?

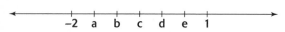

A. $\dfrac{1}{a}$

B. $\dfrac{1}{b}$

C. $\dfrac{1}{c}$

D. $\dfrac{1}{c+d}$

E. $\dfrac{1}{e}$

2. If Janet is n years old, Karen is two years younger than Janet, and Mary is four years more than twice Janet's age, which of the following represents how many years older Mary is than Karen?

A. 2

B. $n-2$

C. n

D. $n+2$

E. $n+6$

3. Janet opened a full 32-ounce container of juice and poured 14 ounces into her glass. Karen drank two-thirds of what Janet left in the container. How many ounces of juice were still in the container after Karen drank her juice?

A. 4

B. 6

C. 10

D. 12

E. 18

4. If $(a-1)(b+2)(c-3) = 0$, what is the smallest value for $a^2 + b^2 + c^2$?

A. 0

B. 1

C. 4

D. 9

E. 14

5. If n is a positive number, which of the following represents $2n\%$ of 150?

A. $3n$

B. $30n$

C. $60n$

D. $75n$

E. $300n$

6. Erica and Niki were the only candidates running for president of the senior class. When the votes were tallied, the ratio of the number of votes that Erica received to the number of votes that Niki received was 3 to 2. If 60 students voted for Erica, how many students voted in the election?

- **A.** 20
- **B.** 40
- **C.** 90
- **D.** 100
- **E.** 150

7. If a and b are positive integers and $(a - b)^2 = 36$, which of the following must be true?

- **A.** $a^2 + b^2 < 36$
- **B.** $a^2 + b^2 > 36$
- **C.** $a^2 + b^2 = 36$
- **D.** $a^2 - b^2 = 36$
- **E.** $a - b = 6$

8. If n is a positive integer, which of the following expressions always represents an odd integer?

- **A.** $n + 5$
- **B.** $2n - 4$
- **C.** $3n + 3$
- **D.** $6n + 3$
- **E.** $n^2 + 1$

9. If a and b are nonzero numbers and $|a+b|=|a|+|b|$, then which of the following must be true?

- **A.** $a = b$
- **B.** $ab > 0$
- **C.** $ab < 0$
- **D.** $a > b$
- **E.** $b > a$

10. In the accompanying diagram, the double line graph shows the revenues and expenses of Concord Electronics for the past five years. Which year had the greatest profit?

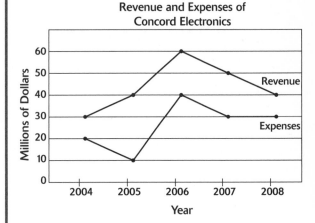

Revenue and Expenses of Concord Electronics

- **A.** 2004
- **B.** 2005
- **C.** 2006
- **D.** 2007
- **E.** 2008

11. If $2a - 2b = 5$ and $a^2 - b^2 = 10$, what is the value of $a + b$?

- **A.** 4
- **B.** 5
- **C.** 10
- **D.** 20
- **E.** 100

12. If n and k are both prime numbers, which of the following is *not* a possible value of nk?

- **A.** 10
- **B.** 13
- **C.** 33
- **D.** 35
- **E.** 49

13. At the beginning of the school year, Caitlin paid $22 for four pens and three notebooks. Two months later, she decided to buy six more of the same pens and five more of the same notebooks before the price changed. If she spent $35 on these additional pens and notebooks, what was the cost of one notebook?

   A. $2
   B. $2.50
   C. $3
   D. $4
   E. $6

14. If n is any integer that has a remainder of 2 when divided by 5, what is the remainder when $3n - 1$ is divided by 5?

   A. 0
   B. 1
   C. 2
   D. 3
   E. 4

15. If the number of bacteria in a Petri dish doubled every hour and if, at noon, there were 800 bacteria in the Petri dish, how many bacteria were in the Petri dish at 8 a.m. that day?

   A. 25
   B. 50
   C. 100
   D. 200
   E. 400

16. In the accompanying diagram, $ABCD$ is an isosceles trapezoid with $\overline{AB} \parallel \overline{DC}$. If $AB = 8$, $DC = 16$, and altitude $AE = 3$, what is the perimeter of trapezoid $ABCD$?

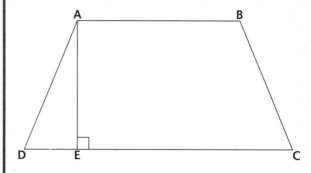

Not drawn to scale

   A. 29
   B. 34
   C. 40
   D. 42
   E. 44

17. Each of the 24 students in Mr. Martin's class plays tennis, soccer, or both. If four students play both sports and eight students play only tennis, how many students play only soccer?

   A. 12
   B. 14
   C. 16
   D. 18
   E. 20

18. A red rectangular box has a volume of 12 cubic inches. If a blue rectangular box is made with each edge twice as large as the corresponding edge of the red box, what is the volume, in cubic inches, of the blue box?

   A. 24
   B. 36
   C. 48
   D. 72
   E. 96

19. In a box, there are ten red balls and eight blue balls. What is the minimum number of balls that have to be removed in order for the probability of picking a red ball at random from the box to be $\frac{2}{3}$?

   A.   0
   B.   2
   C.   3
   D.   4
   E.   6

20. Tom can paint a house in 12 hours, and Hunter can paint the same house in 6 hours. Working together, how long will Tom and Hunter take (in hours) to paint the house?

   A.   4
   B.   6
   C.   9
   D.   10
   E.   18

21. If the average (arithmetic mean) of 6, m, and n is 10, what is the average of m and n?

   A.   4
   B.   12
   C.   18
   D.   24
   E.   36

22. In the accompanying diagram, $\overline{AOB}$ and $\overline{COD}$ are diameters of the circle. If the length of $\overarc{AD}$ is 4π, what is the total area of the shaded regions?

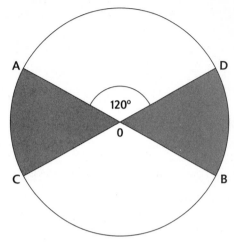

   A. 3π
   B. 6π
   C. 12π
   D. 24π
   E. 48π

Directions (23–37): Each question is accompanied by two statements labeled (1) and (2). Decide whether the data provided in the statements are sufficient to answer the question, and then choose the correct answer choice. When a data sufficiency question asks for the value of a quantity, it is considered sufficient *only* if it is possible to determine exactly one numerical value for the quantity. All given figures lie in a plane and are drawn accurately unless otherwise indicated. All numbers used are real.

23. What is the value of n?

 (1) $|n| = -n$
 (2) $n^2 = 25$

 A. Statement (1) *alone* is sufficient, but statement (2) alone is not sufficient.
 B. Statement (2) *alone* is sufficient, but statement (1) alone is not sufficient.
 C. *Both* statements *together* are sufficient, but *neither* statement *alone* is sufficient.
 D. *Each* statement *alone* is sufficient.
 E. Statements (1) and (2) *together* are *not* sufficient.

24. An urn contains only two kinds of marbles: red and blue. If a marble is picked at random from the urn, what is the probability that the marble is blue?

 (1) There are four blue marbles in the urn.
 (2) The ratio of blue to red marbles in the urn is $\frac{4}{5}$.

 A. Statement (1) *alone* is sufficient, but statement (2) alone is not sufficient.
 B. Statement (2) *alone* is sufficient, but statement (1) alone is not sufficient.
 C. *Both* statements *together* are sufficient, but *neither* statement *alone* is sufficient.
 D. *Each* statement *alone* is sufficient.
 E. Statements (1) and (2) *together* are *not* sufficient.

25. If k is an integer, what is the value of $\frac{1}{4}k$?

 (1) $\frac{1}{2}k = 10$
 (2) $\frac{1}{3}$ of six times k is 40.

 A. Statement (1) *alone* is sufficient, but statement (2) alone is not sufficient.
 B. Statement (2) *alone* is sufficient, but statement (1) alone is not sufficient.
 C. *Both* statements *together* are sufficient, but *neither* statement *alone* is sufficient.
 D. *Each* statement *alone* is sufficient.
 E. Statements (1) and (2) *together* are *not* sufficient.

26. Given that $2x + y = 12$, what is the value of y?

 (1) $y = -2x + 12$
 (2) $x + y = 9$

 A. Statement (1) *alone* is sufficient, but statement (2) alone is not sufficient.
 B. Statement (2) *alone* is sufficient, but statement (1) alone is not sufficient.
 C. *Both* statements *together* are sufficient, but *neither* statement *alone* is sufficient.
 D. *Each* statement *alone* is sufficient.
 E. Statements (1) and (2) *together* are *not* sufficient.

27. What is the value of x?

(1) $\sqrt[3]{x} = -2$

(2) $x^2 = 64$

A. Statement (1) *alone* is sufficient, but statement (2) alone is not sufficient.

B. Statement (2) *alone* is sufficient, but statement (1) alone is not sufficient.

C. *Both* statements *together* are sufficient, but *neither* statement *alone* is sufficient.

D. *Each* statement *alone* is sufficient.

E. Statements (1) and (2) *together* are *not* sufficient.

28. What is the value of the positive integer n?

(1) n is divisible by 5

(2) $10 < n < 30$

A. Statement (1) *alone* is sufficient, but statement (2) alone is not sufficient.

B. Statement (2) *alone* is sufficient, but statement (1) alone is not sufficient.

C. *Both* statements *together* are sufficient, but *neither* statement *alone* is sufficient.

D. *Each* statement *alone* is sufficient.

E. Statements (1) and (2) *together* are *not* sufficient.

29. In the accompanying figure, $ABCD$ is a parallelogram. What is the value of x?

(1) $y = 2x$

(2) $y = 120$

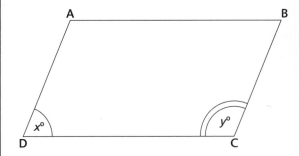

A. Statement (1) *alone* is sufficient, but statement (2) alone is not sufficient.

B. Statement (2) *alone* is sufficient, but statement (1) alone is not sufficient.

C. *Both* statements *together* are sufficient, but *neither* statement *alone* is sufficient.

D. *Each* statement *alone* is sufficient.

E. Statements (1) and (2) *together* are *not* sufficient.

30. In the accompanying figure, is △*ABC* an isosceles triangle?

(1) $m\angle B = (2x - 10)°$

(2) $m\angle C = (x + 30)°$

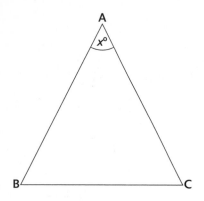

Not drawn to scale

A. Statement (1) *alone* is sufficient, but statement (2) alone is not sufficient.
B. Statement (2) *alone* is sufficient, but statement (1) alone is not sufficient.
C. *Both* statements *together* are sufficient, but *neither* statement *alone* is sufficient.
D. *Each* statement *alone* is sufficient.
E. Statements (1) and (2) *together* are *not* sufficient.

31. Is *n* an odd integer?

(1) $2n$ is an even integer.

(2) $2n - 1$ is an odd integer.

A. Statement (1) *alone* is sufficient, but statement (2) alone is not sufficient.
B. Statement (2) *alone* is sufficient, but statement (1) alone is not sufficient.
C. *Both* statements *together* are sufficient, but *neither* statement *alone* is sufficient.
D. *Each* statement *alone* is sufficient.
E. Statements (1) and (2) *together* are *not* sufficient.

32. In the accompanying figure, points *A*, *B*, and *C* lie on a line. Is *B* the midpoint of $\overline{AC}$?

(1) $AC = 2AB$

(2) $BC = \frac{1}{2} AC$

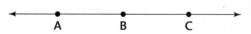

A. Statement (1) *alone* is sufficient, but statement (2) alone is not sufficient.
B. Statement (2) *alone* is sufficient, but statement (1) alone is not sufficient.
C. *Both* statements *together* are sufficient, but *neither* statement *alone* is sufficient.
D. *Each* statement *alone* is sufficient.
E. Statements (1) and (2) *together* are *not* sufficient.

33. Is *n* a positive number?

(1) $2n + 8 \geq 4$

(2) $4n < 3n$

A. Statement (1) *alone* is sufficient, but statement (2) alone is not sufficient.
B. Statement (2) *alone* is sufficient, but statement (1) alone is not sufficient.
C. *Both* statements *together* are sufficient, but *neither* statement *alone* is sufficient.
D. *Each* statement *alone* is sufficient.
E. Statements (1) and (2) *together* are *not* sufficient.

34. In her piggy bank, Kaela has only dimes and quarters, totaling 30 coins. How many quarters does Kaela have in her piggy bank?

(1) There are twice as many dimes as quarters in the piggy bank.

(2) The total value of all the coins in the piggy bank is $4.50.

A. Statement (1) *alone* is sufficient, but statement (2) alone is not sufficient.

B. Statement (2) *alone* is sufficient, but statement (1) alone is not sufficient.

C. *Both* statements *together* are sufficient, but *neither* statement *alone* is sufficient.

D. *Each* statement *alone* is sufficient.

E. Statements (1) and (2) *together* are *not* sufficient.

35. Given that $p > 0$, is $q > 0$?

(1) $p + 2q = 0$

(2) $pq < 0$

A. Statement (1) *alone* is sufficient, but statement (2) alone is not sufficient.

B. Statement (2) *alone* is sufficient, but statement (1) alone is not sufficient.

C. *Both* statements *together* are sufficient, but *neither* statement *alone* is sufficient.

D. *Each* statement *alone* is sufficient.

E. Statements (1) and (2) *together* are *not* sufficient.

36. Is $n = \frac{1}{3}$?

(1) $n > \frac{1}{4}$

(2) $n < \frac{1}{2}$

A. Statement (1) *alone* is sufficient, but statement (2) alone is not sufficient.

B. Statement (2) *alone* is sufficient, but statement (1) alone is not sufficient.

C. *Both* statements *together* are sufficient, but *neither* statement *alone* is sufficient.

D. *Each* statement *alone* is sufficient.

E. Statements (1) and (2) *together* are *not* sufficient.

37. If there are n people in an elevator and their total weight is 900 pounds, what is the value of n?

(1) The average weight of the n people is 150 pounds.

(2) The person with the greatest weight in the elevator weighs 200 pounds.

A. Statement (1) *alone* is sufficient, but statement (2) alone is not sufficient.

B. Statement (2) *alone* is sufficient, but statement (1) alone is not sufficient.

C. *Both* statements *together* are sufficient, but *neither* statement *alone* is sufficient.

D. *Each* statement *alone* is sufficient.

E. Statements (1) and (2) *together* are *not* sufficient.

IF YOU FINISH BEFORE TIME IS CALLED, CHECK YOUR WORK ON THIS SECTION ONLY. DO NOT WORK ON ANY OTHER SECTION IN THE TEST.

STOP

Section 4: Verbal

Time: 75 minutes

41 questions

Directions (1–14): These questions test your ability to recognize correctness and effectiveness of expression. In each sentence, part of the sentence or the entire sentence is underlined. Underneath each sentence, you'll find five ways of phrasing the underlined material. Choice A is the same as the original sentence in the question; the other four choices are different. If you think the original sentence is correct as written, select Choice A; if not, carefully consider choices B, C, D, and E and select the one you think is the best.

In making your selection, follow the requirements of standard written English. Carefully consider the grammar, *diction* (word choice), sentence construction, and punctuation of each sentence. When you make your choice, select the most effective sentence—the one that is clear and precise, without any awkwardness or ambiguity.

---

1. More officers at small community banks, <u>unlike mega-banks, find it necessary to trumpet</u> their fiscal soundness in a climate of understandably uneasy and mistrustful shareholders.

   A. unlike mega-banks, find it necessary to trumpet
   B. unlike the mega-banks, has found it necessary to trumpet
   C. unlike that of mega-banks, find it necessary to trumpet
   D. unlike mega-banks, finds trumpeting necessary
   E. unlike those at mega-banks, find it necessary to trumpet

2. The President's Advisory Board at Learningtree College demonstrated its willingness to listen to the grievances of the student body when it reversed a previous decision and yielded to protesting students <u>demanding that it should rehire</u> a popular political science professor.

   A. demanding that it should rehire
   B. who demanded that it rehire
   C. demanding it should be rehiring
   D. whom demanding that it should rehire
   E. who demanded it to rehire

3. Four members of the State Medical Society, <u>one who</u> is deaf, presented their program for working with special needs children who must be hospitalized for long periods of time.

   A. one who
   B. and including one who
   C. one whom
   D. one that
   E. one of whom

4. Alzheimer's disease, a progressive disease of the brain that is characterized by impairment of memory and a disturbance in at least one other thinking function, <u>an increase</u> in the production or accumulation of beta-amyloid protein that leads to nerve cell death.

    A.   an increase
    B.   causing an increase
    C.   which is a cause of an increase
    D.   results from an increase
    E.   is resulting from an increase

5. Pediatricians urge that all children over the age of 2 be vaccinated for hepatitis A because, without immunizations, children <u>are in danger of contracting</u> the disease and infecting the larger population.

    A.   are in danger of contracting
    B.   are in danger to contract
    C.   are being put in danger of contracting
    D.   have a danger of contracting
    E.   are in danger that they will contract

6. In 1964, when he was 35 years old, Martin Luther King, Jr., won the Nobel Prize, <u>of which he became the youngest male recipient.</u>

    A.   of which he became the youngest male recipient.
    B.   which he became the youngest male recipient.
    C.   in becoming the youngest male recipient of it.
    D.   becoming the youngest male recipient.
    E.   of whom he became the youngest male recipient.

7. Spurred by free texting deals offered by every major communications network, <u>an average of 3,500 text messages are sent and received by American teenagers</u> every day.

    A.   an average of 3,500 text messages are sent and received by American teenagers
    B.   American teenagers' text messages sent and received average 3,500 text messages
    C.   an average of 3,500 text messages sent and received by American teenagers
    D.   American teenagers sent and received an average of 3,500 text messages
    E.   American teenager are sending and receiving text messages which they do at a rate of 3,500 text messages

8. Africa's economic growth and fiscal balance indicators demonstrate a gap between its present stage of development and <u>that of the average</u> for the world's developing countries.

    A.   that of the average
    B.   those of the average
    C.   the average
    D.   averages
    E.   that which is the average

9. <u>Since Europe does not want</u> to emulate the United States and reduce the number of autoworkers, it does not need all the auto plants it has to meet the current demand.

   A. Since Europe does not want
   B. Because Europe does not want
   C. Europe's not wanting
   D. Although Europe does not want
   E. Nevertheless, Europe does not want

10. Tropical waters are not a barrier to the mixing of subpopulations of sharks as scientists previously <u>thought; rather</u> a feeding place during the months when plankton is unavailable in colder waters.

    A. thought; rather
    B. thought; but it is
    C. thought, but rather
    D. thought; instead,
    E. thought; it is that of

11. The early assessments of the chairman's new proposal for <u>implementing the fiscal goals for the next year is not available, but</u> skeptics have already lined up to voice their disapproval.

    A. implementing the fiscal goals for the next year is not available, but
    B. implementing the fiscal goals for the next year are not available, but
    C. implementing the fiscal goals for the next year is not available; yet
    D. putting into implementation the fiscal goals for the next year are not available, but
    E. the implementation of the fiscal goals for the next year is not available, but

12. The philosophical bent of Descartes, <u>while not being wholly selfless—surely he wanted other scholars to start seeing the world as he now could—also underscore their way of thinking</u> as a personal, internal, cognitive experience.

    A. while not being wholly selfless—surely he wanted other scholars to start seeing the world as he now could—also underscore their way of thinking
    B. while not being wholly selfless—surely he wanted other scholars to start seeing the world as he now could—also underscores his way of thinking
    C. while not being wholly selfless—surely he wanted other scholars to start seeing the world as he now could—also underscores the reason why his way of thinking is
    D. not being wholly selfless—surely he wanted other scholars to start seeing the world as he now could, also underscores his way of thinking
    E. while it was not being wholly selfless—surely he wanted other scholars to start seeing the world as he now could—also underscores the way he thought

13. Claiming land under the Homestead Act, Adeline Hornbek came to Colorado with her four children in the <u>1870s, defied</u> traditional gender roles to become the owner of a prosperous ranch.

    A.   1870s, defied

    B.   1870s, but defied

    C.   1870s; defied

    D.   1870s, she defied

    E.   1870s and defied

14. The goal of preservation <u>planning to identify, evaluate, register, and treat</u> the full range of properties representing each historic context, rather than only one or two types of properties.

    A.   planning to identify, evaluate, register, and treat

    B.   planning is to identify, evaluate, register, and treat

    C.   planning to identify, and to evaluate, and to register and treat

    D.   planning: to identify, evaluate, register, and treat

    E.   planning to identify, to evaluate, to register, and to treat

Directions (15–28): These questions are based on the content of the accompanying passages. Carefully read each passage in this section and answer the questions that follow each passage. Answer the questions based on the content of the passages—both what is stated and what is implied in the passages.

Questions 15–19 are based on the following passage.

By 60 million years ago, a distinct line of carnivorous mammals had appeared, the first of them in the shape of a weasel crossed with a cat. They were lithe, stealthy little predators, snaking through the undergrowth and tiptoeing through the canopy, each of them bearing a hallmark adaptation found about halfway back on the jaws. Opposing each other top and bottom, two large cheek teeth—later labeled the carnassials—bore cusps that had been honed to blades, coming together in a scissoring, slicing, meat-cleaving action.

Fore and aft, the carnivore mouth supplied a complete toolbox of the craft, leading the way with incisors for nipping flesh, followed by spiked canines for piercing and stabbing vital arteries and organs, ending in molars for gripping limbs and crushing bone. And invariably along the way there were those shearing carnassials. The teeth were set deeply in thick mandibles, the jaws levered by heavy temporal muscles attached to exaggerated ridges of skull bone. It was the carnivore's Swiss-army-knife alternative to the terror birds' basic maul of a beak.

From some such proto-carnivores arose nine major lines of meat-eaters, all but one still hunting today. They spread across the ecological spectrum, filling the land's top predator niches. These were the ambushing cats and bone-crushing hyenas, lumbering bears and long-distance dogs. One line, on the way to becoming bears, split off and took to the water, feet morphing into the flippers of seals. Another line combined the strength of bears with the running mode of dogs to become the bear-dogs, a hybrid experiment lunging after hoofed prey across the ancient steppes of North America and Eurasia. From little slinking cats of Asia came the lion and tiger, rushing from cover and killing with suffocation throat holds. From North America grew a family of dogs, culminating size-wise in the long-legged, distance-running, gang-tacking wolf.

Excerpt from Where the Wild Things Were *by William Stolzenburg. Permission to reprint granted by Bloomsbury USA.*

15. Which of the following most accurately states the purpose of the passage?

    A.   To compare the structural adaptations of water mammals to land mammals
    B.   To defend a new theory regarding the role of teeth as a defense mechanism in large predators
    C.   To argue against the theory of convergence in the nine major lines of mammals
    D.   To chronicle several events in the evolution of carnivorous predators
    E.   To summarize the catastrophic end to the era of dinosaurs

16. According to the passage the carnassials were

    I.   functionally comparative to the beak of a bird.

    II.   teeth set into the jaws of flesh-eating creatures.

    III. a proto-species of bear-dogs that existed 60 million years ago.

    IV.   an organ designed to digest the ridges of skull bones.

    A.   I and II
    B.   I, II, and III
    C.   II and III
    D.   I, II, III, and IV
    E.   II and IV

17. It can be inferred from the passage that

    A.   none of the currently extant meat-eating species is descended from the original line of carnivores.
    B.   the modern wolf can trace its ancestry back to a weasel-resembling cat.
    C.   no terror-birds lived simultaneously with dinosaurs.
    D.   aquatic mammals are descended from a completely different ancestral line than land mammals.
    E.   structures in different organisms that differ in function never arise from the same progenitor.

18. It can be inferred that the author uses the word *craft* in the first sentence of the second paragraph to refer to

    A.   the ability of a predator to snake through the forest and ambush its prey.
    B.   the proficiency in adjusting to the environment as animals moved from the water onto the land.
    C.   the expertise required to perform experiments in comparative biology.
    D.   the skill with which an animal is able to butcher and devour its quarry.
    E.   the dexterity with which mammals without opposable thumbs can adapt other digits to grasp.

19. It can be inferred from the passage that the author would agree with which of the following statements?

    A. The development of carnassials conveyed an advantage to the species in which they developed in that they allowed them to use their claws to seize prey.
    B. The scanty supply of food on the African plains, not sufficient to provide for big mammalian plant-eaters, was the specific cause of the rise of carnivorous mammals.
    C. The survival of a species can't be predicted from the functional relationships between abundances of species and their resources.
    D. Large carnivores developed structural and behavioral mechanisms that placed them the top of the hierarchy of predators.
    E. Only one remaining ancestral line of the original proto-carnivores is extant today.

Questions 20–21 are based on the following passage.

A comprehensive survey of the United States, at the end of the Civil War, would reveal a state of society that bears little resemblance to the country 50 years later. Almost all those commonplace fundamentals of existence, the things that contribute to our bodily comfort while they vex us with economic and political problems, had not yet made their appearance. The America of Civil War days was a country without transcontinental railroads, without telephones, without European cables, or wireless stations, automobiles, electric lights, sky-scrapers, million-dollar hotels, trolley cars, or a thousand other contrivances that supply the conveniences and comforts of what we call our American civilization. The cities of that period, with their unsewered and unpaved streets; their dingy, flickering gaslights; their ambling horse-cars; and their hideous slums, seemed appropriate settings for the unformed social life and the rough-and-ready political methods of American democracy. The railroads, with their fragile iron rails, their little wheezy locomotives, their wooden bridges, their unheated coaches, and their kerosene lamps, fairly typified the prevailing frontier business and economic organization.

But only by talking with the business leaders of that time could we have understood the changes that have taken place in 50 years. For the most part, we speak a business language that our fathers and grandfathers would not have comprehended. The word *trust* had not become a part of their vocabulary; *restraint of trade* was a phrase that only the antiquarian lawyer could have interpreted; *interlocking directorates, holding companies, subsidiaries, underwriting syndicates,* and *community of interest*—all this jargon of modern business would have signified nothing to our immediate ancestors. Our nation of 1865 was a nation of farmers, city artisans, and industrious, independent businessmen, and small-scale manufacturers. Millionaires, though they were not unknown, did not swarm all over the land. Luxury, though it had made great progress in the latter years of the war, had not become the American standard of well-being. The industrial story of the United States in the 50 years after the Civil War is the story of the most amazing economic transformation that the world has ever known.

20. The author's main purpose in writing this passage is to

    A. suggest that the Civil War was the lowest point in the history of the United States.
    B. summarize the events leading up to and continuing after the Civil War.
    C. indicate a watershed period in the development of the American economy.
    D. bemoan the change from the frontier spirit that characterized the early history of the United States to the impersonal, egocentric modern attitudes.
    E. introduce the tycoons who initiated the growth of the huge conglomerates that built this nation.

21. Which of the following is most likely the title of a longer article in which the passage might have appeared?

    A.   The History of the American Reconstruction

    B.   Twentieth-Century Millionaires

    C.   Transformation from Agricultural Society to an Industrial Nation

    D.   An American Military Chronicle

    E.   Learning the Language of Business

Questions 22–23 are based on the following passage.

Various organizations throughout the United States—including government agencies at national, state, and local levels; nonprofit groups; universities; and corporations—have developed hundreds of environmental indicator sets in recent years to address environmental issues on a variety of geographic scales. Most of the environmental indicator sets were developed for a myriad of purposes, including assessing environmental conditions and trends, raising public awareness, communicating complex issues, and tracking progress toward goals. Some environmental indicator sets are limited to political jurisdiction, such as county, state, or nation; others are limited to natural areas, such as watersheds, lake basins, or ecosystems. Many environmental indicator sets address complex, crosscutting issues—such as ecosystem health—that are affected by environmental, economic, and social factors. For instance, the Great Lakes Water Quality Agreement calls for the development of a set of about 80 eco-system health indicators for the Great Lakes to inform the public and report progress toward achieving the objectives of the agreement. Indicators address specific geographic zones of the entire Great Lakes Basin ecosystem—such as offshore, near shore, coastal wetlands, and shoreline—and other issues such as human health, land use, and societal well-being. The indicator list is continually evolving. Every two years, Environment Canada—the Canadian agency primarily responsible for the preservation and enhancement of the quality of the natural environment—and EPA host a review and discussion of the indicators as required under the agreement, either at the State of the Lakes Ecosystem Conference or through alternate processes. Moreover, some cities, such as New Orleans, Pittsburgh, and Seattle, have developed comprehensive indicator sets that focus on broader issues that incorporate such factors as economic prosperity, social equity, and environmental quality to measure and sustain the quality of life for the citizens in the community.

22. The author would most likely consider all of the following as appropriate purposes for an indicator set *except:*

    A.   To alert the public to the dangers of feral cats to indigenous species of birds

    B.   To count the number of baby chicks in nests of bald eagles

    C.   To note the effect of the encroachment of the suburbs on the natural habitats of coyotes

    D.   To evaluate the effect on fish of pollutants emitted into lakes by motorboats

    E.   To assess the trend toward vegetarianism as delineated in health-food magazines

23. The author refers to the Great Lakes Water Quality Agreement to

    A.   discuss an example of an ecosystem that encompasses multiple systems.

    B.   explain why indicator sets must be limited to a single jurisdiction.

    C.   contrast with complex ecosystems that require multifaceted reviews.

    D.   detail the need to attract more attention to wetlands that are endangered by pollution.

    E.   illustrate the geographical limits of indicator sets that overlap more than one jurisdiction.

Questions 24–28 are based on the following passage.

Nuclear technology was developed for use in war and before its benefits of cheap and abundant power from invisible and seemingly magical forces could be realized, the United States treated the world to the spectacle of human disaster at the hands of this new technology, showing the dark side of a technology which hasn't been able to beat the bad rap, even 60 years later. Had the United States not unleashed the horrible destructive power of the atom bomb on human populations in Japan, would we have learned to accept the inevitable dangers associated with the splitting of the atom as we have with countless other "dangerous" technologies, in exchange for the cheap and abundant power they can provide?

Every significant technology humans have ever developed for war or peace from the time the first Neanderthal rubbed two sticks together and set her cave blanket on fire has had its associated dangers. It is precisely the volatility of natural gas, gasoline, and heating oil that has made them the fuels of choice for everything from transportation to space heating. Yet, no one resisted the refining of crude oil into gasoline for fear of spreading a technology that could be dangerous and even used to make weapons. If we were to look at the number of combustion-related deaths throughout history, they would dwarf those related to nuclear radiation of any kind, including cancers from nuclear contamination; nevertheless, nobody claims we should abandon the internal combustion engine or the burning of coal, oil, or gas for power.

Not a single U.S. nuclear plant has been commissioned since the Three Mile Island incident in early 1979, despite the fact that, at that time, the U.S. had already suffered one drastic energy crisis a few years before and was spiraling headlong toward another when fuel supplies ran short, and oil and gasoline prices spiked during the Iran hostage crisis later that year. While the U.S. retooled its power plants to burn more coal and natural gas and made token investments in renewable energy and conservation, the French were busy constructing a network of nuclear power plants unrivaled by any in the world. Today France is the largest net exporter of electricity in Europe and has some of the cheapest rates in the world for electricity.

Adapted and reprinted with permission of the author, Jonathan Rappe.

24. It can be inferred that the author believes the answer to the question in the last sentence of the first paragraph reveals

    A.   the tendency of Americans to be suspicious of new technologies.

    B.   a proclivity for violence embedded in a culture that romanticizes criminals like Bonnie and Clyde and Jesse James.

    C.   a willingness to acknowledge that progress is inevitably accompanied by risk.

    D.   a contempt for dark forces unleashed in humanity when armed with powerful weapons of mass destruction.

    E.   a rejection of any technology that is intrinsically hazardous.

25. The author's attitude toward nuclear energy is best described as

    A. supportive, yet aware of its inherent risks.
    B. skeptical about its value in the 21st century.
    C. unreservedly militant in his unbridled advocacy.
    D. fearful of the danger that will preclude widespread development.
    E. detached and ambivalent about its ultimate usefulness on a global scale.

26. The example of the Neanderthal serves chiefly to

    A. illustrate an anthropological model of progress that is unhindered by threats of menace.
    B. contrast the simplicity of unsophisticated tool use with the complexity of nuclear power.
    C. show the transformation in humanity's use of energy from nonaggressive to destructive.
    D. chronicle the inception of combustion-related deaths.
    E. draw a parallel to a current phenomenon.

27. What conclusion regarding nuclear energy can be drawn from this passage?

    A. It is tremendously unpopular and universally condemned.
    B. Concomitant mass devastation precludes its use.
    C. Overwhelming public support has mandated its implementation in North America.
    D. Any remaining objections to its use will definitely be eradicated, and proponents will galvanize support.
    E. It has been a boon to the economy in those countries in which it has been utilized.

28. The author uses the example of France to

    A. denounce the underselling of electricity, which has destabilized the world market.
    B. debunk the idea that nuclear energy is an untenable course for the future.
    C. decry the attitude that energy is a constantly renewable resource.
    D. deprecate the pejorative outlook promulgated by American producers of oil and coal.
    E. deny the possibility of nuclear energy becoming a viable alternative to fossil fuels.

Directions (29–41): Analyze the situation in each question and select the answer that is the best response to the question.

29. According to the U.S. Department of Health and Human Services, an estimated 1,700 young people between the ages of 18 and 24 die in alcohol-related accidents each year. In an effort to curb underage drinking, parents, educators, community activists, and concerned young people have formed coalitions to increase educational programs, encourage parents to dialogue with their children, and build peer support for alcohol abstinence. The alcohol industry claims to be onboard with the campaign to stem the surge of teenage drinking.

Which of the following, if true, would most weaken the alcohol industry's claim?

A. Studies of the effects of minimum legal drinking age laws reveal that a higher minimum legal drinking age correlates to decreased traffic accidents.

B. Young people under the legal drinking age of 21 were a major target audience for the industry's magazine advertising.

C. Tacit acceptance of underage drinking as a "rite of passage" contributes to the perception among young people that alcohol is an acceptable part of American culture.

D. Teenagers drink less frequently than adults, but when they do drink, they consume more alcohol than does the average adult.

E. A recent study found that 69 percent of the public believes that alcohol advertising is a significant contributor to underage drinking.

30. To reduce traffic congestion in the inner city, the mayor proposed a plan. He created an advertising campaign to encourage commuters from the suburbs to use public transportation rather than private cars to come into the city. If the plan did not show significant results in a four-month trial period, he implied he would raise tolls on the bridges and tunnels leading into the city by 50 percent. His plan is obviously working because subway ridership is up 11 percent this year.

Which of the following most weakens the mayor's conclusion that his program has changed the habits of commuters?

A. Many drivers have found routes into the city that allow them to bypass the bridges and tunnels.

B. A long-range construction project has closed two major arteries into the city from the suburbs.

C. New seat cushions on the subway, while easier to keep clean than the previous ones, are not as comfortable.

D. The construction of a high-occupancy vehicle lane on one of the main roads leading into the city has cut 10 minutes off the trip for high-occupancy vehicles.

E. Most of the revenue raised from bridge and tunnel tolls has been allocated to public transportation.

31. A town in a small European country is attempting to establish a no-waste, environmentally sound economy by creating a circular ecological system. In theory, it works like this: The waste products of Company A become the raw material for Company B; Company B's waste products become the raw material for Company C; Company C's waste products are the raw material for Company A. This completes the cycle, and a no-waste economy is up and functioning.

If another region wants to implement this system and become ecologically waste-free, which of the following would make the cycle impractical?

A. The waste products of a packaging company are piped into a local farm to be used as fertilizer for crops.

B. Fruit and vegetables from local farms are packaged in biodegradable containers, which can be mulched into ground fill.

C. Some industries in the region export their finished products to neighboring countries.

D. The cost of heating homes in the region will be reduced as waste steam from a nearby refinery is piped into residential areas.

E. Trucks used to transport waste products to recycling stations burn expensive fuel and emit polluting gases.

Questions 32 and 33 are based on the following situation.

The drug Healix, manufactured by Wellco, is used to treat Roth's syndrome. Wellco claims Healix is a far better protocol for the treatment of Roth's than Painfre, a drug manufactured by Pharmco. In fact, Wellco claims that 50 percent of patients who suffer from Roth's get positive results as compared with 20 percent who are treated with Painfre. Pharmco claims Wellco's assertion of superiority is misleading because, in patients who have liver failure, a common complication of Roth's, Painfre is more effective than Healix.

32. Which of the following statements would support Pharmco's claim?

  A. Healix is a drug that must be metabolized by the liver to become active.
  B. Drug trials conducted on Roth's syndrome patients comparing Helix to a placebo showed a positive response in 50 percent to 55 percent of the patients.
  C. Drug trials of Painfre were conducted by pharmacological researchers employed by Pharmco.
  D. Biotechnical research conducted by Wellco was funded by a consortium of physicians who treat patients with liver failure.
  E. The drug trials of Healix were conducted in a double-blind procedure, which is used to guard against experimenter and subject bias.

33. Before a physician could make a well-reasoned decision to prescribe either drug for the treatment of Roth's syndrome, he or she would need the answers to all of the following questions *except:*

  A. How is the positive response to each drug measured?
  B. What percentage of patients can afford to pay the cost of each drug?
  C. What percentage of patients experience adverse events as a result of taking Healix compared to those who take Painfre?
  D. What percentage of patients who experience liver failure without Roth's syndrome require treatment?
  E. What percentage of patients with Roth's syndrome experience liver failure?

34. In seeking reelection in a district with a large elderly demographic, Judge Hawthorne touts his record on age-discrimination cases. He claims that in 57 percent of cases, he has decided in favor of the elderly litigant. According to his campaign literature, this is proof of his commitment to the interests of his constituents.

The chief flaw in the judge's argument is that it does not take into account the possibility that

  A. in many of the judge's cases, elderly litigants sued employers who sought to force them to retire.
  B. the judge himself is over 65 and is, therefore, a member of the group whom he judges.
  C. the evidence indicates that the elderly litigants should have won in more than 64 percent of the cases over which the judge presided.
  D. many of the cases involving the elderly had already been appealed in a lower court.
  E. in cases that do not involve the elderly, the judge has decided in favor of the plaintiff more times than he has decided in favor of the defendant.

35. In the United States, it is illegal to conduct a Ponzi scheme, a fraudulent investment plan that uses investors' money to pay subsequent investors without ever actually investing the original funds. The plan offers high returns in order to entice new investors who will keep the funds flowing into the scheme. But what is the harm? If the plan keeps on going, everyone involved will make money, and no one will get hurt.

Which of the following, if true, most weakens the logic of the plan?

A. A successful Ponzi scheme combines a fake yet seemingly credible business with a formula that is profitable and simple to understand.

B. To enhance credibility, most such scams will provide fake referrals, testimonials, and information.

C. The hallmark of these schemes is the promise of sky-high returns in a short period of time for doing nothing other than handing over money and getting others to do the same.

D. Investors are often encouraged to invest more money into the scheme and to publicize the "great investment program" to their friends and families.

E. Because money travels up the chain, a Ponzi scheme depends upon endless exponential growth to succeed.

36. Grass College, an agricultural college in a rural area, recently sent out the following message to all high school guidance counselors:

"Many prospective students believe that our curriculum is suitable only for those who want a career in agriculture. In fact, we have an excellent liberal arts curriculum. We have spent more money in the last 10 years restructuring the department and refining the course of study than has State University, which attracts most of the liberal arts majors. You should guide your graduates who want a superior liberal arts education to Grass College."

Which of the following, if true, most weakens the argument promulgated by Grass College?

A. Of the students who graduate from agricultural colleges in the United States, 57 percent choose to work in related fields, while 43 percent leave the agricultural field to enter other occupations.

B. Of the 1.5 million bachelor's degrees awarded in the past five years, over 50 percent were concentrated in five fields: business (21 percent); social sciences and history (11 percent), education (7 percent), health professions and related clinical sciences (7 percent), and psychology (6 percent).

C. Liberal arts colleges have a tradition of maintaining smaller student populations with the goal of achieving a lower student-to-teacher ratio and creating a more intimate sense of community than agricultural colleges.

D. Spending huge amounts of money on improving a program usually indicates that it is weak to begin with, and money spent does not necessarily equal excellent quality of results.

E. Over the past five years, State University has increased its enrollment of students from neighboring states who pay more tuition than in-state students.

37. Funk and White's law firm recently relocated its main office from small suburban shopping center to a center city high-rise. Right after the move, three attorneys left the firm. If Black and Gray's law firm wants to retain all its employees, it should maintain its current suburban office location.

   Which of the following arguments uses flawed reasoning that is parallel to the argument above?

   A. Jessica changed her major from psychology to biology. Her GPA went from a 3.6 to a 3.1. Jonathan wants to maintain a high GPA, and he is doing very well in economics. Even if he wants to be physicist, he shouldn't change his major to physics.
   B. Charlie is an attorney who specializes in real-estate law. He recently learned from his friend Myrna that there is an opening in a firm that specializes in corporate real estate, a highly lucrative sub-field. He is going to put in an application at the new firm.
   C. Beth is an advertising sales executive for a major magazine that targets women ages 30 to 45. She has been offered a position with Seth's advertising firm that promotes a line of sports equipment. If she leaves her new position, she'll increase her salary by 25 percent. Beth has decided to leave her secure position and go with Seth's firm.
   D. Alex has recently moved his software company to a new location in a downtown urban setting. Sophie is thinking of moving her dress shop to the same block, but the last occupant in the location was also a dress shop, and it failed. Sophie is not going to move because she thinks a dress shop can't do well in that location.
   E. Ella owns a gym on the top floor of a high-rise building in a major metropolitan city. Noah, the landlord of the building, has offered Ella a larger space where she can expand her gym in a building around the corner from her current location, where a gym previously owned by David went out of business. Ella declined to move because she fears losing her clientele.

38. Country Q derives much of its revenue from taxes collected from major manufacturing companies. The government of country Q has decided to offer large tax breaks to several companies that own factories manufacturing automobile parts. Opponents of the plan argue that this is "corporate welfare" and that the country can't afford the loss of revenue.

   All of the following, if true, would support the government's decision *except:*

   A. The benefits of job creation will more than offset the decline in tax revenues.
   B. Governments of all levels may do this to encourage employment in underdeveloped areas.
   C. Subsidies are given as protection to smaller producers to help them compete with larger companies.
   D. Subsidies may discourage companies from creating innovative responses to compensate for setbacks.
   E. Tax relief will help correct international trade imbalances and help the industry compete with other countries.

39. The Foodie Restaurant recently implemented a new policy of asking customers the names of all members of the party at the time a reservation is made. The management then required all members of the greeting and wait staff to address customers by name. The manager has declared the new policy a success because in the past week, business has increased by 13 percent.

Which of the following, if true, most weakens the manager's conclusion?

A. Foodie Restaurant serves all organic vegetables, a healthy option for families in the area.

B. Last year, Foodie Restaurant was favorably reviewed by food critics in several local newspapers.

C. Foodie Restaurant is located in a trendy downtown area that has been regentrified in the last two years.

D. A new branch of a major department store opened last week on the same street as Foodie Restaurant.

E. Foodie Restaurant hires many local college students and is linked to the food-service program in the Hotel Management Department.

40. The Shakespeare conspiracy theory has lasted for over 400 years. The argument is that a person of so little education and so low a social standing as William Shakespeare could not have written the plays. The plays display too much specific knowledge of the law, of court intrigue, and of manners among the higher classes to have been written by a commoner.

Which of the following is an assumption of the argument?

A. A code embedded in the plays reveals that the true author of the work is Francis Bacon.

B. Writing plays was considered a low-class occupation, well beneath the dignity of the aristocracy.

C. Only a born aristocrat would have the knowledge revealed by the playwright.

D. The lack of references to Shakespeare's authorship in contemporary records is incompatible with Shakespeare's renown.

E. No original manuscripts have survived, an indication that they were destroyed to conceal the identity of their author.

41. In a time when many publishers are concerned about declining readership, some stories published in the newspapers as true have turned out to be fraudulent. It appears that those who are assigned the task of verifying the authenticity of news stories are not working hard enough. This situation proves that publishers are more interested in selling newspapers than in providing the public with the truth.

The conclusion of this argument is based on the assumption that

A. Every piece of news printed in a newspaper must be verifiable.

B. At least 50 percent of all fact checkers are not doing their jobs properly.

C. Fact-checkers are always able to verify every piece of information in an article.

D. When the economy is bad and families are forced to cut back in expenses, fewer people will buy newspapers.

E. It is the responsibility of the publisher of a newspaper to decide what is printed in the paper.

IF YOU FINISH BEFORE TIME IS CALLED, CHECK YOUR WORK ON THIS SECTION ONLY. DO NOT WORK ON ANY OTHER SECTION IN THE TEST.

Scoring the Diagnostic Test

Answer Key

Section 1: Analysis of an Argument

See the "Answer Explanations" section.

Section 2: Integrated Reasoning

1. True
2. True
3. False
4. 1980 to 2000
5. higher than

6. Yes
7. No
8. No
9. E
10. Roadrunner: $12, Coyote: $60

Section 3: Quantitative

Note: PS = Problem Solving, DS = Data Sufficiency, Arith = Arithmetic, Alg = Algebra, Geom = Geometry

1. E (PS, Arith)
2. E (PS, Alg)
3. B (PS, Arith)
4. B (PS, Alg)
5. A (PS, Arith)
6. D (PS, Arith)
7. B (PS, Alg)
8. D (PS, Arith)
9. B (PS, Alg)
10. B (PS, Arith)
11. A (PS, Alg)
12. B (PS, Arith)
13. D (PS, Alg)
14. A (PS, Arith)

15. B (PS, Arith)
16. B (PS, Geom)
17. A (PS, Arith)
18. E (PS, Geom)
19. C (PS, Arith)
20. A (PS, Alg)
21. B (PS, Arith)
22. C (PS, Geom)
23. C (DS, Arith)
24. B (DS, Arith)
25. D (DS, Alg)
26. B (DS, Alg)
27. A (DS, Alg)
28. E (DS, Arith)

29. D (DS, Geom)

30. C (DS, Geom)

31. E (DS, Arith)

32. D (DS, Geom)

33. B (DS, Arith)

34. D (DS, Alg)

35. D (DS, Arith)

36. E (DS, Arith)

37. A (DS, Arith)

Section 4: Verbal

Note: SC = Sentence Correction, RC = Reading Comprehension, CR = Critical Reasoning

1. E (SC)

2. B (SC)

3. E (SC)

4. D (SC)

5. A (SC)

6. D (SC)

7. D (SC)

8. A (SC)

9. D (SC)

10. C (SC)

11. B (SC)

12. B (SC)

13. E (SC)

14. B (SC)

15. D (RC)

16. A (RC)

17. B (RC)

18. D (RC)

19. D (RC)

20. C (RC)

21. C (RC)

22. E (RC)

23. A (RC)

24. C (RC)

25. A (RC)

26. E (RC)

27. E (RC)

28. B (RC)

29. B (CR)

30. B (CR)

31. E (CR)

32. A (CR)

33. D (CR)

34. C (CR)

35. E (CR)

36. D (CR)

37. A (CR)

38. D (CR)

39. D (CR)

40. C (CR)

41. E (CR)

Answer Explanations

Use the rubrics to help you score your essay. Consider the subtopics of the rubrics, and evaluate your essay as objectively as possible. If you can, give your essay to someone else to read (a teacher would be great) and ask for feedback. Essays will, of course, differ, but some of the points you might have made are given in the following outlines.

Section 1: Analysis of an Argument

I. Argument is flawed

    A. Making false assumption: that what applies to one must apply to all (kitchen company vs. bath company)

    B. Generalizing: networking needs of both companies are the same

    C. Ignoring other factors that may be present

II. Alternative explanations

    A. Bathroom company may have changed leadership or designers

    B. Bathroom company may have increased advertising

    C. Bathroom company may have changed product suppliers

III. Questionable statistics

    A. Proof of claim of networking company?

    B. Proof that rise in profits is linked to new networking company?

IV. Conclusion

    A. Summarize main flaws in argument

    B. Summarize examples of faulty logic

Section 2: Integrated Reasoning

1. **True** With increases of 54 percent, 35 percent, 40 percent and 25 percent, Arizona had the highest percent change in all four censuses.

2. **True** Sort on the 2010 population to see which are the 10 most populous states (North Carolina, Georgia, Michigan, Ohio, Pennsylvania, Illinois, Florida, New York, Texas, California) Of those, four showed small increases of less than 5 percent and one, Michigan, recorded a decline.

3. **False** The state with the lowest population of the group in 2000 was South Carolina. In 2010, South Carolina was second lowest, but Louisiana was the lowest.

4. The Consumer Price Index increased most sharply in the period from 1980 to 2000. The CPI increases approximately 100 points from 1980 to 2000, and only about 50 from 1916 to 1980.

5. If the line connecting the values for 1916 and 2000 were used to estimate the CPI for 1990, that estimate would be higher than the actual value. All points except 1916 and 2000 fall below the line, so any point on the line used as an estimate would be higher than the actual value.

6. **Yes** The graph of the percent of each age group reporting retirement as their reason for unemployment does have a shape similar to an exponential growth curve. The bar graph showing the percent of each age group below the poverty level shows the highest percentage of unemployed persons in poverty in the 25 to 34 age group, and declines after that.

7. **No** Family reasons are given most commonly by the 25-34 year old age group, but while the memo suggests that they may choose to give up jobs, there is no direct evidence to say that was the case.

8. **No** It is true that "a large number of workers, especially older workers, are classified as disabled" but illness and injury are reported as causes for unemployment far more frequently by 35 to 64 year-olds than by seniors.

9. **E** The percentage of unemployed people who fall below the poverty level is highest for those under 55, and drops significantly after that. The reason, however, is not clear. The memo suggests that education and resultant lack of job opportunities may be a factor but other factors, like change in life circumstances and social services, may also be at work.

10. **Roadrunner $12, Coyote $60** Because Roadrunner Racers is increasing and Coyote Cars is decreasing, and they will be equal in 6 months, you know that the current price of Coyote is higher. The prices are currently in ratio 1:5, meaning Coyote's price is five times Roadrunner's. In six months, Roadrunner will increase $30, and Coyote will decrease $18, so R + 30 = C - 18, or R = C - 48. The difference between the prices is $48.

Section 3: Quantitative

1. **E** The length of the segment from –2 to 1 is 3. Because the interval from –2 to 1 has been divided into six equal segments, each segment is 0.5 in length and $a = -1.5$, $b = -1$, $c = -0.5$, $d = 0$, and $e = 0.5$. Because a, b, and c are negative and $d = 0$, choices A, B, C, and D will all be negative. Because e is positive, only the value of Choice E is positive. The greatest value must be $\frac{1}{e}$. *(See Chapter XI, Section A.)*

2. **E** Because Janet's age is n, Karen's age is $n - 2$ and Mary's age is $2n + 4$. Because Mary is older than Karen, the difference in their ages is $(2n + 4) - (n - 2)$, which is equivalent to $2n + 4 - n + 2$, or $n + 6$. *(See Chapter XI, Section B.)*

3. **B** Janet left $32 - 14 = 18$ ounces of juice in the container. Karen drank $\frac{2}{3}(18) = 12$ ounces of juice. The number of ounces of juice still in the in the container after Karen drank was $18 - 12 = 6$ ounces. *(See Chapter XI, Section A.)*

4. **B** In order for $(a - 1)(b + 2)(c - 3)$ to have a value of 0, only one of the following three conditions must be met: $a = 1$, $b = -2$, or $c = 3$. If you let $a = 1$ and then choose to let $b = 0$ and $c = 0$, the product of $(a - 1)(b + 2)(c - 3)$ will be 0 and the value of $a^2 + b^2 + c^2$ will be the smallest value possible or $(1)^2 + (0)^2 + (0)^2 = 1$. *(See Chapter XI, Section B.)*

5. **A** Because $2n\%$ is $\frac{2n}{100}$, $2n\%$ of 150 is equivalent to $\frac{2n}{100}(150) = 3n$. *(See Chapter XI, Section A.)*

6. **D** To find the number of votes that Niki received, x, solve the proportion $\frac{3}{2} = \frac{60}{x}$ or $x = 40$. Because 60 students voted for Erica and 40 voted for Niki, the number of students who voted is $60 + 40 = 100$. *(See Chapter XI, Section A.)*

7. **B** Because $(a-b)^2 = a^2 - 2ab + b^2$, you know that $a^2 - 2ab + b^2 = 36$ or $a^2 + b^2 = 36 + 2ab$. Because a and b are positive integers, $2ab$ is positive. Thus, $a^2 + b^2 > 36$. *(See Chapter XI, Section B.)*

8. **D** Test each choice by substituting values for n. Because even and odd results are influenced by whether the number substituted is even or odd, you must use an even number and an odd number when you test. When you substitute 4 for n, $n + 5 = 9$, $2n - 4 = 4$, $3n + 3 = 15$, $6n + 3 = 27$, $n^2 + 1 = 17$. All these results are odd except for Choice B, so you can eliminate Choice B. When you substitute 3 for n in the remaining choices, $n + 5 = 8$, $3n + 3 = 12$, $n^2 + 1 = 10$, and $6n + 3 = 21$. The only expression that represents an odd integer is $6n + 3$.

   Another approach to the problem involves recognizing two principles: (1) the product of an even number and an integer is always even (for example, $2n$ is even) and (2) the sum of an even number and an odd number is always odd (for example, $4 + 3 = 7$, which is odd). In this case, Choice D is $6n + 3$. Since $6n$ is even and 3 is odd, the sum of $6n + 3$ must be odd. *(See Chapter XI, Section A.)*

9. **B** The equation $|a+b|=|a|+|b|$ is true only when both a and b are positive or both are negative. For example, $|3+4|=|3|+|4|$ and $|-3-4|=|-3|+|-4|$. If a and b have different signs, the equation is false—for example, $|-3+4| \neq |-3|+|4|$. Therefore, the choice that must be true is $ab > 0$. *(See Chapter XI, Section B.)*

10. **B** Profit = Revenue – Expenses. According to the line graph, in 2005, revenue was \$40 million and expenses were \$10 million. Profit for that year was \$30 million, the largest for the five years. *(See Chapter X, Section B.)*

	2004	2005	2006	2007	2008
Revenue	\$30 million	\$40 million	\$60 million	\$50 million	\$40 million
Cost	\$20 million	\$10 million	\$40 million	\$30 million	\$30 million
Profit	\$10 million	\$30 million	\$20 million	\$20 million	\$10 million

11. **A** Because one equation has a and b while the other has a^2 and b^2, begin by factoring. Because $(a - b)(a + b) = 10$ and $2(a - b) = 5$ or $(a-b)=\frac{5}{2}$, you know that $\frac{5}{2}(a+b)=10$ or $(a + b) = 4$. *(See Chapter XI, Section B.)*

12. **B** Each choice, except for Choice B, may be expressed as a product of two prime numbers: $10 = 5 \times 2$, $33 = 3 \times 11$, $35 = 7 \times 5$, $49 = 7 \times 7$. Choice B, 13, can never be expressed as a product of primes because 13 is a prime number. (It has only 1 and itself as factors and 1 is not a prime number.) *(See Chapter XI, Section A.)*

13. **D** Let p be the price of a pen and n be the price of a notebook, then $4p + 3n = 22$ and $6p + 5n = 35$. To solve for n, multiply the first equation by –3 and the second by 2 to find that $-12p - 9n = -66$. Add $12p + 10n = 70$, and you get $n = 4$. The number of dollars that one notebook cost was 4. *(See Chapter X, Section B.)*

14. **A** To solve this problem, choose a value for n that has a remainder of 2 when divided by 5. Substitute this value in $3n - 1$ and find the remainder when the result is divided by 5. Because the remainder is 2 when 7 is divided by 5, use $n = 7$. If $n = 7$, then $3n - 1 = 3(7) - 1 = 20$. Because the remainder is 0 when 20 is divided by 5, the value of the remainder when $3n - 1$ is divided by 5 is 0.

   You can also solve this problem by using algebra. You were given that when n is divided by 5, the remainder is 2. Therefore, $n = 5k + 2$, where k is an integer, and $3n - 1 = 3(5k + 2) - 1 = 15k + 5 = 5(3k + 1)$, which is a multiple of 5, and has a remainder of 0 when divided by 5. *(See Chapter XI, Section A.)*

15. B You can solve this problem by setting up a table or by using the formula for finding a term of a geometric sequence. To solve by setting up a table, count back in time from noon to 8 a.m. in one-hour increments. Start with 800 and then take half of the number of bacteria as you counting back in time.

Noon	11 a.m.	10 a.m.	9 a.m.	8 a.m.
800	400	200	100	50

From the table, you can see that, at 8 a.m., the number of bacteria was 50.

To solve using the formula for finding a term of a geometric sequence, start with $a_n = a_1(r^{n-1})$. Because the number of bacteria doubles every hour, $r = 2$. If the first term, a_1, is the number of bacteria in the dish at 8 a.m., then the fifth term is 800, the number of bacteria in the dish at noon. Thus, $800 = a_1 (2^{5-1}) =$ or $a_1 (2^4) = 16a_1$ and $a_1 = 50$. At 8 a.m., the number of bacteria was 50. *(See Chapter XI, Section A.)*

16. B

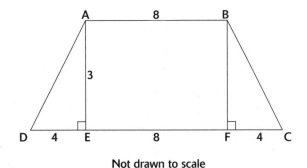

Not drawn to scale

To find the perimeter of trapezoid *ABCD* you need to know the length of *AD*. Because *AD* is also a side in right triangle *ADE*, $(AD)^2 = (AE)^2 + (DE)^2$. To find *DE*, draw an altitude from *B* intersecting $\overline{DC}$ at *F*.

Because the trapezoid is isosceles, $DE = FC$, and because $EF = 8$ and $DE + EF + FC = 16$, the length of $\overline{DE}$ is 4, and $(AD)^2 = 3^2 + 4^2$ and $AD = 5$. Because the legs of an isosceles trapezoid are congruent, the perimeter of $ABCD = 5 + 8 + 5 + 16 = 34$. *(See Chapter XI, Section C.)*

17. A

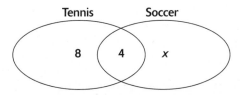

Because four students play in both sports and eight students play only tennis, the number of students who only play soccer is $24 - (8 + 4) = 24 - 12 = 12$. *(See Chapter XI, Section A.)*

18. **E**

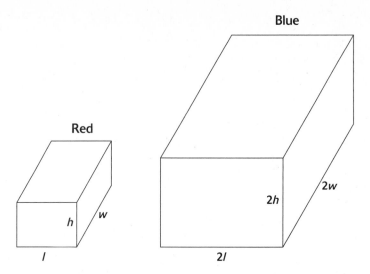

Blue

Red

h w

l

$2h$ $2w$

$2l$

Because the volume of the red box is *lwh* and the edges of the blue box are twice as large, the volume of the blue box is $(2l)(2w)(2h) = 8(lwh)$. The volume of the blue box is eight times the volume of the red box, so $8(12) = 96$. *(See Chapter XI, Section C.)*

19. **C** The probability of picking a red ball equaling $\frac{2}{3}$, implies that the total number of balls in the box has to be divisible by 3. Initially, there are 10 red and 8 blue balls in the box, totaling 18, which is divisible by 3. However, the probability of picking a red ball is $\frac{10}{18}$, which is $\frac{5}{9}$, not $\frac{2}{3}$. The next number divisible by 3 is 15. If there are 15 balls in the box and the probability of picking a red ball is $\frac{2}{3}$, then you have $\frac{x}{15} = \frac{2}{3}$, x being the number of red balls. Solve the proportion and note that $x = 10$. So you need 10 red balls and 5 blue balls. Because there are 10 red and 8 blue balls initially, you must remove 3 blue balls from the box. *(See Chapter XI, Section A.)*

20. **A** Tom can paint a house in 12 hours, so he can paint $\frac{1}{12}$ of the house in one hour. Similarly, Hunter can paint $\frac{1}{6}$ of the house in one hour. If they work together, in one hour they can paint $\frac{1}{12} + \frac{1}{6} = \frac{1}{12} + \frac{2}{12} = \frac{3}{12}$ or $\frac{1}{4}$ of the house. Tom and Hunter can paint $\frac{1}{4}$ of the house in an hour, it will take them $= \frac{1}{\frac{1}{4}}$ or 4 hours to paint the whole house. *(See Chapter X, Section B.)*

21. **B** Knowing the average implies knowing the sum. Because $\frac{6+m+n}{3} = 10$, you know that $6 + m + n = 30$ by multiplying both sides of the equation by 3. Then $m + n = 24$, and the average of m and n is $\frac{m+n}{2}$, which is $\frac{24}{2} = 12$. *(See Chapter XI, Section A.)*

22. **C** Begin by finding the area of the circle. To do that, you need to find the radius. Using the proportion $\dfrac{\text{length of } \overset{\frown}{AB}}{2\pi r} = \dfrac{120}{360}$, you have $\dfrac{4\pi}{2\pi r} = \dfrac{1}{3}$ or $r = 6$. The area of the circle is πr^2 or 36π. Because $\overline{AOB}$ is a diameter, $m\angle DOB + 120 = 180$. Thus, $m\angle DOB = 60$. Also, $\angle AOC$ and $\angle DOB$ are vertical angles, so $m\angle AOC = 60$. Now use a proportion to find the area of sector DOB: $\dfrac{\text{area of sector } DOB}{\text{area of a circle}} = \dfrac{60}{360}$. The proportion is equivalent to $\dfrac{\text{area of sector } DOB}{36\pi} = \dfrac{1}{6}$ or area of sector $DOB = 6\pi$, and the total area of the shaded regions is $2(6\pi)$ or 12π. *(See Chapter XI, Section C.)*

23. **C**

(1) The statement $|n| = -n$ shows that n is a negative number but not the exact value of n. For example, if $n = -3$, then $|-3| = -(-3)$ or if $n = -2$, then $|-2| = -(-2)$. Not sufficient.

(2) The statement $n^2 = 25$ indicates that n could either be 5 or -5. Not sufficient.

Using both statements (1) and (2), you know n is negative and n is either 5 or -5. Thus $n = -5$. Both statements together are sufficient. *(See Chapter XII, Section A.)*

24. **B**

(1) In order to determine the probability of picking a blue marble from the urn, you need to know the total number of marbles in the urn. Not sufficient.

(2) Because the ratio of blue marbles to red marbles in the urn is $\dfrac{4}{5}$, the ratio of blue marbles to the total number of marbles in the urn is $\dfrac{4}{9}$. Thus, the probability of picking a blue marble is $\dfrac{4}{9}$. Sufficient.

Statement (2) alone is sufficient. *(See Chapter XII, Section A.)*

25. **D**

(1) Multiplying both sides of the equation $\dfrac{1}{2}k = 10$ by $\dfrac{1}{2}$, you have $\dfrac{1}{2}\left(\dfrac{1}{2}k\right) = \dfrac{1}{2}(10)$ or $\dfrac{1}{4}k = 5$. Sufficient.

(2) Since $\dfrac{1}{3}(6k) = 40$, you have $2k = 40$ or $k = 20$. Thus, $\dfrac{1}{4}k = 5$. Sufficient.

Each statement alone is sufficient. *(See Chapter XII, Section B.)*

26. **B**

(1) The equations $2x + y = 12$ and $y = -2x + 12$ are equivalent. It is not possible to find the value of y.

(2) Subtract the equation $x + y = 9$ from $2x + y = 12$ and you have $x = 3$. Substituting $x = 3$ in the equation $x + y = 9$, you have $y = 6$. Sufficient.

Statement (2) alone is sufficient. *(See Chapter XII, Section B.)*

27. A

(1) Because $\sqrt[3]{x} = -2$, you have $\left(\sqrt[3]{3}\right)^3 = (-2)^3$ or $x = -8$. Sufficient.

(2) For $x^2 = 64$, you have $x = 8$ or $x = -8$. Not sufficient.

Statement (1) alone is sufficient. *(See Chapter XII, Section B.)*

28. E

(1) If n is a positive integer divisible by 5, then n could be any multiple of 5 beginning with 5, 10, 15, . . . Not sufficient.

(2) If n is a positive integer such that $10 < n < 30$, n could be any integer of the set $\{11, 12, 13, . . . , 28, 29\}$. Not sufficient.

Statements (1) and (2) together give you $n = 15, 20$, or 25, but not the exact value of n. Both statements together are still not sufficient. *(See Chapter XII, Section A.)*

29. D

(1) Because $ABCD$ is a parallelogram, $m\angle D + m\angle C = 180°$ or $x + y = 180$. Substituting $y = 2x$ in the equation $x + y = 180$, you have $x + 2x = 180$ or $3x = 180$ or $x = 60$. Sufficient.

(2) Because $x + y = 180$ and $y = 120$, $x = 60$. Sufficient.

Each statement alone is sufficient. *(See Chapter XII, Section C.)*

30. C

(1) $m\angle A + m\angle B + m\angle C = 180°$. Knowing that $m\angle A = x°$ and $m\angle B = (2x - 10)°$ is not sufficient information to determine the measures of the three angles. Not sufficient.

(2) Knowing that $m\angle A = x°$ and $m\angle C = (x + 30)°$ is not sufficient information to determine the measures of the three angles. Not sufficient.

Using statements (1) and (2) together, you have $x + (2x - 10) + (x + 30) = 180$ or $4x + 20 = 180$ or $x = 40$. Thus, $m\angle A = 40°$, $m\angle B = 70°$, and $m\angle C = 70°$, and $\triangle ABC$ is isosceles. Both statements together are sufficient. *(See Chapter XII, Section C.)*

31. E

(1) The expression $2n$ is always even regardless of whether n is odd or even. For example, if $n = 5$, $2n = 10$, which is even; if $n = 4$, $2n = 8$, which is also even. Thus, there is not enough information to determine whether n is an odd integer. Not sufficient.

(2) The expression $2n - 1$ is always odd regardless of whether n is odd or even. For example if $n = 3$, $2n - 1 = 5$, which is odd; if $n = 4$, $2n - 1 = 7$, which is also odd. Thus, there is not enough information to determine whether n is odd or even. Not sufficient.

Statements (1) and (2) together are still not enough information. Whether n is odd or even, $2n$ is always even and $2n - 1$ is always odd. Both statements together are still not sufficient. *(See Chapter XII, Section A.)*

32. D

(1) Because $AC = 2AB$ and $AC = AB + BC$, you have $2AB = AB + BC$ or $AB = BC$. Thus, B is the midpoint of $\overline{AC}$. Sufficient.

(2) Because $BC = \frac{1}{2}AC$, you have $2BC = AC$ or $2BC = AB + BC$ or $BC = AB$. Thus, B is the midpoint of $\overline{AC}$. Sufficient.

Each statement alone is sufficient. *(See Chapter XII, Section C.)*

33. B

(1) Solve the inequality $2n + 8 \geq 4$ and you have $2n \geq -4$ or $n \geq -2$, which implies that n could be a negative number (such as -1), or 0, or a positive number (such as 3). Not sufficient.

(2) Because $4n < 3n$, n must be a negative number. For example, if $n = -1$, $4(-1) < 3(-1)$, which is equivalent to $-4 < -3$. Notice that if n is a positive number, it is not possible that $4n < 3n$. For example if $n = 2$, $4(2)$ is not less than $3(2)$. Thus, n must be a negative number. Sufficient.

Statement (2) alone is sufficient. *(See Chapter XII, Section A.)*

34. D Let x be the number of quarters in the piggy bank.

(1) Because there are twice as many dimes as quarters, you have $2x + x = 30$ or $x = 10$. There are ten quarters. Sufficient.

(2) If x represents the number of quarters, then $(30 - x)$ represents the number of dimes. Because the coins are worth \$4.50, you have $0.25x + 0.10(30 - x) = 4.50$ or $0.15x = 1.50$ or $x = 10$. Sufficient.

Each statement alone is sufficient. *(See Chapter XII, Section B.)*

35. D

(1) Because $p + 2q = 0$, you have $2q = -p$ or $q = \frac{-p}{2}$. You also have $p > 0$ from the given information and thus, $q < 0$. Sufficient.

(2) Remember that the product of a positive number and a negative number is a negative number, $(+)(-) = (-)$. Because $pq < 0$, and $p > 0$, you have $q < 0$. Sufficient.

Each statement alone is sufficient. *(See Chapter XII, Section A.)*

36. E

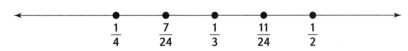

(1) From the statement $n > \frac{1}{4}$, n could be one of the infinitely many possible numbers including $\frac{7}{24}, \frac{1}{3}$, and $\frac{11}{24}$. There is not enough information to determine the exact value of n. Not sufficient.

(2) From the statement $n < \frac{1}{2}$, n could also be one of infinitely many possible numbers. Not sufficient. Using statements (1) and (2) together, you have $\frac{1}{4} < n < \frac{1}{2}$. There are infinitely many numbers between $\frac{1}{4}$ and $\frac{1}{2}$. Both statements together are still not sufficient. *(See Chapter XII, Section A.)*

37. A

(1) Because the average weight of the *n* people is 150 pounds, you have $150n = 900$ or $n = 6$. Thus, there are six people in the elevator. Sufficient.

(2) From statement (2), you know that the heaviest person in the elevator weighs 200 pounds. Therefore, the total weight of the remaining $n - 1$ people is 700 pounds. This is not enough information to determine the value of *n*. For example, you could have $n = 6$ (6 people) with individual weights such as 200, 150, 150, 150, 150, and 100 or $n = 7$ (7 people) with weights such as 200, 200, 100, 100, 100, 100, and 100. Not sufficient.

Statement (1) alone is sufficient. *(See Chapter XII, Section A.)*

Section 4: Verbal

1. **E** Choice A is incorrect because this sentence has an illogical comparison: *officers* are compared to *banks.* Choices B and D have the same error. Choice C uses the singular pronoun *that* to refer to the *officers* rather than the required plural. Only Choice E correctly and logically uses the plural pronoun *those* to refer to the *officers.*

2. **B** Choice B correctly uses the idiomatic phrase *demanded that* (*that* is a relative pronoun that introduces the noun clause *that it rehire*). Choices A, C, and D all incorrectly use *should,* which is already implied by *demanded* or *demanding.* Choice E uses the nonidiomatic phrase *demanded it to.*

3. **E** The subject of the sentence, *members,* should be followed by an appositive phrase that identifies one member of the group. The phrase that best does this is *one of whom.* Choice A is incorrect because it doesn't identify one of a larger group. Choice B uses the wordy and awkward phrase *and including.* Choice C uses *whom* incorrectly as a subject. Choice D awkwardly uses *one that,* which doesn't refer to one of a group.

4. **D** Choice D correctly uses the verb *results* for the subject *Alzheimer's disease.* Choice A is incorrect because the sentence isn't a complete sentence. Choice B improperly suggests the *disturbance* causes the *production.* Choice C is wordy and isn't a complete sentence. Choice E improperly uses the present progressive tense, *is resulting.*

5. **A** The sentence is idiomatically correct. Choice B uses the incorrect idiom, *danger to contract.* Choice C is wordy. Choice D uses the nonidiomatic phrase *have a danger of contracting.* Choice E changes the verbs to the future tense and uses the nonidiomatic phrase *danger that.*

6. **D** Choice D correctly uses the participial phrase *becoming the youngest male recipient* to follow the Nobel Prize. The sentence contains the wordy and awkward phrase *of which he became the youngest recipient* so Choice A is incorrect. Choice B uses the illogical phrase *which he became the youngest recipient.* Choice C is wordy and awkward. Choice E uses *whom* to refer to the *prize; whom* can only refer to people.

7. **D** Choice A has a misplaced modifier: *Spurred . . . network* can be followed only by the words being modified by the participial phrase, in this case, *American teenagers.* Choice C, like Choice A, has the phrase incorrectly modifying *an average.* In Choice B, the text messages are being modified. Choice E is unnecessarily wordy and lacks subject-verb agreement.

8. **A** The sentence has a properly balanced comparison: *its present stage* is compared to *that of* other nations. All the other choices have illogical comparisons. Choice B incorrectly uses the plural pronoun *those* to refer to the singular noun *stage.* Choices C and D illogically compare *stage* to *average* or *averages.* Choice E uses the wordy and nonidiomatic phrase *that which is the average.*

9. **D** The sentence uses the illogical subordinating conjunction *Since* to begin the adverbial clause. The logic of the sentence is contrast, not cause and effect as both choices A and B suggest. Choice C uses the awkward phrase *Europe's not wanting.* Choice E does not make sense with *nevertheless* at the beginning of the sentence; it would only work between the two clauses. Only Choice D correctly begins the sentence with *although,* a word that sets up a contrast between the first clause and the second clause.

10. **C** The sentence needs the construction *but rather* to present a logical contrast from the first situation to the second: *not a barrier, but rather a feeding place.* Choices A and D are incorrect because the semicolon must be used to join two main clauses—the second clause is not a main clause. Choice B incorrectly uses the singular pronoun *it* to refer to the plural noun *waters.* Choice E uses the illogical phrase *it is that of;* there is no noun to be the antecedent of *that.*

11. **B** Choices A, C, and E contain subject-verb agreement errors: The plural subject *assessments* needs the plural verb *are.* Choice D uses the wordy and nonidiomatic phrase *for putting into implementation.*

12. **B** The sentence contains a subject-verb agreement error and a pronoun antecedent agreement error: The singular noun *bent* needs the singular verb *underscores* and the possessive pronoun *his* is needed to refer to Descartes, not the plural pronoun *their.* Choice C uses wordy, awkward, and nonidiomatic phrasing*: the reason why his way of thinking is as a personal, internal, cognitive experience.* Choice D incorrectly replaces the second dash with a comma. Choice E adds unnecessary words: *it was not being* and *the way he thought.*

13. **E** The word *and* is needed to complete the compound predicate *came* and *defied.* Choice A incorrectly uses the comma; Choice B incorrectly uses *but* (no contrast is implied); Choice C incorrectly uses the semicolon; and Choice D is a comma splice error.

14. **B** Choice A is a sentence fragment; it has no verb. Choice B correctly adds the verb *is.* Choices C, D, and E are all sentence fragments; none has a verb for the subject *goal.*

15. **D** The passage gives a chronological overview of the evolution of large carnivorous predators. It doesn't compare structural adaptations (Choice A) or defend a new theory (Choice B). It doesn't argue against convergence (Choice C) or summarize the end of the era of dinosaurs (Choice E).

16. **A** The passage indicates the carnassials were teeth that were functionally similar to the beak of a bird. They were not organs and not a species. Only I and II are correct so Choice A is the right answer.

17. **B** The only statement that can be inferred from the passage is that the wolf evolved from the "cat." The passage states that the weasel-resembling cat was the proto-carnivore that gave rise to the nine major lines of meat-eating mammals. Choice A is incorrect because the passage indicates that eight lines are extant. Choice C isn't stated or implied anywhere in the passage. Choices D and E are inaccurate based on the information in the passage. *(One line, on the way to becoming bears, split off and took to the water, feet morphing into the flippers of seals.)*

18. **D** The author uses the word *craft* to refer to "a complete toolbox of the craft, leading the way with incisors for nipping flesh, followed by spiked canines for piercing and stabbing vital arteries and organs, ending in molars for gripping limbs and crushing bone." Thus, the *craft* is the ability to butcher and devour meat. All the other choices are inaccurate.

19. **D** The author suggests that large meat-eating predators rose to the top of the food chain. This can be inferred from the last paragraph: "From some such proto-carnivores arose nine major lines of meat-eaters, . . . filling the land's top predator niches." Choice A is inaccurate because it refers to claws, which aren't mentioned in the passage. Choice B may be true, but it isn't discussed in the passage.

Choice C is most likely inaccurate, but it, too, isn't discussed in the passage. Choice E is inaccurate because the passage states that of the nine lines, all but one is extant. That means eight lines are still in existence.

20. **C** The author's primary purpose is to indicate a critical period of time in the history of American business. Choices A and B emphasize aspects of the Civil War, not relevant to the author's purpose. Choice D is inaccurate. Choice E is off topic; the author does not refer specifically to any tycoon.

21. **C** Because the focus is on the dramatic changes in American society following the Civil War, the excerpt is most likely from a larger work about the transformation from an agricultural society to an industrial one. Choice A is too narrow a topic. Choice B has the wrong focus. Choice D is off topic, and Choice E is too specific.

22. **E** The passage implies that an indicator set is a collection of environmental factors that can include physical, biological, and chemical indicators. All the choices except Choice E, which only refers to eating trends, are examples of indicator sets.

23. **A** The author refers to the Great Lakes Water Quality Agreement, which encompasses a "set of about 80 ecosystem health indicators," indicating a complex ecosystem. Choice B is inaccurate, and Choice C contradicts the information in the passage. Choice D may be a true statement, but it is not the author's purpose in the passage. Choice E is not supported by any evidence in the passage.

24. **C** The clue to this answer is embedded in the question: "would we have learned to accept the inevitable dangers associated with the splitting of the atom. . . ." Choices A, B, and D are not supported by any evidence in the passage. Choice E is the opposite of the author's point.

25. **A** The author believes that nuclear energy is a source "of cheap and abundant power" but that the public is unjustifiably threatened by its inherent danger. He is not skeptical of its value (Choice B) or militant in his advocacy (Choice C). He is not fearful (Choice D) or ambivalent (Choice E).

26. **E** The author uses the example of Neanderthal to show that all sources of powerful energy have associated dangers; thus, he draws a parallel to the current situation in which a form of energy (nuclear power) has the potential for danger. Choice A is contradicted by the evidence in the passage. Choices B and C are inaccurate. Choice D is tangentially related to the point but is not his purpose here.

27. **E** The only statement that is supported by the passage is that nuclear energy has been effective in France. Choices A and B are too extreme. Choice C is inaccurate. Choice D is too extreme and not supported by the text.

28. **B** The author uses the example of the successful use of nuclear energy in France to show that nuclear energy is a viable resource. He doesn't denounce France for providing a cheap source of electricity (Choice A). Choice C may be true, but this is not his purpose in referring to France. Choices D and E are not supported by evidence in the passage.

29. **B** The alcohol industry claims it is supportive of the efforts to curb teenage drinking; however, if it targets young people in its advertisements, it is counteracting its purported goals. All the other choices are true statements, but they aren't relevant to the argument.

30. **B** The mayor's conclusion is based on the assumption that his plan changed the habits of the commuters. If construction has closed two main arteries into the city, however, it is very likely that commuters have switched to public transportation. This would also explain the increase in ridership and weaken the mayor's conclusion. Choice A doesn't weaken the conclusion; choices C, D, and E are irrelevant.

31. **E** The waste-free, environmentally sound cycle can only work if all components contribute to the concept. If transporting the products is wasteful and polluting, the cycle is disrupted, and the no-waste policy is ineffective. Choices A, B, and D all contribute to the no-waste economy. Choice C is irrelevant.

32. **A** Pharmco's claim is legitimate because Healix must be metabolized by the liver to become active. In patients with liver failure, the drug won't become effective. Choice B doesn't address the claim. Choices C, D, and E all deal with the drug testing and are not relevant to Pharmco's claim.

33. **D** A physician would need to know the answer to all the choices except D. Choice D is not relevant to the physician because he or she is dealing with the treatment of Roth's syndrome, not with that of liver failure.

34. **C** The judge is basing his claim on the percent of cases won; however, the statistic can be misleading. If the elderly litigants should have won in more than 57 percent of the cases, then the statistic cited doesn't support the judge's claim that he is committed to his elderly constituents. Choices A, B, D, and E are irrelevant to the judge's claim.

35. **E** The logic of the Ponzi scheme is that new investors continue to pour money into the fund. Eventually, either the pool of investors will run dry, or investors will begin to take money out at a rate greater than money going into the fund. An endless exponential growth must eventually collapse (Choice E). Choices A, B, C, and D are all characteristics of a Ponzi scheme, but they don't indicate the cause of its failure.

36. **D** The argument equates money spent with successful results; it is not a necessary conclusion. The department most likely was weak to begin with, a condition that would explain the needed expense. Choices A, B, C, and E are all irrelevant to the argument.

37. **A** This is an example of faulty reasoning: The assumption that one cause necessarily and consistently produces the same effect. The parallel argument in Choice A makes the same faulty assumption: Change equals loss. The other choices are not parallel to the situation in the argument. Choice B doesn't involve loss. Choice C predicates change equals gain. Choice D offers a situation that has a logical precedent: A previous dress shop failed. Choice E also has a logical precedent for a decision.

38. **D** All the choices except Choice D support the decision to offer tax breaks. Choice D indicates a shortcoming of the plan.

39. **D** The manager attributes his profitable week to one cause: his new greeting plan. However, a new department store opening on the block could also account for increased revenue. Choice A isn't relevant to the week's profits. Choice B refers to an event that took place last year, not last week. Choice C also refers to a previous time period. Choice E is not relevant.

40. **C** The argument assumes that a common person could not have the knowledge needed to write the plays. Choice A is irrelevant. Choice B contradicts the assumption. Choices D and E are not relevant to the specific argument.

41. **E** An assumption of the argument is that the publisher is the one who makes the decisions about what stories get printed. In most cases, this is the job of the editor rather than the publisher. Choice A is not an assumption of the conclusion. Choices B and C are not true. Choice D is not relevant.

Scoring Worksheets

Analytical Writing Assessment Scaled Score and Approximate Percentile	
Analytical Writing Assessment Scaled Score	**Approximate Percentile**
6	90
5	60
4	24
3	10
2	3
1	2
0	0

Quantitative		
	Number Correct	**Number Incorrect**
Problem Solving (22 questions)		
Data Sufficiency (15 questions)		
Total		

Quantitative subtotal (number correct) = _____

What Your Quantitative Score Means				
	Excellent	**Above Average**	**Average**	**Below Average**
Problem Solving	18–22	15–17	9–14	0–8
Data Sufficiency	12–15	9–11	6–8	0–5

Verbal		
	Number Correct	**Number Incorrect**
Sentence Correction (14 questions)		
Reading Comprehension (14 questions)		
Critical Reasoning (13 questions)		
Total		

Verbal subtotal (number correct) = _____

What Your Verbal Score Means				
	Excellent	**Above Average**	**Average**	**Below Average**
Sentence Correction	12–14	9–11	6–8	0–5
Reading Comprehension	13–14	11–12	7–10	0–6
Critical Reasoning	11–13	7–10	5–6	0–4

Quantitative subtotal + Verbal subtotal = Total score

_____ + _____ = _____

Note: Use your total score to locate your approximate percentile ranking in the following chart.

Total Score and Approximate Percentile Ranking		
Total Score (Quantitative and Verbal)	**800-Point Scale**	**Approximate Percentile**
64–78	710–800	91–99
53–63	660–700	81–90
45–52	610–650	71–80
37–44	580–600	61–70
32–36	550–570	51–60
26–31	510–540	41–50
22–25	470–500	31–40
18–21	430–460	21–30
7–17	380–420	11–20
0–6	200–370	0–10

Notes

Notes

Notes

Notes

Notes

Notes